Wakefield Diocese

Wakefield Diocese

Celebrating 125 Years

Kate Taylor

© Kate Taylor 2012

First published in 2012 by the Canterbury Press Norwich
Editorial office
3rd Floor, Invicta House,
108–114 Golden Lane,
London EC1Y 0TG

Canterbury Press is an imprint of Hymns Ancient & Modern Ltd
(a registered charity)
13A Hellesdon Park Road, Norwich,
Norfolk, NR6 5DR, UK

www.canterburypress.co.uk

All rights reserved. No part of this publication may be reproduced,
stored in a retrieval system, or transmitted,
in any form or by any means, electronic, mechanical,
photocopying or otherwise, without the prior permission of
the publisher, Canterbury Press.

The Author has asserted her right under the Copyright, Designs and
Patents Act, 1988, to be identified as the Author of this Work

British Library Cataloguing in Publication data

A catalogue record for this book is available
from the British Library

978 1 84825 253 0

Typeset by Regent Typesetting, London
Printed and bound in Great Britain by
CPI Group (UK) Ltd, Croydon

Front cover photographs: Wakefield Cathedral by Kate Taylor,
children's workshop in the Chantry by Ali Bullivent, landscape near
Holmfirth by Brian Holding
Back cover: The Cathedral Sanctuary by Harriet Evans

Contents

List of Illustrations   viii
Foreword by the Bishop of Wakefield   xi
Acknowledgements   xiii
Introduction   xv

Part I The First Fifty Years, 1888–1938   1

The Origin of the Diocese	1
The Diocese	6
The Bishops	8
The Cathedral	11
A House for the Bishop	15
The Principal Administrative Bodies	17
Other Diocesan Organizations	22
New Churches, New Mission Rooms and New Parishes	23
The Union of Benefices	33
The Two Religious Communities	34
Missionary Work Overseas and at Home	37
The Diocese in the First World War	40
District Visitors, Women Workers and Deaconesses	41
Moral and Social Responsibility	43
Anglo-Catholicism and the Gradual Acceptance of Ritualist Practices	47
Patronage	50
The Sanderson Bequest	53
The Golden Jubilee and the Death of Bishop James Seaton	55

Part II The Diocese between 1938 and 1967 — 57

Introduction	57
The Bishops	59
New Churches and an Old Chapel	64
Bishop Hone's Primary Visitation	66
The Impact of the Second World War	69
The Call to Worship and Witness	72
The End of the War, the Diocesan Appeal for £250,000, the Renewal of the Cathedral Bells, and Bishop Hone's Retirement	73
More New Churches, Dual-Purpose Buildings, and Mission Halls	75
From Fire and Flood	79
Reordering at St Thomas the Apostle, Heptonstall	80
The Union of Parishes, and Redundant Churches	81
New Parsonage Houses	85
The Diamond Jubilee	85
Other Festivals and a Celebration of Television	86
The 250th anniversary of the Society for the Propagation of the Gospel	87
The Industrial Christian Fellowship	88
Other Evangelizing Efforts	89
The Parish and People Movement	90
Christian Stewardship	92
Deaconess Aglen and the Board of Women's Work	92
The Introduction of Further Anglo-Catholic Features and Practices	93
New Secondary Schools	93
Some Other Post-war Changes	95
Ecumenical Moves	96
The Wakefield Diocesan Committee for Religious Drama	97

CONTENTS

Part III Years of Challenge and Change, 1968–2013   103

Introduction   103
The Bishops   105
Bishop Treacy's Primary Visitation   111
The Change to Synodical Government   118
Local Government Reorganization   120
The Changing Position of Women: Readers, Deaconesses,
    Deacons and Priests, and other Appointments   120
New Forms of Ministry   130
Campaigns and Celebrations   144
Ecumenical Steps   168
Social Responsibility and Community Service   177
The Link Dioceses – Mara, Faisalabad and Skara   190
Catholic and Charismatic Renewal and New Forms of Worship   191
The Reordering of Churches   199
The Cathedral   207
The Mirfield Centre   211
Changes to the Parish Structure   212
Parsonage Houses   221
Redundant Churches   222
The Dioceses Commission   229

Appendix: The Diocesan Journals   232
Bibliography   236
Index   239

List of Illustrations

Page
x   Portrait of Bishop Stephen Platten by David Poole
xviii   Map of the diocese in 1888
xx   Map of the diocese in 1926
4   Halifax Minster, *Chris Lord Photography*
8   Bishop How
9   Bishop Eden
11   Wakefield Cathedral about 1900
12   The procession on 25 April 1905
13   The memorial to Bishop How
14   The Cathedral Sanctuary, *Harriet Evans*
16   Bishopgarth
22   Church House
27   St Saviour's, Thurlstone
33   Holy Cross, Airedale
36   The quarry at the House of the Resurrection
39   The Church Army Van
46   Bishop Seaton in 1937 with Basque refugees
53   St Luke's, Grimethorpe
56   Sir William Cartwright, Chairman of the County Council, and his lunch guests, 25 May 1938
59   Bishop Hone
61   Bishop McGowan
62   Bishop Wilson
64   St Paul's, Old Town, Barnsley
65   Work on the new front for the Chantry Chapel on Wakefield Bridge, 1939
71   Emergency wards which were provided for wartime casualties at Pinderfields Hospital and remained in use for a further sixty years
74   In the cathedral bell chamber, *Liz Preston*
76   St Francis's Church, Fixby
80   St Andrew's after its removal from Ferry Fryston to Ferrybridge

LIST OF ILLUSTRATIONS

- 81   The reordered St Thomas's, Heptonstall, *Phil White*
- 83   The interior of Holy Trinity, Wakefield
- 91   Noel T. Hopkins
- 94   Holy Trinity School, Illingworth, about 1976
- 95   The House of Mercy, Horbury
- 98   Bishop Ramsbotham
- 100 Bishop's Lodge
- 105 Bishop Treacy
- 106 Bishop James
- 111 Bishop Robinson pledging support for Wakefield City of Sanctuary
- 119 Bishop Platten, *Harriet Evans*
- 121 Margaret Bradnum
- 138 David Wheatley in the chapel of Holgate's Hospital
- 152 Bishop Hope
- 156 Members of the Mothers' Union carry banners into the football ground for the centenary celebrations, *Roy Clements*
- 162 Bishop McCulloch bearing the Christ our Light candle
- 172 The church in West Bretton
- 178 The Chapel provided in the Retreat House when it became St Peter's Convent in 1989
- 187 St Peter's, Gildersome
- 201 Ground plan of the reordered Dewsbury Minster
- 202 The Heritage Centre, Dewsbury Minster, *Gillian Gaskin*
- 205 The controversial extension at All Hallows, Almondbury, *Brian Holding*
- 208 The Treacy Hall from Cross Street, *Brian Holding*
- 209 George Nairn-Briggs as Dean of Wakefield conducting the wedding in Wakefield Chantry Chapel of Pat Langham and Nev Hanley, *John Briggs*
- 210 HM Queen Elizabeth II at Wakefield Cathedral, *The Wakefield Express*
- 218 St James's, Midhope
- 227 All Souls, Haley Hill
- 228 St Mary's Community Centre, Chequerfield
- 229 St James the Great, Castleford

Portrait of Bishop Stephen Platten

Foreword

There has been a good tradition of both cathedrals and dioceses producing histories of their development. With those dioceses established in the past 150 years, this tradition has been less universal. Wakefield is but one good example of this. The diocese was set up in 1888 as a rather tardy response to the Industrial Revolution in this part of West and South Yorkshire, formerly part of the West Riding. Since then there have been notable developments and transformations both within the Church of England and in wider society. In these pages Kate Taylor charts this history with the twin skills of a scholarly mind and an attractive style.

The year 2013 marks the 125th anniversary of the Diocese of Wakefield, and in these potently nostalgic days even such an apparently inauspicious anniversary plays its part. It seemed appropriate, then, on this anniversary, to commission a history. This is now still more appropriate with the possibility that the three dioceses of Bradford, Ripon and Leeds, and Wakefield will all lose their individual identity if the proposals of the Dioceses Commission are implemented.

I would like to give my warmest thanks and pay tribute to Kate Taylor, who has gained some distinction as a local historian, particularly in the field of theatre history. She has completed this history as 'a labour of love' with enormous energy and great skill – not to mention fun. Her visits to Bishop's Lodge to read through records have been a pleasure for us all. We offer this history both as a contribution to this coming anniversary and also to the wider knowledge of the growth and development of the Church of England in this part of West and South Yorkshire.

+Stephen Wakefield
Easter 2012

Acknowledgements

My thanks must go first to Bishop Stephen Platten for inviting me to write this history and for his unfailing encouragement and support. I am grateful too to Anne Dawtry and June Lawson for reading the draft manuscript and for their constructive comments.

I have been privileged to see the material held by Bishop Seaton's family and to read the unpublished memoir of Bishop Hone. I am grateful to both their families for their kindness.

The greater part of this account has been distilled from primary source material, including the Bishops' Acts Books, held at various premises in Wakefield, and my thanks must go to the staff at Bishop's Lodge, Church House, Messrs Dixon, Coles and Gill, Huddersfield Library Local Studies Department, Wakefield Library Local Studies Department, and the West Yorkshire Archive Service, who have all been tirelessly helpful. I have also made considerable use of local newspapers. Further points have come from very many people, within the diocese and beyond, who have provided information and insights. They include John Allen, James Allison, David Andrew, Janice Barker, Jane Bower, Linda Box, Margaret Bradnum, Paul Brier, Maureen Browell, Christine Bullimore, John Bullimore, Matthew Bullimore, Gill Butterworth, Ian Byfield, Jane Chesman, Roy Clements, Helen Collings, Mary Cooper, +Stephen Cottrell, Paul Crabb, Martyn Crompton, Jane Dickinson, Patrick Duckworth, Margaret Dye, +Christopher Edmondson, Ashley Ellis, Bryan Ellis, Lesley Ennis, David Fletcher, Brenda Frank, +Robert Freeman, Brian Geeson, Richard Giles, John Goodchild, Lisa Grant, Jonathan Greener, Pamela Greener, Irene Greenman, George Guiver, John Harris, Ruth Harris, Robert Hart, Steven Haws, Anthony Howe, Freda Jackson, Brunel James, Guy Jamieson, Alison Jewell, Adrian Judd, Celia Kilner, Felicity Lawson, John Lawson, Bryan Lewis, Jenny Lowery, Tony Macpherson, +Nigel McCulloch, Robin Mackintosh, John Maiden, Deidre Morris, Diana Monahan, George Nairn-Briggs, Peter Needham, David Nicholson, Catherine Ogle, Howard Pask, Elsie Peace, Philip Pearce, Matthew Pollard, Brenda Ratcliffe, Michael Rawson, Malcolm Reed, Mother Robina CSPH, Catherine Robinson,

WAKEFIELD DIOCESE

+Tony Robinson, Martin Russell, Tim Sledge, +Brian Smith, Christine Smith, Susan Starr, Christine Stearn, Richard Steel, Michael Storey, Dick Swindell, Isabel Syed, Barbara Tom, Timothy van Carrapiett, David Ward, Philip Wells, David Wheatley, Susan Whitwam, Michael Wood, Vicki Yates, and Michael Yelton. I am immensely indebted to them all. A substantial debt is due to Bishop Platten and Jane Butterfield for devising the index.

Kate Taylor
2012

Introduction

The 125 years since the Diocese of Wakefield was formed have seen immense changes both within the Established Church and within society. They have seen two world wars, a proliferation of faiths (in particular of Islam within the diocese), a decline in people coming forward for ordination, a radical change in the status of women within the Church, and an accelerating decline in church-going. The Church has moved from being relatively inward looking to a position where community involvement of many kinds has become something of an imperative. Among the many remarkable changes it is worth noting that a suggestion in 1907 for intercessions 'to stay the advance of Moslem activity and its false teaching by the missionary zeal of the Church' would have been wholly unacceptable as an official recommendation a hundred years later.

There has been a substantial increase in mission focus. Before the Second World War, churches devoted considerable time and money in efforts to support the various missionary societies which undertook work overseas. In 1981 Bishop Colin James remarked, 'Not so long ago we used to think of mission as something we in the west did to others in foreign parts. Then we awoke to the need of mission in de-Christianized England too.'

Writing at the time of the ninetieth anniversary of the founding of the diocese, John Lister, Provost of Wakefield Cathedral, said that its history had seen 'a complete revolution in thought and social patterns'.

The first fifty years of the diocese saw a steady drive towards the provision of more churches – some with their own new parishes – and mission rooms. They also saw the struggle to retain church schools and press the claims of religious education. Later years have seen considerable retrenchment with the union of benefices, the creation of team parishes and group ministries, and the redundancy of no small number of church buildings.

In 1973, Eric Treacy, Bishop of Wakefield since 1968, looked back on forty years in the ministry to identify some of the changes he had seen in that comparatively short period. In 1933, the majority of clergy were from public schools and the ancient universities, he said. The Church was unselfcritical and, he argued, only a little sensitive to issues of human welfare.

There had been an 'astonishing change' in the relationships between the different Christian denominations, and prejudice had gone. There had, even forty years earlier, been a lack of understanding between the Catholic and Evangelical wings of the Established Church itself. Now he found mutual respect. In the 1930s there was still an earnest desire to convert the heathen in foreign parts. Forty years later there was an acceptance of peaceful co-existence with the 'other great religions', though Treacy regretted that this had robbed missionary work of some of its dynamic. He discerned a change, too, in the relationships between bishops and their clergy. Bishops had been remote figures, 'inaccessible and often incomprehensible'. Motor cars and telephones, he thought, had been among the catalysts for change. In the 1970s bishops had become 'everybody's men'. They were to be 'grabbed' for every kind of occasion, perhaps because of the lack of other public figures to take a place on platforms. But in the 1970s he also found the Church in flux. 'Forty years ago men were ordained to a Church which was stable, which had a well-established place in the life of the community,' he said. And went on, 'Men who seek ordination today are entering the ministry of a church in which nothing is certain, which is far from well-established, in which things are constantly changing. They give themselves to the service of a Body which offers less security than almost any other field of employment.' In his Memoir, written in 1955, Wakefield's fourth bishop, Campbell Richard Hone, spoke of the problems he encountered in the 1940s when the majority of candidates for ordination were 'from lower middle-class homes, good and sincere for the most part but with little evidence of outstanding ability, or theological knowledge'.

The 125 years saw a gradual but marked change in the role of lay people in the Church nationally which was reflected in the diocese. This has included the introduction of lay ministers and the emergence from parish laity of those seeking ordination as self-supporting priests. Recent years have seen, too, a broader embrace of cultural forms, in particular wider styles of music, and art (including art installations), and a widening of cultural and social concerns.

The major problems facing the diocese at the end of the twentieth century and the beginning of the twenty-first were those facing the Church nationally: declining congregations except (perhaps) in evangelical churches, the lack of clergy and certainly the lack of money to pay them, the refusal of some Anglo-Catholic parishes to accept women priests and their insistence on having a separate bishop, a diminishing liberal influence and the difficulty and reluctance of some parishes to pay the parish share.

INTRODUCTION

On a much more positive note, many churches which were once open only on Sundays are buzzing with activity throughout the week. Provision ranges from lunch clubs for the elderly to activities for the whole family, such as Messy Church, or ones directed particularly at children, such as Kidz clubs.

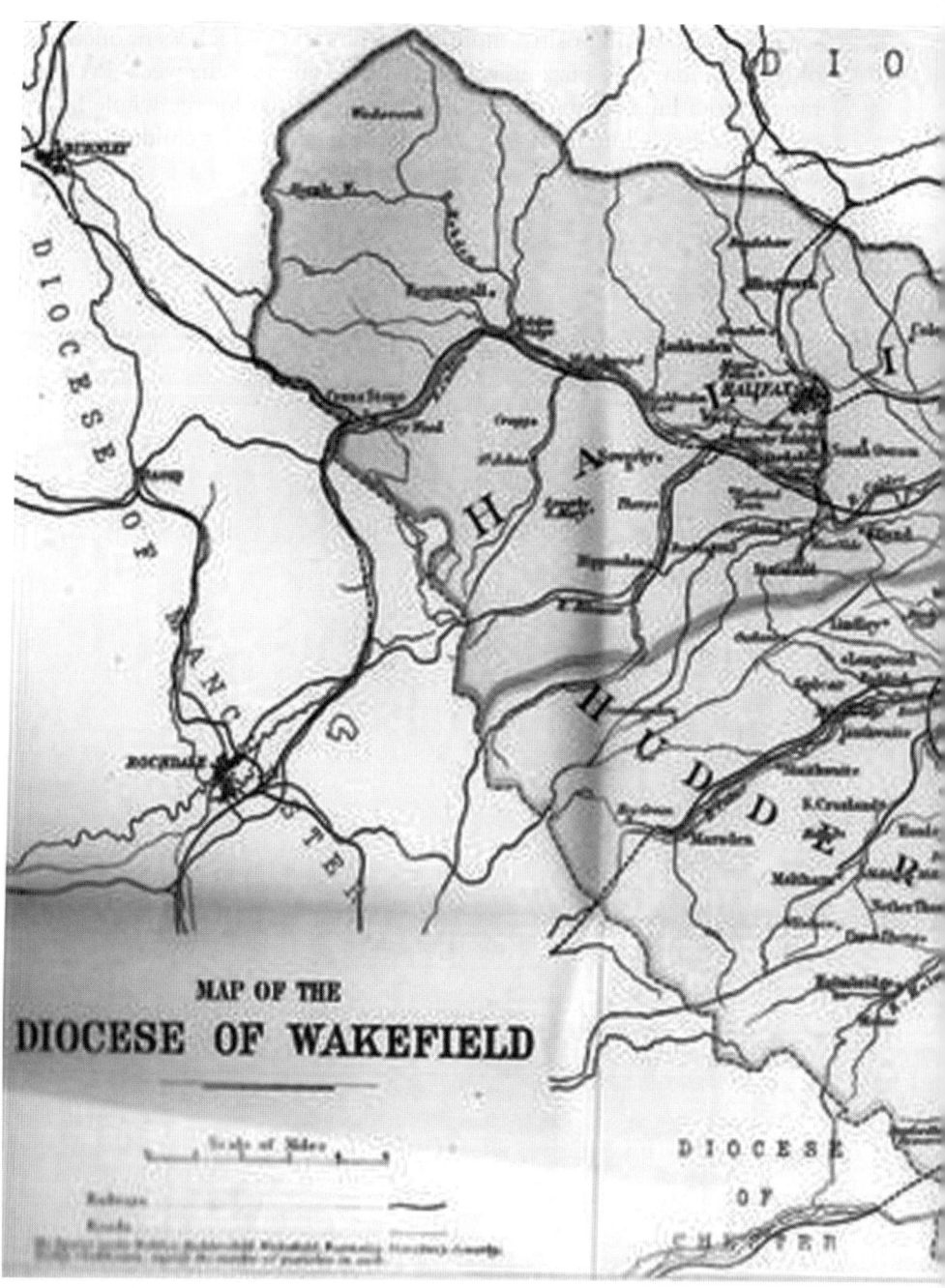

Map of the diocese in 1888

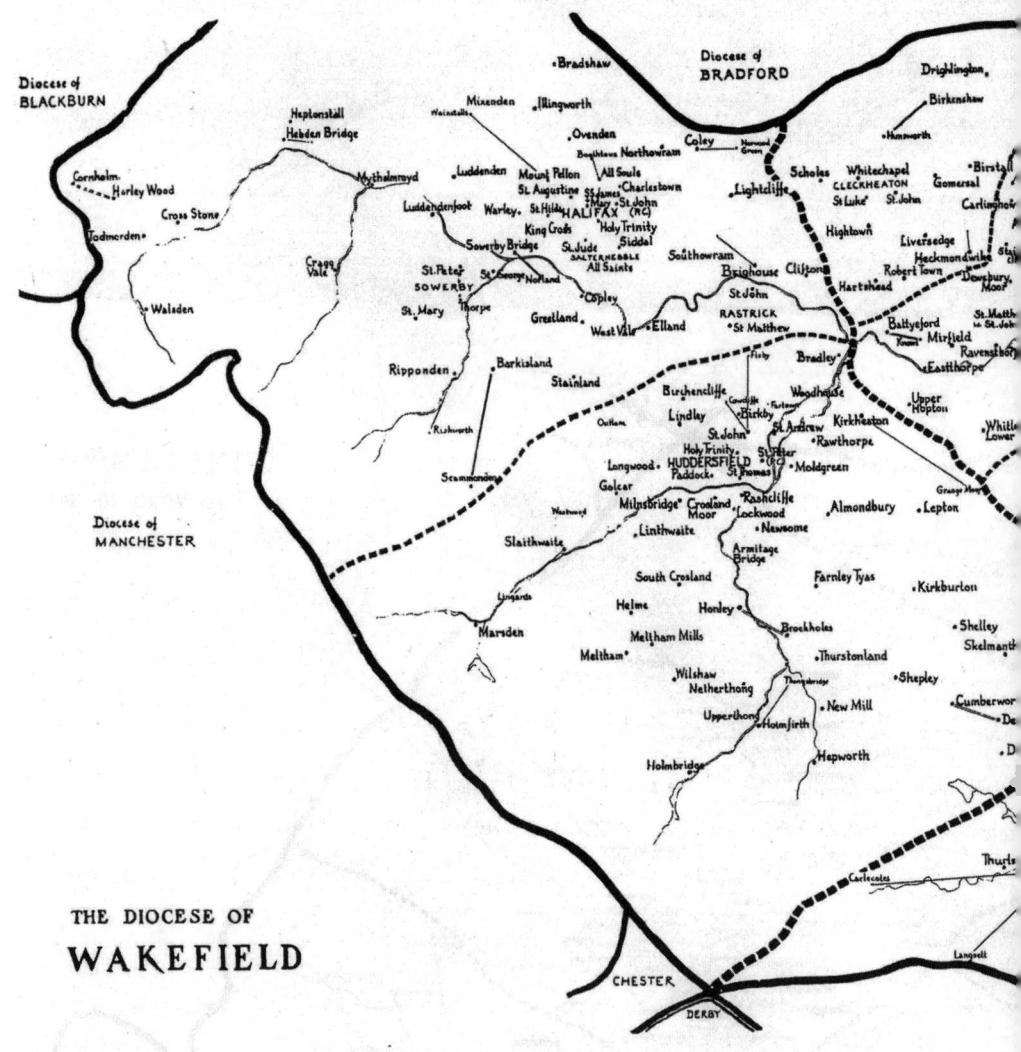

Map of the diocese in 1926

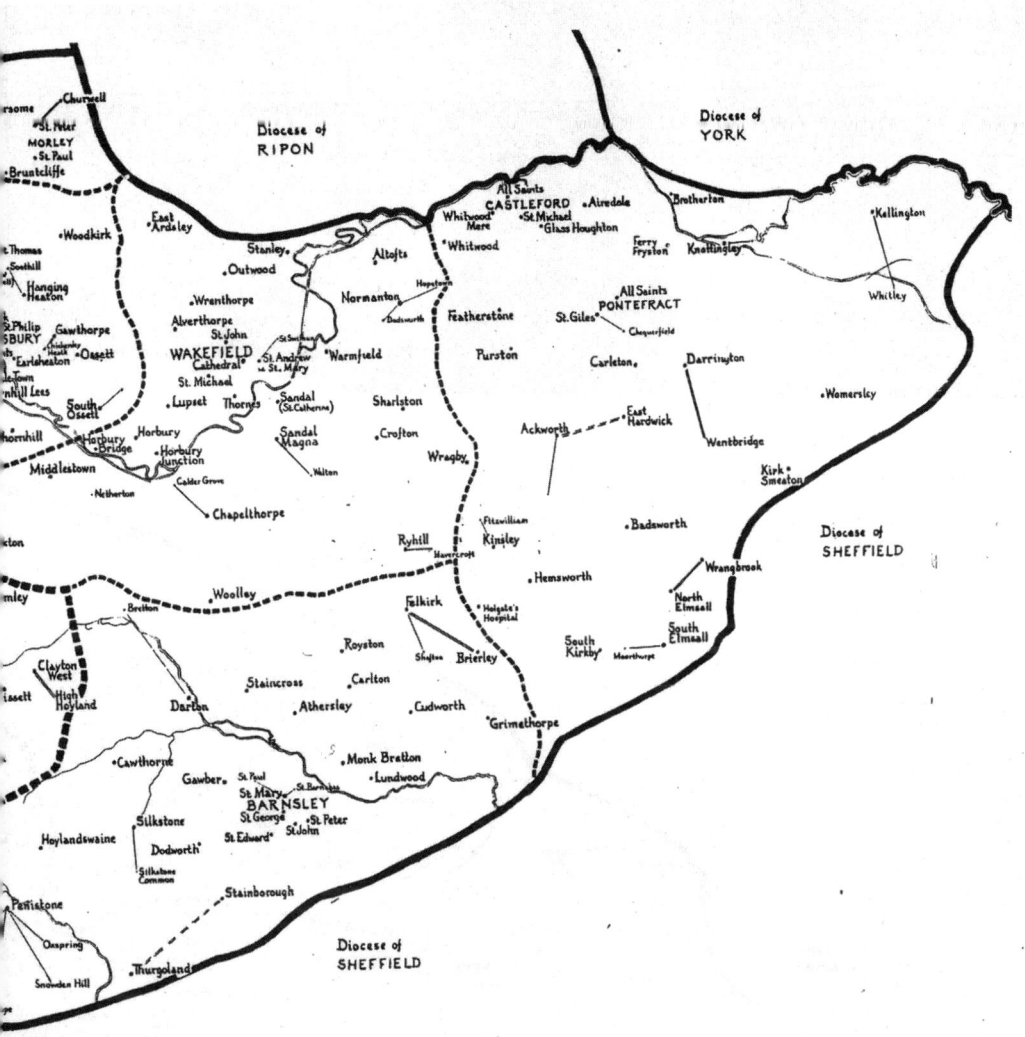

PART I

The First Fifty Years, 1888–1938

The Origin of the Diocese

The Diocese of Wakefield was established in 1888, taking in a substantial area from the southern end of the Diocese of Ripon. It had been a long time coming!

Between the sixteenth and nineteenth centuries, no new bishoprics had been established in the Church of England. Then came the Dioceses of Ripon (1836) and Manchester (1845). By 1875, the population of the Ripon Diocese had doubled, from 800,000 at its inception to 1,600,000. With a vast distance to cover and with so many parishes to visit, the health of the second Bishop of Ripon, Robert Bickersteth, was under strain. Moreover, Nonconformity was flourishing. It was later said that the immense success of early Methodism in the Calder valley owed something to the deadness and dullness of church life in the area, but it must have owed considerably more to the influence of the 'wealthy capitalists and employers of labour' who, Francis Pigou, Vicar of Halifax in 1875–88, observed, were a strong influence on the spread of Nonconformity in the area. Evidence suggesting that smaller diocesan units resulted in greater numbers of men coming forward for ordination and in more candidates for confirmation was a further incentive to create additional dioceses.

The genesis of the Diocese of Wakefield falls into two distinct phases: the first culminating in the Act of Parliament of 1878 which authorized the establishment of a Wakefield see; the second, dating from 1884, bringing the Diocese into being by the Order in Council of 17 May 1888.

For any new diocese to be created a very substantial capital sum was needed to endow the bishopric. The Bishoprics Act of 1878 specified a minimum income of £3,500 a year.

Although there had been earlier suggestions that a new see should be created with Halifax as its cathedral city, it was the death of Charles Musgrave, Vicar of Halifax and Archdeacon of Craven, in April 1875 that prompted moves to create a further bishopric in southern Yorkshire with Halifax parish church as the cathedral. It was thought that some

£100,000 would be required. The Halifax living was a substantial one. There seemed a possibility that some of the endowments of the benefice could be appropriated, by means of an Act of Parliament, towards financing the bishopric. A leading advocate of a Halifax diocese, industrialist Sir Henry Edwards (1812–86), who had represented Halifax in Parliament in 1847–52, suggested that, rather than appropriating funds from the living, the diocesan of the new see should also be the Vicar of Halifax. The idea was canvassed at a meeting in London attended by several Members of Parliament, but the scheme came to nothing and later in 1875 Francis Pigou was appointed to the Halifax benefice. However, when the Ecclesiastical Commissioners set up a committee to define the boundaries of the proposed bishoprics of Truro and St Albans, it was asked to look at the need nationally for other new bishoprics. The committee included the Conservative West Riding Member of Parliament, Lieutenant Colonel Walter Spencer Stanhope. Its initial recommendations were for sees centred on Liverpool, Newcastle and Southwell. When, following its deliberations, the Bill was first drafted in 1877, a diocese of South Yorkshire had been added which would have included Sheffield (not part of the Diocese of Ripon) as well as Halifax and Wakefield and places between. The prospect of being severed from York did not appeal to the church people of Sheffield and, when the bill finally came before Parliament, Sheffield had been dropped from it but the South Yorkshire scheme remained. The Government's first intention was to identify Wakefield as the cathedral city. Following an intervention from Sir Henry Edwards, the Bill proposed either Wakefield or Halifax as the cathedral city, leaving the final decision to the Queen in Council.

There was what the *Wakefield Herald* described as a 'monster meeting' in Wakefield on 23 May 1877, with leading civic as well as church figures there, to seek formal support for 'the superior claims of the town'. The Mayor of Wakefield, Alderman W. H. Gill, took the chair. The Vicar of Wakefield, Norman J. D. Straton, and Wakefield's Conservative Member of Parliament, Thomas Kemp Sanderson, were on the platform together with Lieutenant Colonel Stanhope. Alderman Gill referred to his meeting with the Home Secretary to press the claims of Wakefield. Stanhope expressed concern that, if the see were centred on Halifax, the bishop would have a lower status than the vicar as the latter had some thirty livings in his gift and the new bishop would certainly have far fewer. Wakefield people had already undertaken a major restoration of the parish church. There had been no comparable work at Halifax. Sanderson, pointed out than in 1836 there had been the possibility of Wakefield being the cathedral city rather than Ripon. Moreover, Wakefield was not, like

Halifax, merely 'on a railway branch line'. A sum of £100,000 was again identified as necessary to endow the bishopric. A number of Wakefield people promised individual donations of £1,000. Sanderson proposed, 'Inasmuch as the Bill empowers Her Majesty by Order of Council to make choice between Wakefield and Halifax as the cathedral city for the proposed new diocese, this meeting desires to express its sense of the superior claims of Wakefield and hereby prays Her Majesty to select the former place.' It was, of course, carried.

A similar meeting in the New Assembly Rooms in Halifax on 25 May, convened by Sir Henry Edwards, was less well attended. Edwards explained how he had lobbied successfully to have the option of Halifax added to a bill that originally referred only to Wakefield. The meeting secured unanimous support for a motion urging that Halifax be chosen as the cathedral city, citing the possibility of an easy adaptation of the parish church and the strategic situation of Halifax geographically and in terms of railway communication within the projected diocese. But the *Halifax Courier* noted 'something like mutiny in the Halifax Camp' because a number of the poorer vicars in the Halifax area thought that any surplus money that might still be appropriated from the vicar's endowments should be directed to improving their livings rather than financing a bishop. The paper foresaw that the cathedral would as a consequence be in Wakefield. A committee was appointed, with Edwards among its members, to promote the claims of Halifax. Edward Balme Wheatley-Balme (1819–96) however, who was not at the meeting, sent a message that he would give £5,000 towards the bishopric fund whichever town was chosen.

Wheatley-Balme, who lived at Cote Wall, Mirfield, was ultimately the single most significant donor to the bishopric, giving some £10,000. When, before the diocese could be founded, the Ecclesiastical Commissioners required four guarantors to ensure that a house would be provided for the bishop, he was one of these. When the Wakefield Diocesan Conference was first set up, Bishop How chose him as one of his personally nominated ten members.

Huddersfield was never in serious contention as the cathedral city, and a meeting of Huddersfield clergy, again in May 1877, accepted that the honours would go to Wakefield.

The persistent advocacy of Wakefield's MP, Thomas Kemp Sanderson, went a long way to furthering Wakefield's cause where the two Radical Halifax members (James Stansfeld, a radical protestant dissenter, and John Dyson Hutchinson) remained detached. Pigou noted that they were more interested in pursuing the disestablishment of the church than in creating a new diocese. Pigou was asked by the then Home Secretary, Richard

Assheton Cross, to give his opinion on the relative merits of the two towns for the see. At their meeting he was told by Cross that the petition of the clergy against Halifax, fearing that money that might have been used to improve their benefices would be diverted to the bishopric fund, sealed its fate. The claims of Wakefield were preferred. When Sanderson was given the Freedom of the City of Wakfield in 1895, the citation referred to its being 'in great measure' due to him that Wakefield had been chosen for the cathedral.

The Bishoprics Act, passed in 1878, provided specifically for a Bishop of Wakefield as well as for the anticipated sees of Liverpool, Newcastle, and Southwell. The cathedral would be, 'Such church at Wakefield as may be determined by order of Her Majesty in Council subject to the rights of the patron and incumbent.' The new bishopric was to have such a part of the endowment of the Bishopric of Ripon as would bring in £300 a year.

Halifax Minster, Chris Lord Photography

The historic significance of Halifax Parish Church was recognized when in 2009 it was given minster status. The accolade was celebrated at a service in November.

But although an Act of Parliament now provided for the South Yorkshire see, for some years the matter was dropped. There was an economic recession affecting both agriculture and commerce. Although the Diocese of Liverpool was formed in 1880 and that of Newcastle in 1882, there was no progress for some years on the Wakefield scheme.

Two things in 1884 prompted a second campaign to secure the new diocese. The first was the establishment that year of the Diocese of Southwell. The second was the death of Bishop Bickersteth and the appointment of William Boyd Carpenter who was consecrated on 25 July 1884, to the Ripon see. One of the key figures in reviving the scheme and in ensuring a successful conclusion was the Vicar of Wakefield, Norman Straton, who, new to Wakefield in 1875, was by 1884 one of the leading churchmen in the Ripon Diocese and had become a Canon of Ripon in 1883. The other most significant figure was Joshua Ingham Brooke, who had been Rector of Thornhill since 1867, and Rural Dean of Dewsbury since 1871, and was, like Straton, a Ripon Canon.

In 1884, Straton conceived the idea of bringing the (national) Church Congress to Wakefield in 1886 as a means of promoting the Wakefield scheme and adding to the funds. The Congress founded in 1861 in Cambridge, was a voluntary gathering bringing together Anglican clergy and lay people, and embracing Evangelicals, Ritualists and the broad church party. Straton obtained support at a public meeting in August 1884 to request the Bishop of Ripon to secure the next Congress for his diocese.

At Bishop Boyd Carpenter's first Diocesan Conference, held in Leeds on 11 October 1884, Francis Sharpe Powell, a former Member of Parliament for the West Riding who had strongly supported Halifax's claims in 1875, raised the subject of the division of the diocese and ensured the carrying of a motion asking the bishop to name a committee to raise the necessary funds.

Boyd Carpenter paid his first visit as bishop to Wakefield on 21 January 1885 to attend the annual Church Institution soiree. The event became not so much a social event as a campaign meeting at which the bishop was urged to exercise his good offices to secure the swift division of his diocese, in particular by driving the fund-raising. That June, Boyd-Carpenter wrote to all his clergy urging them to 'do all in their power' to secure the completion of the Wakefield Bishopric scheme. He subsequently visited many centres in the Ripon Diocese to foster the setting up of local fund-raising committees.

By the time of the Ripon Diocesan Conference in October 1885, Straton and Brooke as secretaries of the Wakefield Bishopric Fund had contacted all those who had offered subscriptions during the earlier campaign and succeeded in obtaining promises of £24,365. Straton was able to say, 'Those who have hitherto regarded the erection of the Wakefield bishopric as an event which might possibly occur in the distant future must now be aware that it has come within measurable distance.'

The Church Congress, held in Wakefield in 1886, amply demonstrated the facilities Wakefield could offer as the diocesan cathedral city. It opened with a reception in the recently built Town Hall on 5 October followed by processions to the parish church, St John's and Holy Trinity where services were held simultaneously. The trade floor of the Corn Exchange was converted into the Congress Hall. The Music Saloon in Wood Street and the Church Institute in Marygate were taken over by caterers. The offices of the Wakefield Charities in Market Street became a press room and the postmaster ensured that reports could be sent by electric telegraph to all parts of Britain. One of the country's leading clerical outfitters exhibited his garments in the Co-operative Society's store in Bank Street.

The Wakefield scheme had nothing like the financial support from wealthy merchants or landowners that other nineteenth-century bishoprics enjoyed. Wheatley-Balme was the only individual to contribute more than £1,000. Much of the money came from subscribers giving no more than a guinea. District Visitors and other collectors brought £645 from people who had little beyond pence to give. Offertories were held in many of the parishes of the Ripon Diocese. The sum from Huddersfield parish church was the second largest and amounted to £184. At Wakefield parish church the offertory was, at £175, the third largest. From Halifax, perhaps reflecting the disappointed hopes there, the offertory was fifty-second from the top of the table, a mere £18.

By 1888, the Wakefield Bishopric Fund had raised £83,510 19s 5d of which £79,857 was invested as an endowment. The Order in Council creating the bishopric was signed on 17 May 1888. It specified that All Saints parish church should be the cathedral.

The Diocese

The new diocese was created largely from the Ripon Archdeaconry of Craven but taking in also the parishes of Crofton, Warmfield and Woolley from York's Pontefract Rural Deanery. It lay between Heptonstall, to the north-west, Halifax, Drighlington and Morley to the north, Penistone and Barnsley to the south, Ripponden and Marsden to the west and Warmfield and Wakefield to the east, and included the industrial towns of Batley, Brighouse, Dewsbury, Halifax, Holmfirth, Huddersfield, Mirfield and Ossett, The two greatest centres of population were Halifax and Huddersfield.

It had 167 benefices including the chaplaincies of West Bretton, and Stainborough. Between 1836 (when the Diocese of Ripon was founded) and 1888, 105 churches in the new diocese had been consecrated. Eighty-two of these were new parish churches. Thirteen were parish churches that had been rebuilt or built on new sites. A further eight were mission churches or chapels of ease. The most recent of the new parish churches were St John the Baptist, Daw Green (1886), Hartshead St Peter with Clifton (1886), St Mark's, Huddersfield, and St Anne's, Southowram (1887). St Luke's, Sharlston, which was a daughter church in the parish of Warmfield, was also consecrated in 1887.

Those advowsons that had been held by the Bishop of Ripon or the Archbishop (as Bishop) of York were transferred to the successive bishops of Wakefield.

The diocese had six rural deaneries, more or less comparable to those taken from the Archdeaconry of Craven. The Ecclesiastical Commissioners had intended it to have a single archdeacon. However, the clergy in the new area petitioned them for a second and an Order in Council of 17 November 1888 provided for Archdeacons of both Halifax and Huddersfield, each to receive £200 a year from the Ecclesiastical Commissioners. Straton, the Vicar of Wakefield, and the other of the two secretaries of the Wakefield Bishopric Fund, was promptly appointed as the Archdeacon of Huddersfield to be followed, when Straton became Bishop of Sodor and Man in 1892, by the new Vicar of Wakefield, William Donne.

The Rural Deaneries of Halifax, Birstall and Dewsbury came within the Archdeaconry of Halifax, and those of Huddersfield, Silkstone and Wakefield were allocated to the Archdeaconry of Huddersfield. (The Halifax Rural Deanery, by then with some fifty parishes, was given a second Rural Dean in 1914 for an experimental period.)

The November 1888 Order allowed for twelve honorary canons which were to include the four priests who had been Canons of Ripon or York but were now in the Wakefield Diocese. The two Archdeacons were instituted and the first eight Canons installed on 4 December 1888.

There was already one Religious Order – the Community of St Peter, Horbury – within the boundaries of the diocese. When the Community of the Resurrection moved to Mirfield in 1898, it gained a second.

The boundaries of the diocese changed as populations continued to grow and new dioceses were formed. The major change came in 1926 under the Pontefract and Hemsworth Deaneries Transfer Measure, when the diocese was extended and the Rural Deaneries of Hemsworth and Pontefract, which had been until then in the Diocese of York, were added. This brought a further thirty-five parishes into the diocese. The Rural

Deanery of Silkstone was then renamed Barnsley, and the Rural Deanery of Pontefract was created. Midhope, which came into the Diocese of Sheffield at its foundation in 1914 but which was run in plurality with Penistone, was transferred to the Diocese of Wakefield in June of that year. Five years later, in 1919, the parishes of Tong and Wyke were transferred from Wakefield to the new Diocese of Bradford. When the Diocese of Blackburn was formed in 1927, from a part of the Diocese of Manchester, the parishes of Todmorden and Walsden were added to the Wakefield Diocese and the patronage of the two parishes was vested in the Bishop of Wakefield instead of the Bishop of Manchester.

Shortly after the 1926 extension of the diocese, the Archdeaconry of Huddersfield became the Archdeaconry of Halifax, and the hitherto Archdeaconry of Halifax became the Archdeaconry of Pontefract. The extension of the diocese provided an entitlement to six further honorary Canons.

The Bishops

Bishop How

Wakefield had three bishops in its first fifty years, William Walsham How in 1888–97, the long-serving George Rodney Eden, who was bishop in 1897–1928, and James Buchanan Seaton who died as the diocese celebrated its jubilee in 1938. After its major extension in 1926 made the assistance of a suffragan bishop highly desirable, Campbell Richard Hone, already the Archdeacon of Pontefract, became the first Bishop of Pontefract in 1931.

Wakefield's first bishop, William Walsham How (1823–97), had spent twenty-eight years as Rector of Whittington, Shropshire (his father had purchased the advowson) before, styled Bishop of Bedford, becoming a suffragan to the Bishop of London and Rector of St Andrew Undershaft in 1879. He was consecrated in St Paul's Cathedral on 25 July. In 1888, at sixty-four, and now a widower, How recoiled from the prospect of 'spending his declining years in a region of smoke, of coal pits, and mill chimneys' and shrank from the heavy task of organizing a new diocese, but regarded it as his simple duty to accept the challenge. He had a friend there already in Joshua Ingham Brooke, the Rector of Thornhill, whom he promptly appointed as his Archdeacon of Halifax. Another friend, William Foxley Norris, was presented by Sir John Ramsden to Almondbury in 1888. How's son Henry became Vicar of Mirfield in 1889. How had been educated at Shrewsbury School and Wadham College, Oxford, before going on to Durham for a course in Theology. He was, for a new diocese, primarily a safe pair of hands. He was of high-church leanings but was not an out-and-out Tractarian: he conducted retreats and held quiet days, but he abhorred some of the ritual associated with the Oxford Movement. The education and welfare of children were among his prime concerns and he was one of the original figures named as a trustee for the National Society for the Protection of Children when it gained its royal charter in 1895. It was under his influence that the Church of England Society for Waifs and Strays founded a boys' home, Bede House, in College Grove Road, Wakefield in 1892. He died on 10 August 1897 while on a fishing holiday in Ireland. Today he is best known for his hymns, in particular 'For all the saints who from their labours rest', which he wrote at Whittington and which was first published in 1864 in *Hymns for Saints Days and other Hymns.*

Unlike Bishop How, George Rodney Eden (1853–1940) had an accelerated career, at least until he reached Wakefield. He came from what used to be termed 'a good family', his grandfather, Sir Robert Eden, being the third baronet of West Auckland. He was educated at Richmond (Yorkshire) and Reading and gained a scholarship to Pembroke College, Cambridge. In 1879, shortly after his ordination as a priest, he was invited to serve as the chaplain to Joseph Barber Lightfoot, Bishop of Durham. Four years later he was presented to the living of Bishop Auckland. In 1890, he was consecrated at Canterbury as the Suffragan Bishop of Dover. He was

Bishop Eden

still only forty-four when he was enthroned at Wakefield on 4 November 1897. He took his seat in the House of Lords on 27 February 1905 where he was regarded as an authority on education. He was for a time chair of the Education Committee of the Church of England National Assembly. In Wakefield, Eden was in the forefront of some of the social movements. With Walter Moorhouse, he established the Wakefield Sanitary Aid Society. Pressure from this body contributed to the local authority's decision to clear the slums and build housing estates. With Edwin Hirst, he set up the Wakefield Garden Suburb Trust, acquiring a tract of land to the north of Dewsbury Road and then selling individual plots at modest prices to artisans or men from the lower middle class. An able administrator, he served at least once as secretary of the Lambeth Conference, staying for some weeks at Lambeth Palace. He retired in 1928 and spent some time in voluntary ministerial work in Egypt. An obituary in the *Cathedral News* in February 1940 spoke of the 'keenness and shrewdness of that fine face and clear-set eyes'. A memorial was unveiled in the cathedral at the time of the Diocesan Conference on 8 October 1942.

Wakefield's third bishop, James Buchanan Seaton (1868–1938), a bachelor and a moderate Anglo-Catholic in the *Lux Mundi* tradition, died in office. Seaton was a Yorkshireman to the extent that during the summer, he followed the fortunes of the county cricket team closely. He was born in Leeds and was educated at Leeds Grammar School where he gained a scholarship to Christ Church, Oxford in 1886. He took a Second in 'Greats' in 1890, and returned for a period to teach at Leeds Grammar School. He was made deacon in 1892 and priest in 1893. In 1893–96 he was a curate at Oswestry parish church. For the next four years he was the Vice-Principal of Leeds Clergy School (Leeds Theological College) before becoming Vicar of Armley in 1905–09. He spent the next five years in South Africa as Rector of St Mary's and Archdeacon of Johannesburg before returning to Oxfordshire in 1914, as the Principal of Cuddesdon Theological College and Vicar of Cuddesdon. He was made an honorary Canon of Christ Church, the Oxford cathedral. Appointed as Bishop of Wakefield in 1928, he was consecrated on 1 November in York Minster and enthroned on 30 November. Spoken of as a man of 'deep humility and boundless kindness and thoughtfulness', Seaton was able to relate easily to the miners and mill workers of his diocese as well as to the professional classes, and made himself readily accessible to all. Seaton's contribution in all his different spheres of work was not that of great achievements conceived and carried through, nor yet original enterprises in any particular direction. It was always and everywhere the same, namely himself and his personality. At the enlargement of the diocese in 1926, he set out to recruit more clergy and to obtain a suffragan bishop. He knew all his clergy well and entertained them at Bishopgarth. It seemed that he hated committees but loved working with young people. He held youth weekends at Bishopgarth for both males and females, hosting up to fifty at a time. He lived simply. He used to have his meals at a window in his study. He loved the Bishopgarth garden and enjoyed weeding the lawns. He 'seldom said or did things that interested the press', and was not a good platform speaker. He was, however, a keen supporter of the work of the church overseas and the translation of one of his young clergy to the See of Gambia must have given him immense pleasure.

The Cathedral

Under the Order in Council of 17 May 1888, Wakefield's medieval parish church became the cathedral of the new diocese. Bishop How's first ordination, of four deacons and two priests, took place there ten days later, even before his enthronement.

Wakefield Cathedral about 1900

The installation and enthronement of the first bishop on 25 June 1888 was a major event both for the town and for the diocese, celebrated by the Mayor and Corporation as well as by the churches. It included a reception in the Town Hall when a series of illuminated addresses were read, and a lunch, presided over by the Archbishop of York, William Thomson, in the Corn Exchange before the procession to the new cathedral.

As a consequence of now having a cathedral, Wakefield became a city by Letters Patent dated 11 July 1888.

At Bishop How's enthronement, the Archbishop of York pointed out that the cathedral was inadequate for its new purpose and also urged the church people from across the diocese to support it financially. The first of his points was met when the extension to the east was completed in 1905 as a memorial to How. The second remained a perennial problem.

Planning for the cathedral extension began within two months of How's death. An appeal was launched for £50,000, and John Loughborough Pearson, architect of the new cathedral at Truro, was commissioned to provide the designs, although the work was completed after his death under the direction of his son Frank. The slope of Kirkgate allowed Pearson to provide a crypt with a chapter house and vestries. The high-gothic scheme included lengthening the chancel, creating the Chapel of St Mark beyond it at the eastern end, and building north and south transepts. The foundation stone was laid by the Archbishop of Canterbury, Frederick Temple, on 18 June 1901. Work was soon to be suspended until further money was raised. Eventually £48,286 was subscribed and the extension was consecrated on St Mark's Day, 25 April 1905.

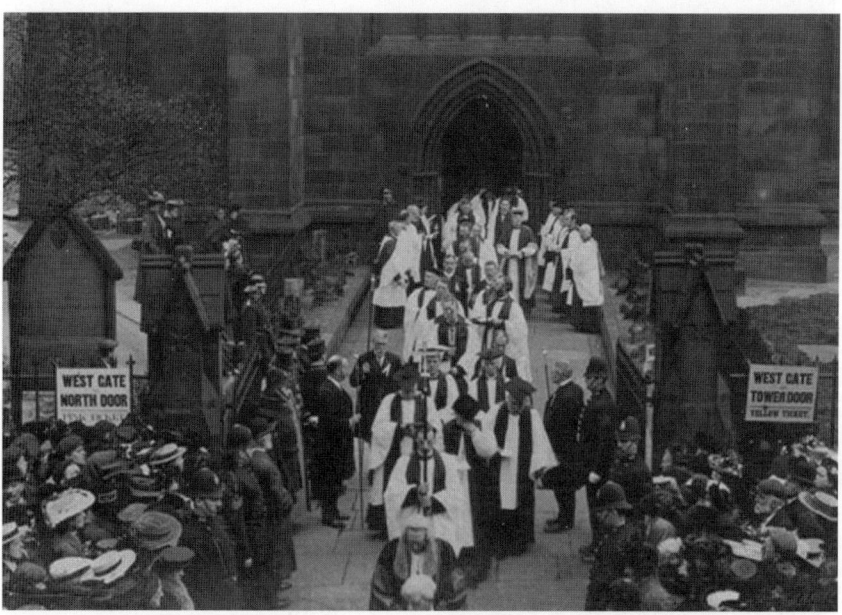

The procession on 25 April 1905

The numerous niches on the outside of the vast east wall never held the figures for which they had been designed. The new chancel was consecrated on 27 December 1905.

The clerk of works was a Mr Crooks from Bristol Cathedral, and the main contractors were Armitage and Hodgson. The extension furnishings, including carpets from the East, were overseen by a ladies' committee headed by the bishop's wife, Constance Mary Eden. An altar cloth was worked by the Sisters of St Peter's Convent. A monument to How in the form of a white marble tomb chest with a recumbent effigy by J. Nesfield Forsyth was placed in the south transept.

The memorial to Bishop How

Later memorials to the successive bishops and to some archdeacons have been placed within the extension. A memorial window to the diocese's first registrar, William Francis Lovell Horne, who died in 1911, was added to St Mark's Chapel.

Prior to the completion of the extension, Bishop Eden set up a committee to consider 'the mutual relations of the diocesan and parochial authorities in Wakefield Cathedral'. A memorandum of 1905 focused on the lack of endowments, the adjustment of the legal position of cathedral and parish church, and the liabilities for the maintenance of the extension which could not 'fairly be met by the parish only'. In a lecture in 1908 on the cathedral, William Donne claimed that the extension cost £110 a year to maintain but that there had not been much support from the diocese.

A Cathedral Management Committee was set up in 1910 under the chairmanship of the bishop, with equal representation from the cathedral and from the diocese

The Sanctuary was enhanced in 1912 by the addition of stone canopied sedilia and a credence on the south side with a bishop's and chaplain's seat opposite them. The bishop's seat was flanked by the figures of St Paulinus and William Walsham How. Designed by Frank Loughborough Pearson and executed by Nathaniel Hitch, they were given as a memorial to the baronets Robert and Tristram Tempest of Tong Hall.

The Cathedral Sanctuary, Harriet Evans

It is thought that a great stone cross was erected towards the end of the tenth century close to the cathedral site, marking a preaching station. Such a cross was found in 1861 at a butcher's shop in Westgate where, lying on its side, it was used as a doorstep. It was taken some years later to the Yorkshire Philosophical Society's museum in York. In 1933 a replica of the cross was provided by Wakefield Historical Society and placed in the south transept.

Unlike the old cathedrals, Wakefield was and is a parish church as well as the mother church of the diocese. The Vicar of Wakefield had to serve as a parish priest, with attendant civic as well as pastoral responsibilities, but was also a significant figure at diocesan level. In the early years, both Norman Straton and his successor, William Donne, had the diocesan status of archdeacon. No subsequent vicars of Wakefield did. Under the Cathedrals Measures of 1931 and 1934, and an Order in Council of 1937, the Vicar of Wakefield gained the title of Provost, adopted at the time by the heads of all the new cathedrals, defining an office 'which would be distinct from that usually associated with Crown patronage'.

Before the Reformation, the parish church had had a Lady Chapel, founded in 1322. When this was revived in 1935 it was fitted up with an altar provided as a memorial to Canon McLeod who had been the Vicar of Wakefield from 1919.

St Mark's Chapel gained new features in 1943, making use of a bequest by Miss Margaret Percy Tew. The beaten-metal altar front and carved and gilded reredos were designed by Sir Charles Nicholson. The altar rails, again designed by Nicholson, were made by Robert Thompson of Kilburn and bear his trademark mouse.

A House for the Bishop

At the suggestion of Bishop William Boyd Carpenter, a separate fund was established in 1885 to provide a house for the bishop. Fund-raising was led by Carpenter's wife who enlisted an impressive team of other women to canvass individual rural deaneries and run bazaars. By February 1888, a little over £10,000 had been raised. It was an open question as to whether a house would be bought or built. The purchase of Thornes House, Wakefield, was an early suggestion.

When Bishop How first came to Wakefield, he stayed at Thornhill Rectory, which had been made available to him by his old friend, Canon Brooke. He moved quite soon to a house in South Parade, Wakefield, rented from Michael Edwin Sanderson, later to be the diocese's greatest benefactor. In 1889, he moved to Overthorpe, Thornhill. He found living in either Wakefield or Thornhill inconvenient as almost every journey across the diocese meant changing trains at Mirfield junction, described by his son as 'the gloomiest and draughtiest of all stations'. How would have liked to live in Mirfield and a substantial property, Hall Croft, became a candidate but the Ecclesiastical Commissioners were anxious for the bishop to live nearer to, or in, his cathedral city. By 1890, a three-acre site had been acquired in the highly respectable St John's area of Wakefield. William White, a colleague of George Gilbert Scott, was commissioned as the architect, and the foundation stone of the new brick Gothic 'palace' was laid on 24 October 1891. How moved into the mansion in 1893. The name Bishopgarth was chosen by the four men who had guaranteed to the Ecclesiastical Commissioners that a house would be provided. The term 'garth', derived from a Norse word for a yard and could mean an enclosure or a Manor House. The name was given to a hymn tune composed in 1897 for Queen Victoria's jubilee by Arthur Sullivan to How's words 'O King of Kings whose reign of old hath been from everlasting'.

Bishopgarth

Bishopgarth was fitted with electric lighting in 1908, long before many of the parish churches.

Bishop How's successor, George Rodney Eden, lived at Bishopgarth for some twenty years. However, in August 1918, he announced that high taxation and the high cost of living made it impossible for him to continue in residence there. It was immediately requisitioned by the Ministry of Pensions but was later let to the West Riding County Council. Eden moved to the Manor House at Heath where he remained for the rest of his period as bishop. A chapel was created there and, *inter alia*, was used for at least one confirmation service. James Seaton, Wakefield's third bishop, lived at Heath for a short while but in April 1929 he declared his intention to move to Bishopgarth. He died there in 1938. As Archdeacon of Pontefract, Campbell Richard Hone had bought Woodthorpe Lodge with nine acres of grounds, a paddock, some woodland, a lawn and both flower and kitchen gardens. When he followed Seaton as Bishop of Wakefield in 1938, he insisted on remaining there. He described Bishopgarth as 'a most inconvenient and badly planned house', with 'dark passages and small cubicle rooms for ordination candidates, a range of necessary rooms under the roof and awkward larders and kitchens'. His wife said that it was 'quite impossible' and that she could not manage it with all its inconveniences and the shortage of servants. Renamed Bishop's Lodge, the house at Woodthorpe was bought by the Ecclesiastical Commissioners. All subsequent bishops have lived there. Bishopgarth was sold to the West Riding County Council.

The Principal Administrative Bodies

In October 1888, Bishop How held a meeting of clergy and laity in the Wakefield Church Institute to establish the principal Diocesan societies: these were the Wakefield Diocesan Church Extension Society (which was to assist with funding both churches and parsonage houses), the Diocesan Board of Education (which was to contribute towards school buildings, teachers and the teacher training college at Ripon), and the Bishop of Wakefield's Spiritual Aid Fund (for increasing stipends, providing visiting clergy during the sickness of an incumbent, helping to fund temporary rest for overworked clergy, and assisting infirm or aged clergy to retire). The Board of Education worked conjointly with the Ripon Diocesan Board of Education until January 1890.

An appeal was made at the October meeting (and many times subsequently) for donors to the funds who might give a single capital sum or promise an annual subscription. The initial subscription list was short and the sums promised, typically of the diocese, only modest. The donors could indicate which of the three funds they were supporting and it was soon clear that most regarded the Spiritual Aid Fund as the most important. In their first year the Church Extension Society received £742, the Board of Education £597, and the Spiritual Aid Society £3,650, including one donation of £1,000 earmarked for the parish of St Luke's, Heckmondwike.

In May 1908, the different funds were brought together under the new umbrella of the Wakefield Diocesan Fund and the office of Organizing Secretary was established. A Diocesan Loan Fund was founded in 1911 to further assist church extension.

Wakefield Diocesan Church Organization Society was founded in 1894 as a limited company to hold trusts and land on behalf of the diocese. It became, *inter alia*, the trustee of parochial property used partly for religious and partly for secular purposes since this could not be vested in the minister and churchwardens but only in an incorporated body.

Bishop How held his first (and apparently only) synod on 29 April 1889. Some 250–300 clergy walked in procession, to the gaze of numerous bystanders, wearing their surplices, college hoods and caps, from the Church Institute in Marygate to the cathedral for a communion service led by How and the two Archdeacons. From the pulpit, How observed that he saw no need for the synod to meet either regularly or frequently. He referred to the importance of the laity in diocesan affairs. He spoke of the necessity, among the clergy, for personal holiness, pastoral activity, and their own daily prayer. He referred to the disputes over ritual then dividing the church, called for tolerance of the different positions and said that 'there are but few now who rejoice in the spectacle of prosecution of ritual offenders' although he added that, in his view, ritualism went against the spirit of loyalty to the church.

At the afternoon meeting in the Church Institute, How returned to the matter of the laity and spoke of having decided at the outset of his tenure to set up a Diocesan Conference. The Conference, presided over by the bishop, was to be the principal forum of the diocese and was to have no more than 460 members. Clerical members included the Archdeacons, Rural Deans, Proctors in Convocation, and all beneficed clergy. Unbeneficed clergy who had held the bishop's licence as priests for two years, were also included. The Diocesan Chancellor and the Registrar were among the lay members, together with one representative from each parish, with a second from parishes with a population of over 4,500. Lay members were to be elected triennially in each parish by male communicants aged over twenty-one. The bishop could himself nominate ten people – clerical or lay – as members. The Conference was to elect a standing committee to be charged with its general business.

The first Conference was held on 22 and 23 October 1889, in the hall of Wakefield Mechanics Institute (popularly known as the Music Saloon although strictly the term applied only to its upper floor hall). The bishop spoke of the Conference aims to make the Church in the diocese as efficient as possible and to raise the 'lofty standard of religion and of spiritual life among the people'. A committee was appointed to draw up a scheme for the Diocesan Board of Education which would be needed in January 1890 when the new diocese became independent of the Ripon Board.

Throughout the period under consideration and indeed until it was replaced in 1971 by Synodical government, the Conference normally took place annually over two days in October, meeting in various halls and churches across the diocese. It received reports from all diocesan organizations and heard papers on key issues affecting the Church nationally or at diocesan level.

The Conference also passed resolutions on many issues, including pending parliamentary action. Early in its life, for example, there was a special meeting in April 1883 to debate a motion opposing the Welsh Suspensory Bill which was to disestablish the Church in Wales. Education was a major and perennial issue in the first decades of the diocese. In 1908, at the time of an Education Bill aimed at reversing some of the provisions of the 1870 Education Act, the Conference placed on record its 'deliberate conviction that there is no hope of any arrangement of the Education Question affording any permanent settlement or lasting peace, which does not secure – as far as it is possible to secure it – the opportunity of full church teaching for all children whose parents desire it, given by qualified teachers who are themselves members of the Church'.

From time to time the Conference focused, too, on social questions. The 1907 Conference, for example, heard a paper on housing reform (a matter in which Bishop Eden was especially interested) by Canon Moore Ede of Gateshead, who referred to the value of town planning, to co-operative house building on lines known as Tenants Limited, and to garden cities. In 1923, the Conference focused on birth control and the instruction of the young in the 'laws' of sex.

Licensed but unbeneficed priests living at the Community of the Resurrection in Mirfield were included in the membership of the Conference. This brought it one of the best minds in the Church at the time, Walter Howard Frere (1863–1938), an outstanding liturgical scholar who had been one of the six original members of the Community and who was the Superior at Mirfield in 1902–13 and 1916–22.

Changes in the diocesan organization reflected those at national level. Prompted, it seems, by the great Pan-Anglican Congress of 1908, the two Archbishops set up a committee to look into the organization and financing of the churches. In the light of the committee's recommendations, the financial organization of the Wakefield Diocese was reshaped. Canon Richard Phipps, who had come to Wakefield as a curate at the cathedral in 1892, resigned the living of Brighouse in 1912 to become the Wakefield Diocesan Secretary, and, in anticipation of the national scheme, he masterminded a restructuring of the financial organizations of the diocese. Under his guidance, and after agreement at the 1912 Diocesan Conference, the over-arching Wakefield Diocesan Board of Finance was established, to take control from 1 January 1914, of the Wakefield Diocesan Education Society and the Wakefield Diocesan Fund (which held both the Wakefield Church Extension Fund and the Spiritual Aid Fund). From then onwards, the Conference, which was the supreme authority in matters of finance, had responsibility for determining the sum needed each year for diocesan expenditure.

The new scheme set out seven areas of church work and the diocesan bodies which would come under each:

- Training for the ministry
  Ordination Candidates' Fund.

- Maintenance of the ministry, clerical and lay
  The Bishop of Wakefield's Spiritual Aid Society.
  The Wakefield Church Extension Society (object iii).

- Provision of pensions for the ministry
  The Wakefield Clergy Pensions Fund.

- Provision for widows and orphans of the clergy and for necessitous clergy
  The West Riding Charitable Society Ripon and Wakefield section.
  The Queen Victoria Clergy Fund.
  (Neither of these was strictly diocesan but could be used by the Board of Finance as distributing agencies.)

- The erection of church buildings
  The Wakefield Church Extension Society.
  The Wakefield Diocesan Loan Fund.
  The Cathedral Sustentation Fund.

- Religious education of the young
  The Wakefield Diocesan Education Society.
  The Diocesan Association of Church Schools.
  The Wakefield Diocesan Sunday Schools Association.

- Provision for expenses of diocesan and central organizations
  General Purposes Fund.

The Conference had the responsibility of appointing the Board of Finance.

Until 1912, giving by parishes towards the expenses of diocesan administration was entirely random (or so it seems). The sums contributed were very widely varied depending in part, but in part only, on the size and affluence of the parish. In 1911, the smallest sum contributed, 19s 4d, came from Farnley Tyas. The parish of Dewsbury gave £58. At the 1911

Diocesan Conference the scheme for quota payments was introduced, with parishes being assessed against a variety of criteria and then informed of the size of contribution required in the following year 'to meet the diocesan and central needs of the church'. Free-will offering schemes were strongly recommended. The system was, inevitably, widely resented albeit utterly essential. In 1930 a report was made to the parochial church council of Holy Trinity, Wakefield, observing that Holy Trinity had always considered the payment of the quota as its first duty. The note adds the wry observation that it was 'almost alone' in the diocese in taking this view initially.

In 1913, Phipps, who had private means, moved into Manygates House, Sandal, a substantial dwelling lying in some six acres of parkland and 'pleasure grounds'. In the absence at the time of any other diocesan administrative base, the house became the centre for meetings of the Diocesan Board of Finance and other committees.

Diocesan conferences gained a place in the national administrative structure in 1920 when the Church Assembly was established after the seminal report of 1916, *Church and State*, had argued that Parliament had 'neither the leisure, fitness nor inclination to perform efficiently the functions of ecclesiastical legislature'. The Assembly was made up of a House of Bishops, a House of Clergy and a House of Laity. Under the Church Assembly (Powers) Act of 1919 it could pass measures which, if approved by Parliament, received Royal assent, just as Acts of Parliament would do, and became part of the statute law of England. Effectively the state church gained a high degree of self-government. Diocesan conferences elected their representatives to serve for three-year periods in the House of Laity. Parochial Church Councils and the attendant Electoral Rolls became mandatory. The number of parochial representatives on the Diocesan Conference depended from 1921 on the size of the electoral roll rather than on the number of communicants.

The Diocesan Board of Patronage was established in 1920. The Diocesan Dilapidations Board came into being in November 1923 under the new Church Assembly's Ecclesiastical Dilapidations Measure of that year. Its concern was with the state of repair and the maintenance of parsonage houses. It had to appoint surveyors, and any further alteration to the houses could be made only with the Board's consent. It was accepted that the Board might itself have to instigate repairs and would then need to recover costs.

The diocese had perhaps no permanent office until 1923 when it made use of 5a South Parade, although certainly for a time in the 1890s its administrative headquarters was in Manor House Yard, close to the cathedral. Then, in 1925, through the gift of Miss Mary Thompson, it acquired 1 South Parade which was given the name of Church House. The house was both opened and dedicated, by Bishop Eden, on 4 November.

There were very few synods. The first since the time of Bishop How was held on 10 and 11 May 1921, when Bishop Eden expressed concern at the comparatively small number of candidates from the diocese coming forward for ordination, and went over the resolutions from the Lambeth Conference and York Convocation.

Church House

Other Diocesan Organizations

Bishop How established a Diocesan Lay Readers Association (for men only) in 1889. Anyone with a licence from Ripon would be granted his licence. Others could get one, it was announced, by passing a simple examination on the Bible and the prayer book and by satisfying the bishop as to his moral character and fitness for the office. All Lay Readers would get a licence which would hold good throughout the diocese and, if an incumbent requested it, would also be given a commission to exercise the office in a particular parish. Perhaps it should be noted that, although 'Reader' has always been the formal designation, until recent years 'Lay Reader' was much more commonly used within the diocese, even in issues of the *Diocesan Gazette* and the *Wakefield Diocesan News*. For the sake of consistency, 'Reader' has been adopted hereafter.

The Diocesan Council of Girls' Friendly Societies was established in 1891 by Edith How, the bishop's daughter-in-law, who came with her husband to live at Bishopgarth with the widowed bishop.

A Diocesan Board of Missions was formed in 1905. It was designed to promote the work within the diocese to support missionary work abroad and, to this end, to plan missionary exhibitions and festivals within the diocese.

The Diocesan Sunday School Teachers' Association was founded on 27 June 1908, bringing together a number of smaller bodies.

Bishop Eden formed the Diocesan Board of Readers in 1921. At the time he explained, 'In the increasing scarcity of clergy, we are convinced that a real call is coming, especially to our educated laymen, for all earnest and sincere church people to take an active part in the evangelistic work of the church.' The aim of the Board was to raise standards and to arrange and supervise conferences. A first diocesan admission service for Readers was held at the cathedral on 6 May 1922. Sixty-six Readers were admitted into the new office. Each attended in the Chapter House to sign a new roll and make a declaration. They were presented by Archdeacon Harvey as the Warden of Readers. W. H. Coles served as the registrar for the new organization. Bishop Eden said that the service marked an epoch in the long and chequered history of the Readers' movement which had been revived in the 1870s. Formerly it was only a diocesan office. Now Readers were admitted into a Corporate Body for the whole Church of England.

In 1930, Bishop Seaton formed a Diocesan Council of Youth.

New Churches, New Mission Rooms and New Parishes

The fundamental concerns of the diocese in its first fifty years were the provision of further churches to serve a growing population and the clergy to staff them, and the gathering of the flocks to attend them. Pressures for new churches came from the spread of housing into the suburbs, the emergence of council-housing estates, and the development of a new community serving a colliery. The churches might be built for new parishes, or in areas designated as conventional districts which might later become independent parishes, or chapels of ease (consecrated buildings in the same parish as, but at a distance from, a parish church) or as mission churches (licensed for worship but not consecrated). Where there was little hope of finance for a church building, Commissioners looking at the needs of the diocese advocated the opening of mission rooms.

Not infrequently, new congregations were brought together in these mission rooms, perhaps making use of an existing church school. A temporary mission chapel might follow. As funds slowly accumulated (or if a prosperous benefactor emerged) a permanent church might ensue. The lack of money, in particular, meant that the fulfilment of new-church schemes might take a long time, as much as twenty years or more.

While the landed classes had been generous in building and endowing churches in the area in the past, the new diocese now enjoyed relatively little of their support. Some still gave sites for new churches (Lord Dartmouth, for example, provided the site for St Andrew's at Bruntcliffe) but these might come, too, from industrial concerns or from a local authority which had acquired land for housing.

The process of church building and of establishing new parishes had continued independently of the expectation of a new diocese so that Bishop How's earliest act of consecration, on 27 May 1889, was of one of the churches planned before the see was created. St Luke's, Heckmondwike, was on a site given by the Low Moor Iron Company. The parish had been formed in 1878. Services had taken place first at the National School and then in a temporary iron church. Typically for the period the church was designed (by Medland Taylor of Manchester) in a Gothic style, specified at the time as 'geometrical decorated'. An endowment had been provided by Mrs Woodhead of Moor House.

Lack of funding meant that a church might be partially completed years before the overall design was accomplished. An example of the not unusual struggle was the forty-year gestation of St Peter's, Barnsley. Its history went back to 1872 when a schoolroom was built on Doncaster Road as a mission for St Mary's, Barnsley's parish church. Two years later a visiting priest conducted a mission in the vicinity which resulted in the drawing together of a congregation. One of St Mary's curates, John Lloyd Brereton, was given charge. Plans for a church were drawn up by the Hampstead architect Temple Lushington Moore (1856–1920), but fund-raising was dismally slow. By 1883, a large enough endowment had been amassed to provide a stipend of £150 a year and the new parish was formed with Brereton as its first vicar. Three years later, in 1886, a temporary nave was built on the site planned for the church, next to the schoolroom. By 1892, a more extensive and permanent building could be envisaged and the cornerstone was laid in January of that year. At the time, Brereton referred to the 'slow and uphill struggle' and observed that when he had first gone there, the local people had little idea of what a church was and thought it was something for the upper classes. In October 1993, Bishop How consecrated the still-temporary nave and the newly added chancel, side aisles and vestries. With the church still unfinished in 1908, a public meeting was held in Barnsley's Arcade Hall when the Rector of Barnsley, Canon Foxley Norris, said that the parish still had only half a church and no parsonage house and that out of a stipend of £160 the vicar was spending £40–£50 on rented accommodation. A committee was established with representatives from the church councils of each of the Barnsley parishes to remedy the situation. The foundation stone of the new nave was laid on 2 July 1910 and the completed church was consecrated on 14 December 1911.

Each of Wakefield's first three bishops set up a Commission of Enquiry into the 'wants and requirements' of the diocese, How in January 1889 within a year of his installation, Eden in 1907 when he had already been in the diocese for nine years by which time many of the proposals of How's Commission had been met, and Seaton in 1929 when, with a somewhat changed brief, the Commission was asked to report on cases where existing churches and mission rooms appeared to be unnecessary.

How's Commission included both his archdeacons, all six rural deans, a further member of clergy from each of the deaneries, and a number of lay people. It considered not only the need for more churches but the situation in regard to church schools, and the question of whether there were advowsons which could be transferred to the bishop. Its report, which was published in March 1890, noted that it was always difficult to secure the endowments required for new parishes and that the funds at the disposal of the Ecclesiastical Commissioners to contribute to them had been seriously diminished. Hence the Report, published on 5 March 1890, recommended the formation of only a modest number of new parishes. Two further parishes were needed in the Dewsbury Deanery, where steps had already been taken to create one at Bruntcliife, to serve Purlwell, and Gawthorpe with Chickenley Heath. In the Halifax Deanery they were needed to serve a rapidly developing suburb in the Queen's Road area, and in the centre of Todmorden. Both Marsh and Crosland Moor, in the Huddersfield Deanery, warranted new parishes. St Jude's, a newly built chapel of ease at Salterhebble, which was almost ready for consecration, might also serve a new parish. Adjustments were suggested to the boundaries of other parishes and the Report recommended the creation within existing parishes of further chapels of ease, mission churches and mission rooms. A new parish of Horbury Junction had been formed, with services held in a mission room, but a new church was needed.

Bishop How, in a rather low-key manner, issued an appeal for £50,000 to meet the recommendations in the Report. Typically it met only a modest response. In its first year it raised £13,670 but by the time of the 1898 conference it had realized only £27,000. It was wound up the following year.

Very gradually most of the recommendations were met. St Jude's was consecrated on 30 November 1890 and the area became a district chapelry in January 1891. The church of St Mary the Virgin, Horbury Junction, the third Anglican church in the village of Horbury, was consecrated on 10 October 1893. The new parish of Crosland Moor was established by Order in Council in 1893 after Sir Joseph Crosland offered £1,000 towards building the church. Bishop How did not live to see the church itself, however. The memorial stone for St Barnabas was laid by Bishop Eden on 4 August 1900. The church was consecrated on 4 October

1902. (Its west end was completed, although without its planned tower, in 1958.)

Before his death in 1897, Bishop How had licensed or consecrated more than twenty chapels of ease, mission churches or mission rooms. Some were merely rooms within a church school, as at Northowram, some were temporary iron churches erected cheaply in the hope that, in due course, a new church would be built and possibly a new parish established, and some were handsome daughter churches like St Aidan's, Skelmanthorpe. This had been designed by George Frederick Bodley (1827–1907) for the parish of Scissett. It was consecrated on 28 September 1895 and became a separate parish in 1900. The last church that How consecrated, in 1896, was St Saviour's, Heckmondwike, which was provided by Edward Wheatley-Balme as a chapel of ease, and which replaced an iron church. Iron churches, popular and cheap, were eminently capable of recycling. This one had come from St Luke's Cleckheaton in 1889 and went on to Jeremy Lane, Heckmondwike, for use as a Sunday School room.

One of How's last acts was to agree with Edward Simpson of Walton Hall the site for St Paul's mission church in Walton. It was another iron building and had been constructed in London and brought in sections by rail to Walton. It was dedicated on 10 January 1898 by Bishop Eden.

In August 1900, Lord Savile laid the memorial stone of All Saints, the chapel of ease at Elland. It was the new peer's first visit to the diocese since he had acceded to the title, and a formal address of welcome was given. The architect was E. H. Fellowes Prynne but the intention, not unusually, was to build just the chancel, with vestries below it, and the first part of the nave. The north and south transepts would follow when finances permitted. For a time in 1903 work came to a standstill because of lack of money but in November 1903 the chancel and transepts were dedicated by Archdeacon Brooke. A debt of £5,000 meant that there could be no consecration. When consecration came, in May 1912, the church was spoken of as 'a noble ideal pursued with faith and tenacity, through almost unspeakable difficulties'.

In the Halifax Deanery, a separate scheme for church extension in the town and district was inaugurated at a meeting on 6 November 1900. Its objects were to obtain sites, build and enlarge churches and mission churches, and make grants towards the stipends of additional clergy. It was accepted that in regard to the last item it would co-operate with the Diocesan Spiritual Aid Society. In consequence, in 1902, the Halifax and Rural Deanery Church Extension Society was formed and proposed the creation of a new parish carved out of King Cross and Mount Pellon (already mooted by How's Commissioners), a new parish near Brighouse

Station carved out of the parish of Rastrick, and a stone church to replace the iron one at Siddal. It identified the need for mission rooms at Bailiff Bridge, Norwood Green, Hove Edge, Wainstalls, Luddendenfoot and Midgley.

In some few places, new churches were provided without struggle by individual benefactors. How's Commissioners' Report had noted the desire for a mission church at Cornholme, Harley Wood, at the northwestern end of the diocese. An iron chapel opened there in 1896. The handsome stone church of St Michael and All Angels, which replaced it, designed by C. Hodgson Fowler, was consecrated on 27 September 1902, the full cost being borne by Mrs A. Master-Whitaker, wife of the Vicar of Helme, who secured an endowment of £120 to provide for a Curate in Charge. Cornholme became a district chapelry a year later.

At Thurlstone, in the geographically vast parish of Penistone which covered thirty-four square miles and had a population of over nine thousand living in scattered hamlets, a chapel of ease was, the Commissioners had said, 'much needed'. It had to await benefactors. The sisters Mary and Hannah Bray, who died in 1895 and 1897, left the residue of their estates in trust to the Vicar of Penistone and the Bishop of Wakefield (in all some £5,000) towards it. Captain Vernon Wentworth of Stainborough Hall (Wentworth Castle) made a grant towards the provision of a Curate in

St Saviour's, Thurlstone

Charge. St Saviour's was another of the churches designed by C. Hodgson Fowler. Its foundation stone was laid on 5 November 1904. The church was consecrated on 9 December 1905. Fowler's plan had been for a tower at the west end of the church. However, this was never built and the west end was 'temporarily' completed (it still is) with a brick wall where the rest of the church is in the local millstone grit.

If St Peter's, Barnsley, took many years to complete, the church of St Edward the Confessor, serving the Kingstone area at the western end of the town, was, as it were, handed to the diocese on a plate. It came quite independently of any recommendation by How's Commission. It was surely the most sumptuous of the new churches in the diocese, and was built and endowed by Edward Lancaster of Keresforth Hall in memory of his parents. Early English in style, it was modelled on a church in Southport designed by same architect, Goodwin S. Packer. The memorial stone was laid by Lancaster's daughter, Mrs Fanny Jane Shaw, on 5 October 1900, and the completed building was dedicated and consecrated by Bishop Eden on 13 November 1902. The church, which had a clerestory, side aisles and a mosaic-floored chancel, was designed to seat 400, with a large crypt containing a meeting room with stage, and a vestry with a robing room. Another ground-floor vestry was converted into a Lady Chapel in 1910. No expense was spared on the materials. It had granite columns, pews of pitch pine, choir stalls of oak, an octagonal alabaster pulpit and matching octagonal font by Norbury, Paterson and Co. of Liverpool. There was a reredos in English alabaster and Italian marble by Harry Henry and Son, Exeter. Lancaster also provided a seven-bedroom vicarage. A good deal of house-building was taking place in the area and a new parish was formed from parts of St George's and St John's.

Neither of the new parishes proposed at Purlwell and the Queen's Road area of Halifax had come into being when, after nine years as its bishop, Eden commissioned a new report in 1907 on the needs of the diocese. In the period since Bishop How's Commission had reported, the diocese had gained three 'fully equipped' parishes, five chapels of ease, and twenty-one mission churches and mission rooms. There had also been an increase in the number of curates and Readers. Among the mission churches was St Hilda's, King Cross, which had been opened in 1898 as a memorial to Bishop How. In 1909 Eden's Commissioners recommended this as the church for the previously suggested parish in the Queen's Road area. The need for a parish at Purlwell was also reiterated. But otherwise, rather than proposing further new parishes, the Report advised that 'at least' three conventional districts – lying within an existing parish but with their own Curates in Charge – should be formed. These were needed where a colliery or mill had developed its own population. In due course they might become separate parishes. The Report looked for the completion of three partially built churches and the provision of nine parsonage houses, including one for each of the two new parishes and others for parishes where no parsonage had yet been built or to replace an existing but insanitary house. It urged that steps should be taken towards the erection of four more chapels of ease, ten mission churches (six of them taking the place of existing mission rooms) and twenty-three new mission rooms. One parish was to be taken back into the parish from which it had been divided. Three existing parish churches, which were now too small for an expanding population, should be replaced by new churches. The report also recommended some rearrangement of parish boundaries and some rearrangement of parishes within rural deaneries. It noted that the present supply of clergy was totally inadequate and that fifty-seven parishes needed further staff. A body of special-service clergy was needed, too, for hospitals and other public institutions. The Report was of course followed by an appeal for the money, this time with a rather greater fanfare!

How's appeal for funds to meet the recommendations of his Report had been launched quietly. Not so Bishop Eden's! Randall Davidson, the Archbishop of Canterbury, came to Wakefield in the summer of 1910 to initiate it. He stayed at Bishopgarth overnight before being given a civic welcome in the Council Chamber of Wakefield Town Hall on the morning of 25 June. A public lunch for 500 people, with a menu described by the *Wakefield Herald* as 'recherché', took place on the ground floor of the Corn Exchange before the company moved upstairs to the assembly room for the formal speeches. The event, possibly the last such occasion in the diocese, was attended by many of the leading aristocracy and gentry from the county. They included Earl Fitzwilliam, the Earls of Dartmouth, Harewood and Scarborough, Lord Allendale, Lord Savile, Lord St Oswald, Sir George Armytage, Sir Edward Green, Sir Thomas Pilkington, Sir John Ramsden, Sir Walter Stanhope, and the Right Honourable Charles George Milnes Gaskell. Davidson referred to a link between himself and Wakefield when he spoke of a predecessor, Archbishop Potter, who had been a Wakefield man, and remarked that he had a portrait at Lambeth Palace of Potter as a boy of eight evidently reading from a Greek Testament. Bishop Eden spoke of the need to raise some £6,500 a year – more than twice the current level of donations – to provide a further £3,000 for the Spiritual Aid Fund, £1,500 for the Church Extension Fund, and £2,000 towards Education.

Among the parish churches that Eden's Commissioners identified as too small was St Paul's at King Cross, Halifax. The parish had been taken from the parish of Halifax in 1846 and the church had been consecrated in 1847. Although parts of the parish had been taken into St Hilda's and St Jude's, it still had some 15,000 or 16,000 inhabitants. The original church seated 450. Its replacement, on a nearby site, was designed by Sir Charles Nicholson and was his first major commission in the diocese. The new St Paul's was consecrated on 26 October 1912.

When Bishop Eden consecrated St Matthew's, Northowram, on 31 May 1913, he noted that it was the third church in the Borough of Halifax that he had consecrated in three years. Hitherto, the old school had served as a mission church. The church was the gift of George Watkinson (d.1961) who had been the curate at Coley but who became the first vicar of the new parish. The cost of the tower was defrayed by his brother, S. L. Watkinson. The architects were Walsh and Nicholson of Halifax and the style was described as 'Halifax vernacular' or fifteenth-century English Gothic, and subsequently as 'Arts and Crafts Gothic'. The nave and aisles were lined with diamond-shaped brown quarry tiles from Nostell. The site had been a quarry.

The war and the ensuing depression led to a period of stagnation before further churches were built. By 1924, shortly before its major expansion, the diocese had 177 parishes (those worked in plurality counting as one). Ten had a population of over 10,000 while, at the other end of the scale, fourteen had a population of under 1,000, Wilshaw being the smallest at 232.

New house-building programmes prompted the building of St Cuthbert's, Birkby, in 1925, with the intention of creating the first new parish in the diocese for many years. The architect was A. H. Hoare who, more than a decade earlier, had designed St Andrew's, Purlwell. The foundation stone was laid by Lord Halifax on 2 May of a church which would initially have just a chancel, a part of the nave, and part of the south aisle. The partially built church, with a temporary west end, was consecrated on 23 August 1926 and the area, until then a conventional district, became a separate parish in 1933. (The west end was completed in 1956.)

Local authority building schemes, providing substantial housing estates, brought a new challenge to the diocese. Wakefield Corporation embarked on its great Lupset estate in the early 1920s. A three-acre site was given by the vendors of the Snapethorpe estate, the Old Roundwood Colliery Company, and earmarked in 1926 for an Anglican church (Methodist and Roman Catholic churches were also built to serve the estate) and an appeal was launched for funds in May 1928 when the area had 1,400 new houses and a population of over 7,000. Initially only a parish hall-cum-mission room was built. The church itself, in a modern style breaking away from the Gothic, was built from stone from a demolished woollen mill and from the old Wakefield Registry of Deeds building in Kirkgate. When it was consecrated, in October 1936, it was the first church to be consecrated in the Borough of Wakefield for sixty years. The new parish was formed from parts of Alverthorpe, St Michael's and Thornes.

Meanwhile, Bishop Eden retired in October 1928. He had consecrated two last churches in the preceding June, St John the Divine, Rishworth, and St John the Evangelist, Staincross. The latter, which then gained its own parish, had been built as a chapel of ease for Darton, and Bishop How had dedicated its chancel on 27 April 1897.

The first consecration by Eden's successor, Bishop James Seaton, on 20 March 1929, was of St Michael's Castleford, in the area which had come into the diocese only in 1926.

When Seaton set up a Commission, on 9 August 1929, to inquire into the needs of the diocese, the emphasis was different from the two earlier ones, reflecting the changed times. In addition to looking at further church extension, it was to report on cases where existing churches and mission rooms appeared to be unnecessary. It was, as the previous Commissions had done, to advise on possible rearrangements of parish boundaries and rural deaneries, but it was also to enquire where paid lay workers might be usefully employed. It completed its report in two years. It noted that since Eden's 1909 report, eleven new parishes and two new ecclesiastical districts had been formed. Nine new parish churches had been built and consecrated and there had been four new district churches, and eight mission churches or mission rooms. There were three instances of the union of parishes. Twenty-four new vicarage houses had been built or bought.

In 1932, despite the difficult economic climate nationally, Bishop Seaton made an appeal for £35,000 – the report had suggested a figure of £45,000 – to fulfil the new recommendations. In less than three years, on 6 April 1935, he was able to hold a service in the cathedral celebrating the realization of that sum. 'No appeal in this diocese', Seaton claimed, 'has been ever supported by so many individuals, rich and poor, young and old.' Others attributed its success to Seaton's friendly personality and ready availability. Many organizations, like the Mothers' Union, the Girls' Friendly Society, and the Church Lads' Brigade, as well as parishes and individuals, had contributed. Addressing the congregation, Seaton outlined what had already been achieved. Holy Cross at Airedale had been consecrated. Building had begun at St George's, Lupset. St Barnabas, Barnsley had been completed. An iron church, transferred from Pontefract, had been sited at Three Lane Ends, Castleford (and dedicated as St James the Great) as a mission chapel for All Saints, Whitwood Mere

(Hightown). It was prompted by changes to the parish boundary and plans by Castleford Urban District Council for a housing estate. There were 'school churches' at Lundwood and Wrangbrook, a mission building had been acquired at Rawsthorne, endowments had been provided for six curates, and five further sites had been obtained for church or school building.

The village of Upton had developed as a consequence of the opening of the colliery there. The colliery company provided a site for the church cum schoolroom at Wrangbrook in the parish of South Kirkby. Colonel Sir Maurice Bell, one of the directors of the company, laid the foundation stone of a new, small and modern church building on 4 May 1931. It was dedicated to St Michael.

The building of the vast Airedale estate by Castleford Council brought an urgent need for a new church there. The township had come into existence in 1921. A temporary iron church had been acquired from Castleford in 1922 when the area was still in the Diocese of York. Initially a conventional district, with a Curate in Charge, it became the separate parish of Airedale with Fryston in 1930. Appealing for funds for a permanent church, Bishop Seaton called it 'the most immediately urgent need in the diocese' and urged all those who bought Airedale coal to make a donation. The building of the church of the Holy Cross was remarkable! News that Fryston Hall was to be demolished prompted the purchase of its stone for £300. The stone was taken to the site for the new church with the help of volunteer labour, including that of coal miners. The Ionic columns were re-erected at the front of the church. The Marquess of Crewe laid the foundation stone on 18 March 1933 and the church was consecrated on 14 July 1934. The church was designed by Sir Charles Nicholson and the pews were by the 'mouse man', Robert Thompson of Kilburn. Many parishioners had come to Airedale from County Durham and the stoup was made of stone from Durham Cathedral.

John Charles Sydney Daly, the energetic young man who had come to Airedale as Curate in Charge in 1929, moved on less than a year after the consecration of the church. He was consecrated as the first Bishop of Gambia and Rio Pongas on the Festival of Philip and James, 1 May 1935, at All Hallows by the Tower, London. Daly had been at King's College, Cambridge and the Dean of the College preached on the occasion. Fifty people from Airedale attended. 'All must have felt that they were taking part in a gallant adventure of the Church of England,' the Dean observed.

The offertory at the 1935 service of thanksgiving for the success of Seaton's appeal was for the Gambia Diocese.

Holy Cross, Airedale

The Union of Benefices

Rationalizing by uniting benefices has occurred since the sixteenth century. While the spate of unions of benefices in the diocese did not come until the latter part of the twentieth century, some few unions actually took place or were explored much earlier. The union was normally preceded by a Commission of Inquiry and required an Order in Council to confirm it. In rural areas, benefices might be united where the population was too small to warrant the maintenance of separate parishes. In urban areas, already in the 1920s the clearance of housing from town centres might provide a case for uniting adjacent benefices. Under the Union of Benefices Act of 1921, St Mark's, Huddersfield, was united in 1922 with the mother parish of St Peter, and St Luke's, Norland, was united with Christ Church, Sowerby Bridge. In 1924, having been overseen by the Vicar of Penistone for at least fifty years, the benefices of Midhope and Penistone were united.

Bishop Seaton promoted a Public Inquiry in the mid 1930s, during the building of the Lupset housing estate, into the advisability of uniting

Christ Church, Thornes, with St James's, Thornes, in Wakefield. The scheme was rejected at the time but Seaton warned that the removal of much of the population of Christ Church (through slum clearance) would mean that the possibility must be revisited.

The Two Religious Communities: the Community of St Peter, Horbury, and the Community of the Resurrection

Although the Community of St Peter, Horbury, and the Community of the Resurrection at Mirfield lie within the diocese, neither is a diocesan body. But their contribution to the work of the diocese warrants their place in this history.

The Community of St Peter, the first religious community in the north of England since the Reformation, was founded in 1858 by the high-church incumbent of Horbury, John Sharp. He had been prompted by his cousin, Harriet Louisa Farrer, to bring together women 'pledged to devote themselves to rescue and preventive work', who could run a refuge for girls and young women. More will be said of this long-lasting venture later. As the Community grew, Sisters were sent, or daughter-houses founded, to oversee penitentiaries or rescue houses elsewhere, including Carlisle, Chester, Croydon, Freiston in Lincolnshire, Joppa (Edinburgh), Leeds, London, Rushholme (Manchester), Sheffield, and Wolverhampton. Some of their number also worked in more local parishes of high-church inclinations, visiting and teaching. They served in all three Horbury parishes, at Middlestown, and as far afield as South Elmsall, and All Saints, Leeds. At Horbury Bridge, as well as teaching in the Sunday School, they managed a night school for girls. In the early 1920s they also assisted with parish work at two London churches and at St Peter's, Folkestone. From 1925, invited by the parochial church council, the cathedral staff included two of St Peter's nuns. They lived in Wakefield at St Gabriel's House, Rishworth Street, which was dedicated on Lady Day, 25 March. At the cathedral they cared for the altar vessels and the vestments, cleaned the silver, looked after the linen and arranged the flowers. But they also worked with young people in the Sunday Schools and undertook pastoral work in the parish. Between 1900 and 1908, when it ceased to hold women prisoners, nuns from St Peter's served as visitors at Wakefield Prison. From 1922 they also visited Armley Gaol. In 1900–20, Sisters managed the County Home, Stafford, for discharged women prisoners. The Community of the Holy Paraclete at Sneaton Hall, Whitby, was founded from St Peter's where a small school, later to be called St Hilda's, had been started in 1875. Shortly after the outbreak of the First World War, the school was refounded at Whitby by some of the Sisters from Horbury who had taught there and who formed the nucleus of the new Order. During 1905–30 Sisters managed a High School and undertook missionary work at Nassau in the Bahamas.

Retreats for clergy, for their own Associates, and for others, were provided at the Convent from 1865. In 1915, they began offering retreats to working women and girls. In the 1920s they provided a retreat house at Balhousie Castle, Perth.

The nuns served the Church in two other ways. They had begun providing embroidered vestments, altar linen and banners (including some for Miners' Unions) in 1868 and the work continued until well after the Second World War. They also baked communion bread which was sent to cathedrals and churches all over England and to at least one prison, as well as abroad.

Problems developed in the last years of Bishop Eden's episcopacy and in Bishop Seaton's first years which led to a change at the convent. The management of the House of Mercy became unsatisfactory and the imposition of a harsher Rule for the Order led to the Community's Manchester house forming a separate order of St Peter Chains. The Superior at Horbury, Mother Sarah, and a number of the Sisters, departed in 1932 to their London house in Eaton Square and, at Seaton's request, Sisters from the Manchester Community moved to take charge at Horbury. The *Wakefield Diocesan Gazette* of November 1932 reported that the work of the House of Mercy was now in the hands of the Community of St Peter Chains. The departing Sisters formed a new Community at Laleham Abbey.

In 1924, at the time of the revival, initiated by (Alfred) Hope Patten, of the shrine of Our Lady, three Sisters from Horbury went to Walsingham to assist with the new hospice for the anticipated pilgrims. During 1932–47 the work at Walsingham was continued by members of the Laleham community.

The Community of the Resurrection, Mirfield

The way of life and the achievements of the Community of the Resurrection at Battyeford, Mirfield, are told in the account written by Alan Wilkinson to mark its centenary, but the author focuses on its work outside the diocese, and especially in South Africa and the former Rhodesia, rather than on its significance more locally. He refers briefly to its 'close connections' with the Community at Horbury but without amplification. The Community of the Resurrection had been founded in 1892 at Pusey House, Oxford, by its principal, Charles Gore, and five other public-school and Oxford men intent on forming a group of celibate priests who would retain their individualism yet share a corporate life of fellowship and prayer and who would engage in pastoral, evangelistic, literary and educational work. In its early years the Community was unsettled, but the idea of having a House in a working-class parish had appealed since its inception. Walter Howard Frere, another founder member, urged the need to settle in a permanent home in the north of England. Although other areas were considered (the Bishop of Manchester made it plain that he did not want the Community in his diocese, presumably because of the controversies that Anglo-Catholicism aroused), when Mirfield was suggested by Henry Walsham How, the Community accepted it. Hall Croft, the great house once preferred by Henry's father, was still available. It was taken on a lease in 1898 and the Community was able to buy it, with nineteen acres of land including a quarry, in 1902. Henry's father, Bishop How, died in 1897 but Bishop Eden was happy to countenance its arrival and blessed the house when the Community moved in. Among those present was James Seaton who was at the time a member of the wider body, the Society of the Resurrection.

The quarry at the House of the Resurrection

The Mirfield Community contributed to the work of the diocese in many ways. Members led three of the four Reading Circles which were formed in 1902 for diocesan clergy. In 1903, the Community converted the stable block and founded the College of the Resurrection with the aim of providing training for the ministry for men of little means. It was opened by Bishop Eden on 25 April when he referred to the declining numbers of men entering the service of the Church compared with the increase in the population itself. The following year the College was affiliated to the University of Leeds. While it trained men for work in the Church anywhere, many of its students got their first experience of ministry in local parishes, and good numbers of them went on to serve in the Wakefield Diocese. The quarry, which provided stone for the expansion of the Community's buildings, formed a splendid amphitheatre. Local people went there in crowds each year for the Community's annual Commemoration Day. On 19 June 1909, the new Archbishop of York, Cosmo Lang, making his first visit to the diocese, spoke at a great gathering in the quarry which had been lent for the occasion to the Wakefield Diocesan Union of Men's Bible Classes.

In 1915, the Community opened a retreat wing which served groups from the diocese and well beyond.

Priests at the Community who were licensed to preach within the diocese were de facto members of the Diocesan Conference. They might simply take occasional services or provide pastoral care for a lengthier period: in the last years of the First World War, for example, Father Gerard Sampson took charge of St Saviour's, Ravensthorpe. Frere, who was the Superior during 1902–13 and 1916–22, before he became the Bishop of Truro, in particular contributed very substantially to aspects of the work and thinking within the diocese. He also drew up the constitution for the Order of the Holy Paraclete. In the period of tension between Seaton and the Superior of the Horbury Community, Frere, then at Truro, was something of a sounding board for the Bishop and offered advice. Priests, including Frere, returning to Mirfield from serving abroad as bishops, proved very useful in assisting the Bishops of Wakefield. In 1934, Bishop Seaton authorized both Frere and James Oakey Nash, formerly Bishop of Capetown, to undertake episcopal duties.

Some members of the Community were keenly interested in the revived shrine at Walsingham; Frank Biggard gave the address when the extension to the Pilgrim Church there was blessed in June 1938. Later, in the 1940s, when he was the Superior at Mirfield, Raymond Raynes gave extensive counsel and support to Hope Patten in his (difficult) negotiations with the Laleham nuns.

Missionary Work Overseas and at Home

There is some justification for including in the same section both the support given to overseas missions and the numerous missions and other initiatives to reach out to people within the diocese, since both had the same purpose – the spread of Christianity – and, at least at one period, both activities came under the remit of the Wakefield Diocesan Board of Missions.

Support in the area for missionary work overseas was well established long before the diocese was formed. Some parishes had their own favourite cause. Others supported the well-known national missionary societies like the Church of England Zenana Missionary Society, the Society for the Propagation of the Gospel, the Church Missionary Society and the Oxford Mission to Calcutta.

In June 1905, under the aegis of the new Diocesan Board of Missions, the diocese held it first United Missionary Festival. Bishop Eden spoke of the event as a 'fresh start' in the history of missionary efforts in the diocese, emphasizing the need for proper organization at diocesan level. The objects of missionary work, he suggested, should be to bring together different bodies of Christians working abroad, the upbuilding and development of native churches, and more direct organization of native work in Colonial dioceses.

In June 1917, there was a Missionary Pilgrimage to the diocese to enlist support for foreign missions. The Pilgrims were led by Alice Parker, who was on furlough from the mission field in Japan.

The most ambitious and extensive missionary endeavour for work overseas came in 1925–28, with the national World Call to the Church urging each parish across the country to gain more knowledge of the work of the church overseas and to do whatever they could on its behalf. Six reports were issued, each on a different geographical area of the mission field. The expectation was that the reports would be discussed at parish or deanery level and would stimulate giving financially and inspire individuals to find a vocation in missionary work. The Wakefield Diocese was asked to raise an additional £5,000 in 1926 for missionary work and to find twelve more workers for mission fields. Bishop Eden commissioned a team of Messengers to visit individual parishes to further the Call. A group of students came on a ten-day campaign in 1926, visiting each deanery and working in forty-seven parishes in all. They also visited Barnsley and Penistone Grammar Schools, Hemsworth and Pontefract Secondary Schools, and Wakefield Central School in Ings Road. The World Call provided the focus for the Diocesan Missionary Service in the cathedral on 28 January 1928. The Call encouraged more priests to serve overseas. James Blair, who had been ordained in Wakefield Cathedral in 1929, for example, joined the Oxford Mission to Calcutta in 1932 and twenty years later was enthroned as the Bishop of Calcutta.

However, holding missions at home was at least as important as supporting missionary work overseas. These were perennial albeit sporadic. Over the years, many parishes in the diocese held missions, over a long weekend or perhaps for a week or fortnight at a time. The missions were conducted by visiting clergy, university students, brethren from the Community of the Resurrection, or Church Army officers. Alternatively parish clergy might themselves conduct services in the open air or in unusual venues where non-church-goers might be found and with which they would certainly be more familiar. In 1893, Wakefield Cathedral held the first of its services in the wooden circus nearby, a building close to the market area and dedicated normally to equestrian shows or music-hall style programmes. In individual towns different churches might work together to target non-church-goers, in particular workpeople in factories. The establishment of mission rooms, and in some cases mission churches, in the first decades of the life of the diocese was designed to convert the non-attender. From 1893, the Church Army had a van in the diocese, licensed by Bishop How and with the then Bishop's Chaplain, Richard Phipps, as its adviser. The van supported missions in any parish where the incumbent would welcome it. It is last referred to in Church Army Archives in 1937–38.

The Church Army Van

The first major mission in which the diocese as a whole took part was the National Mission of Hope and Repentance, a call in 1916, during the First World War, from the two archbishops 'to clergy and churchpeople to co-operate in some simultaneous and combined effort to bring the message and power of Christianity more effectively to bear upon our people in every parish in the land'. It was 'a summons to every churchman to recognize his vocation as a member of a great corporate body'. It aimed to bring religion into every home. Bishop Eden wrote in the *Diocesan Gazette* of the need to 'put more aggression into our religion'. The Mission aimed to recall the nation to higher ideals. He said, 'The sense of brotherhood has been grievously impaired by violent competition, party spirit, selfish and class interest, and neglect of the poor. The idolatry of wealth has come between us and God.' He looked for a campaign to persuade people to come forward for confirmation and to recall lapsed communicants. A committee was set up to promote the Call. Preparatory retreats for clergy were arranged, two of the three being at the House of the Resurrection in Mirfield. Retreats for Women Workers were provided at the House of Mercy in Horbury. Canon How (son of Wakefield's first bishop), who chaired the Committee, explained the need for repentance: for the sins of intemperance, unchastity, injustice, worldliness, love of pleasure, lack of zeal, selfishness, and essentially the failure to heed Christ's call. In September 1916, a team of Bishop's Messengers was commissioned at a service in Huddersfield Parish Church. As well as speaking in churches and church halls, some of them visited working men's clubs.

The Diocese in the First World War

The years of the First World War were, inevitably, difficult for the diocese. It was reported in January 1918 that thirty-six parochial clergy from the diocese had been appointed as chaplains to the Forces. The number rose to fifty after the 1918 Military Service Act raised the age for conscription to fifty-one. Four were killed. In addition fourteen members of the Community of the Resurrection also served as chaplains. Guidelines were formulated for the lay administration of consecrated buildings where there were no ordained clergy available. Vast military training camps were established by the War Office at Ripon, Richmond and Masham, and the Wakefield Diocese – especially the Church of England Men's Society – was asked to help both to finance and to run recreational huts where there were to be facilities for acts of worship as well as for games such as billiards. Volunteers assisted the men stationed there to write letters home. Wakefield's main contribution was the provision of a huge sectional building in Clotherholme Road, North Camp, Ripon. This was opened on 21 February 1916 by Lady Armytage attended by Bishop Eden. It was a wooden building measuring 140 feet by 30 feet with an administration block of 80 feet by 25 feet. It had a large recreation room, a refreshment bar, and three rooms with billiard tables.

The Church Extension Fund gave £100 towards a chapel at Halifax War Hospital in 1916.

District Visitors, Women Workers and Deaconesses

Records show that, in terms of church attendance, women far outnumbered men. Tables showing the numbers coming forward for confirmation reveal about twice as many females as males. On the only occasion when the figures for the electoral rolls were recorded separately, in 1922, they included 21,960 men and 34,569 women. Women had, however, only a secondary status – much needed for pastoral work but excluded from sacramental roles and largely from administrative ones, too.

In the years before the Second World War, parochial District Visitors – probably always women – served in great numbers. In 1915, the first year for which records survive, there were 1,038. In 1930, there were 1,490 and in 1938 there were 1,135. The system had been established nationally in the nineteenth century. Evidence from parish magazines shows that they each had a small area, perhaps just one or two streets in an urban parish and a cluster of houses in a rural one. They called at intervals on all the households in their district, whether the members were church people or not. They probably got to know their clients well. Although it was not their principal function, where possible they collected money for church work, including funds for the Church Missionary Society. Primarily, however, District Visitors took clothing and blankets and harvest produce to the needy, distributed tracts, urged parents to bring children for baptism, suggested that older children and young people attend confirmation classes, and, importantly, knew those who were ill, when they might distribute vouchers for nourishing foods such as beef tea. Until the coming of the National Health Service in 1948, hospital treatment was costly, but those of the well-to-do who played a major part in sustaining local hospitals, had the right to introduce people for free care; the District Visitors regularly sought these 'recommends' for those in their patch and also found a means of sending some few for a convalescent stay at the seaside. All but a handful of such Visitors were unpaid.

In contrast to the District Visitors, there were very few Women Workers. These were expected to undergo a modicum of training and to give many more hours to the work. Unless they had private means, they might well be paid. In 1900, the Diocese of Ripon established the Grey

Ladies settlement in Bingley for the training of women church workers. Bishop Eden attempted something similar. In 1901, he founded a Home in Westgate, Wakefield, which would serve as a hostel for trainee women. Courses of lectures were provided for the resident women. A Miss Beresford from Bedale was placed in charge of the Home and took up residence there. Canon Foxley Norris was appointed as the non-resident warden. The Home had a management council made up entirely of men. Such women as came into residence were expected to pay a guinea a week for their board. The bishop envisaged that the centre would undertake work among the factory girls who loitered in city-centre streets in the evenings. A club ran 7pm–9.30pm nightly for girls and young women, offering a chance to learn needlework, to play table games, or to listen to a Woman Worker read. Women from the parish of Wakefield helped to run it. Their role included cutting out clothes, so it would seem that some dressmaking was attempted. It was expected that Women Workers would also be attached to a parish, for daytime pastoral work. Parishes were asked to donate £10 a year to the Home. It was reported in 1902 that Miss Beresford paid visits to 'a large colliery village' once a week where she ran a mothers' meeting and visited from house to house. She also ran a mothers' meeting at the Westgate Home.

The Home was not a success, failing to draw more than half-a-dozen women at most, and it closed in 1904. But an Association of Women Workers was formed in its place. Sporadic courses of lectures continued and there were occasional conferences. In 1910, Bishop Eden offered to grant a diocesan licence 'to those ladies who are able voluntarily or at a salary to devote their whole time or such a specific portion of their time as shall be deemed adequate to the work of the church'. To qualify they had to be recommended by a parish priest and accepted by the bishop, to have had adequate training in the particular departments of work to which they proposed to devote themselves, and to satisfy the bishop in an examination of general knowledge of the Bible and prayer book, and technical knowledge of some special branch of church work or social service. It seems likely that the Association died with the outbreak of war. However, there were still some Women Workers: in his memoir, Wakefield's fourth bishop, Bishop Hone, recalled a Mary Ashton assisting him with visiting and with the pastoral care of young women during the war when he was Vicar of Brighouse.

Just as there were few Women Workers, so too there were never many deaconesses. In 1930, when the Lambeth Conference sought to determine what deaconesses might do, there were only 260 in the Church of England as a whole. The Order had been founded in 1861 and deaconesses were normally paid a stipend. The first reference to one in the Wakefield Diocese was in 1896 when Edith May was serving at St John's, Wakefield. Records show individual deaconesses working at St Mary's, Luddenden, in 1915, St Michael's, Castleford, in 1926, St Paul's, Armitage Bridge, in 1931, and St Mary's, Mirfield, in 1938. There is little evidence of what they did. However, the 1930 Conference referred to them as assisting the minister in preparing candidates for baptism and in the administration of baptism itself, officiating at the churching of women, and reading Morning and Evening Prayer in church, although excluding such parts as were reserved to the priest. Very importantly they could not assist in any way with the service of communion. It seems likely that much of their work lay in teaching in Sunday Schools and in visiting.

Moral and Social Responsibility

The principal social concern in the early years of the diocese was intemperance. The Church of England Temperance Society had been founded in 1862. Branches were formed in many parishes. Some churches had Bands of Hope or ran a Church Lads' Brigade, which was an offshoot of the Temperance Society. The Wakefield Diocesan branch of the Temperance Society was founded in 1892, and in 1896 offered a salary of £50 a year for a two-year appointment of an organizing secretary. In May 1899, a provisional committee was formed in the Wakefield Deanery, with Archdeacon Donne as its chairman, to work towards employing a Police Court Missioner who would support people brought before the Petty Sessions or leaving prison, to try to restore them to a wholesome and sober life. The first Missioner, Thomas Way, appointed towards the end of 1899, visited the West Riding magistrates' courts in Wakefield and Dewsbury and the borough courts in Batley, Dewsbury, Morley, Ossett and Wakefield. In his first three months, he worked with seventeen 'cases', primarily people charged with drunkenness, but also those charged with assault, theft or vagrancy. In the next few years, two further Missioners were appointed, one of whom, Thomas Grundy, was also charged with supervising the newly established Labour Home in Ramsden Street, Huddersfield. This catered for twelve male residents. It was replaced in July 1908 by a much larger purpose-built home in The Shore, where twenty-four men could be accommodated in second-floor cubicle bedrooms. There was also modest accommodation for women. Grundy can have been only in his very early twenties when he was first brought to Huddersfield. When he died in 1919 at the age of forty-five, he was still the superintendent of the Labour Home.

The success of the Police Court Missioners nationally in drawing offenders away from a life of crime led to the founding of the Probation Service under the 1907 Probation of Offenders Act. Each of the Wakefield diocesan Missioners gained appointment as a Probation Officer in their existing areas. Their new position gave them both a right and a duty to attend the courts where before they had been admitted only with a magistrate's permission. However, they retained their role, with some additional payment, as Police Court Missioners since the work was deemed to be more extensive than that of a Probation Officer. The Mission work was strictly undenominational, Missioners making no distinction among their offenders in terms of their creed, sex or crime. Their work was varied: one report in 1906 showed one of the diocesan Missioners visiting an employer to save an offender from dismissal, and finding work for a girl who had fled the blandishments of a brothel-keeper.

The other pressing problem, at least in the eyes of the Church, was prostitution. Police Court Missioners reported numbers of girls who were seen as 'rescue cases'. In 1917, Bishop Eden set up a provisional committee to enquire into the rescue work already in progress in the diocese and to draw up a constitution for a Diocesan Council for Preventive and Rescue Work. Its report noted that the diocese already had within its borders penitentiaries and 'rescue' homes in the form of the House of Mercy at Horbury, founded in 1858 and run by the Community of St Peter, the St John's Industrial Training Home for Discharged Female Prisoners, in Wakefield, and St Margaret's House, Halifax. St John's Home, purpose-built in 1872, was the successor to a Refuge for Women which had been opened in 1842. At the House of Mercy some seventy or eighty girls and young women, who might come from anywhere in the country, were kept on average for two years. St Margaret's, which had three permanent beds and two emergency beds, provided a shelter and temporary home for women and girls under the age of thirty. It was managed by a committee of church people together with representatives of the Halifax Board of Guardians. The Worker there routinely visited the workhouse hospital and gave help to girls leaving its Lock Ward. Maternity cases were sent to St Faith's in Leeds, provided that the necessary fees were available. At Barnsley, where an organization had been formed in 1881, there were two strands to the care of vulnerable girls, one preventive and the other rescue work. There was a small Home, run on undenominational lines, for girls aged twelve to sixteen taken from 'undesirable' surroundings and then trained for domestic service. It could take only six or so at a time. The Shelter was run by a Church Army Sister and took in anyone homeless or in difficulties. It ran a Bible class and a club for needlework and gymnastics. It cost some £300 a year to run and received substantial support from local people including some who were not members of the Established Church. In 1917 it was, additionally, providing a club for soldiers' wives (some of whom, albeit not necessarily in Barnsley, were tempted into adultery or prostitution while their husbands were on active service). The Church Army Sister visited police courts and lodging houses on the lookout for the vulnerable.

Meeting in July 1917, the provisional committee, whose members included the Mother Superior of St Peter's Convent and a Miss Arnold of Barnsley Rescue House, agreed that no further penitentiaries were required but noted the need for small shelters in Wakefield and Dewsbury, that Barnsley wanted a small maternity home and that Dewsbury needed a trained rescue worker. There was seen to be a demand for the systematic visiting of churchwomen who were in prison, and of patients in Poor Law hospitals. The committee also recommended a rescue house and trained worker at Huddersfield. The new Council for Rescue and Preventive Work first met in March 1918. Its objects were 'to promote a healthy public opinion on all moral questions and to assist all institutions which exist for preventive, rescue and penitentiary work on church lines within the diocese by advice and grants'. It had eighteen members, eight of whom were female. These included Miss Arnold and Mrs Jaeger of the Barnsley Rescue House, Mrs Marchetti of St Margaret's House, the Mother Superior of St Peter's Convent, and four who were wives, daughters or unmarried sisters of diocesan clergy.

The Council held an overview of developments within the diocese and at times took action itself. Soon after it was formed and following an initiative by one of the Council's members, Mrs Tupper-Carey, who was the wife of the Vicar of Huddersfield, it launched an appeal for £2,000 to lease Woodhouse Hall, Almondbury, Huddersfield. This could be rented at £70 a year, to care for up to twenty illegitimate babies born to girls who had been taken into the rescue homes within the diocese. It became St Katharine's Hostel. Again in 1918, the Council agreed to contribute £5 a year towards what became Hope Hospital in Chapeltown and was to be supported financially primarily by local authorities.

From 1921, St John's Home came under the direct care of the Council. An article in the *Wakefield Diocesan Gazette* in 1923 reported that it was the only Home of its kind in the north of England and there were forty girls in training, learning cooking, housework, knitting and laundry work. Many girls went on to domestic service, sometimes abroad. Some voluntary teaching was undertaken by staff (all of whom were female) from Wakefield Girls High School. In 1937, its status changed. The number of girls entering the Home had fallen because girls in trouble were now being taken before children's courts and then sent to Approved Schools which had been introduced nationally in 1933 as a replacement for Reformatories. St John's therefore sought and gained recognition as an Approved School itself but, although now serving the Home Office, it remained under the care of the Diocesan Council. A new rescue house in King's Mill Lane, Huddersfield, named Springfield, was opened on 7 December 1923 by Archdeacon Harvey. The extension in 1926 brought Pontefract into the diocese. A rescue house, the Haven, had been founded there in 1915 by the Pontefract Centre for Preventive and Rescue Work and had been run, at least from 1917, by Church Army Sisters. In 1925, at the time that the Church Army Sisters were withdrawn, a new house was acquired in Linden Terrace. It was dedicated as St Giles's Haven, on 8 February 1926, and was managed until 1930 by members of the Community of St Peter, Horbury. Subsequently a lay supervisor was appointed.

In 1932, the Council for Rescue and Preventive Work was, in the light of a decision by the Archbishops' Advisory Council, renamed the Council for Moral Welfare Work.

During the Spanish Civil War, the West Riding saw Basque children come as refugees in the autumn of 1937. Bishop Seaton was among those who welcomed them.

Bishop Seaton in 1937 with Basque refugees

Anglo-Catholicism and the Gradual Acceptance of Ritualist Practices

The ritualism associated with the Oxford, or Anglo-Catholic, Movement was by no means unknown in the West Riding before the diocese was created. For example, Edward Akroyd, who had built the church at Copley in 1865, withdrew his support from his vicar, the Reverend J. B. Sidgwick, in 1872 because he was becoming too 'high' for his tastes. In 1879, he sold the patronage of All Souls, Haley Hill, the church he had built in 1859, to the Simeon Trustees to ensure that it remained evangelical. The Trust had been established by Charles Simeon (1759–1836), a man of national standing as a leader of the evangelical revival. The Vicar of Penistone, Canon Turnbull, was a member of the Anglo-Catholic English Church Union and wrote sympathetically about the use of the confessional in an issue of his parish magazine for which he was strongly criticized by Penistone historian, John Dransfield. He would have gone much further, so Dransfield says, had it not been for the strength of the Penistone branch of the Protestant Church Association. Some of the Anglo-Catholic churches within the area which was to form the diocese, were at times pilloried in the local press for the curious dress of their incumbents and curates, the rituals of their services and the decor of their churches. But ritualist practices, especially those associated with the communion service, were, under the infamous Public Worship Regulation Act of 1874, also a civil offence. Clergy, albeit not in the Ripon Diocese, had been imprisoned. When the Reverend Sydney F. Green was sentenced to gaol in 1881 and subsequently deprived of his living, Frederick Dykes (brother of the hymn tune composer) resigned from his position as choirmaster at Wakefield Parish Church in protest.

The years 1887–92 saw no less a person than the Bishop of Lincoln, Edward King (1821–1910), charged by lay people within his diocese with unacceptable practices, and judged by the Archbishop of Canterbury's court and ultimately by the Privy Council. But for what, exactly? He mixed water with the wine before consecrating it; he had lighted candles on the altar even though it was daylight; he made the sign of the cross during the absolution and the benediction; but, much worse, he stood and knelt on the west side of the altar, with his back to the congregation, when he consecrated the elements, instead of on the north side; moreover, he initiated the singing of the Agnus Dei after the prayer of consecration. He was also, it seems, the first bishop since the Reformation to wear vestments. His effective exoneration brought to an end the ritualist trials but did nothing to appease the firmly evangelical. The Simeon Trustees, and no doubt other patrons, insisted that their protegees continued to celebrate communion from the north side of the altar. The use of incense, crucifixes rather than simple crosses, portraits or statues of the Virgin and Child, the figure of Christ on the chancel screen, the existence of a reredos, sculptures or pictures depicting the Stations of the Cross and, of course, the dedication of a Lady Chapel, were widely resisted.

It would be fair to say that Anglo-Catholic churches were in the minority and their rituals rare in the diocese in 1888.

In March 1899, Bishop Eden responded to a Home Office inquiry about the use of confessional boxes to the effect that there were none in the parish churches of his diocese.

From time to time the diocese attracted the hostile attentions of the members of the Protestant Truth Society, or Kensitites, sometimes known as the Wycliffe Preachers, which had been founded in 1890 by the Protestant extremist John Kensit (1853–1902) to oppose Anglo-Catholicism. In June 1907 a group of them gathered at Battyeford, for example, to express their condemnation of the Community of the Resurrection.

Gradually, however, as the details of the granting of faculties show, elements of ritualism became a little more widely accepted, especially from the 1920s, though never by the most firmly evangelical churches and their members.

In 1913, there was some controversy when an anonymous benefactor offered a pair of candlesticks to Halifax Parish Church and also proposed converting the Rokeby Chapel into a side chapel for communion. The majority of the congregation were in favour but there were those who suggested they might never take communion in the church again.

By 1917, it seems that practices associated with the Anglo-Catholic wing of the church were accepted, at least by the press which had hitherto mocked them. When Canon Ernest Winter, who had been Rector of Elland for almost twenty-five years, died in January 1917, the *Yorkshire Post* reported the funeral arrangements uncritically. It observed that on the evening before the funeral, his body was taken into the church, 'clothed in priest's eucharistic vestments'. Six candles were placed round his coffin which was covered with a violet pall. Vespers for the dead were said and men from the parish kept vigil through the night. There were requiem services at 5am and 7.20am before the funeral service itself. Incense was used during the offertory at the funeral and the body was censed. Winter had been described as 'devoted to the Catholic presentment of the church'.

There was a controversial discussion at the Diocesan Conference in 1919 over alterations in services and in the ornaments of churches.

Agreement was finally reached that 'any definite departure from the usual custom which obtains in a parish church in regard to the appointed ornaments and services of public worship should not come into effect without the consent of the incumbent and a two-thirds majority of the parochial church council'.

Holy Trinity, Wakefield, founded by evangelicals in 1838 as an alternative to the 'high' parish church, became Anglo-Catholic in 1925–26 under the Reverend A. E. C. Morgan. He had a new altar built with a reredos bearing carved figures of the crucifixion, 'the blessed Mother', Mary Magdalene and the four Evangelists. He also had a small recess formed under the south window of the sanctuary for a credence and piscina. There were those among the former churchwardens and older members of the congregation who strongly objected. 'It had not been that kind of worship in that church in the past,' they argued. By 1930, and probably earlier, Morgan was celebrating 'choral Eucharist' and marking such festivals as the Purification of the BVM (*sic*). A Lady Chapel was added to the church in 1930, and at Easter 1931 an account in the parish magazine tells us that 'the High Altar was beautiful with Arum lilies and the Lady Chapel stood out with Madonna Lilies'. The writer, Dorothy Una Radcliffe, gave £20 towards the cost of the Lady Chapel.

As the cathedral city of the diocese, Wakefield was the target of a campaign in 1926 by the Wycliffe Preachers. The Kensitites were concerned that a proposed revision of the Book of Common Prayer would legitimize the Catholic practice of the 'reservation of consecrated elements'. They feared the return of the doctrine of purgatory, the confessional box, the veneration of relics and the worship of the Virgin Mary, and argued that it was Protestantism that gave the British their 'moral fibre'. Their meeting, in Unity Hall, ended with a declaration of loyalty to the principles of the Reformation and a call to the Bishop to vote against any revision of the prayer book.

The first formal assembly of Anglo-Catholics in the diocese was at Elland in 1925. In June 1926 the group met in Wakefield. The day began with Eucharist in the cathedral 'with full Anglo-Catholic ceremonial including incense'. The celebrant was the Vicar of Wakefield, William Arthur Macleod. After lunch at the Church Institute, the party gathered in Unity Hall with the Vicar of Horbury, Canon Hill, in the chair. The meeting opened with the hymn, written in 1906 by Vincent Stuckey Stratton Coles (1845–1929), 'Ye who own the faith of Jesus', which has the refrain 'Hail Mary full of grace'. The principal speaker emphasized the Ritualists' wish to include the beauties of art and music in their services and their opposition to the 'gloomy' views of Puritans.

The Lambeth Conference of 1930 called for co-operation among the different 'schools of thought' within the church.

By 1930, and perhaps before, the hearing of confessions was given a regular place in the cathedral's week. Macleod organized the reservation of the sacrament, in St Mark's Chapel, from February 1930 An aumbry for this purpose was blessed on 17 February. In Holy Week, the stations of the Passion were marked, and both Corpus Christi and the Visitation of the B V Mary (*sic*) were celebrated. Elsewhere in the diocese the next few years saw more faculties granted for the installation of statues of the Virgin and Child, aumbries, reredoses and processional crosses. In May 1931 St Paul's, Birkenshaw, obtained a faculty for a Vessica with a figure of the risen saviour. A faculty was granted to All Hallows, Kirkburton, in 1932, for the restoration of the ancient chapel of St Nicholas.

Noel T. Hopkins, who served at the cathedral as the Vicar of Wakefield and subsequently as the Provost in 1933–62, and who prompted the reinstatement of the Lady Chapel there, was an Anglo-Catholic who had been strongly influenced by Charles Gore (1852–1932), one of the founders of the Community of the Resurrection. In 1938, Hopkins wrote two sympathetic articles for the *Cathedral Magazine* on 'Sacramental Confession'. The centenary of the Oxford Movement was celebrated in the diocese in the summer of 1933 with a service in the cathedral on 11 July. The tribute paid to its founders focused on their legacy of 'a greater sense of the supernatural and a fuller use of sacramental aids for holiness of life'. The evangelical Church Association provided an opposition meeting.

Faculties for Lady Chapels were granted to a number of churches in the 1930s. A Lady Chapel, built by volunteers, was dedicated at St James's, Chapelthorpe in the summer of 1934. In 1936, the Lady Chapel at St James's, Flockton, provided in memory of Lady Beatrice Lister Kaye, was dedicated.

Patronage

The exercise of patronage was a major factor in influencing the churchmanship of a parish.

There was concern when the diocese was established that the bishop would hold the patronage independently of only fourteen of the 167 benefices, giving him few opportunities to choose priests himself. Nine vicars had, between them, the patronage of a further eighty benefices. The Vicar of Halifax alone had the gift of some thirty-one livings. Laymen, especially the landed gentry, were patrons of twenty-three livings: Sir John Ramsden held All Hallows, Almondbury, and the two Huddersfield parishes of St Peter and St John the Evangelist. Lord Savile was the patron of St Michael's, Emley, and St Michael's, Thornhill. Walter Spencer Stanhope of Cannon Hall was the patron of St John's, Hoylandswaine. All Saints, Darton, was in the gift of Wentworth Blackett Beaumont of Bretton Hall, and the Countess of Cardigan and Earl Wilton made the presentation to All Saints, Batley in turn. The Rawson family were patrons of St John the Divine, Triangle.

Bodies of trustees had a further fifteen livings. Both the Peache Trustees and the Simeon Trustees had had a policy of buying up advowsons where the opportunity came, in order to ensure the livings went to men of an evangelical or low-church persuasion rather than to Anglo-Catholics. The Peache Trustees administered the advowsons established or bought up by Mrs Rebecca Disney Robinson, the well-to-do widow of a former incumbent of Woolley. These were Christ Church, St Andrew's, and St Mary's, Wakefield, and St Helen's, Sandal. St James's, Flockton, was held by the trustees of the Carter Charity.

There were single livings in the gift of the Lord Chancellor, the Duchy of Lancaster, and Keble College, Oxford. Keble had been founded only in 1870 but the benefactors of the parish of St John the Evangelist, Horbury Bridge, most notably John Sharp, the Vicar of Horbury, had decided by 1879 to nominate the Warden and scholars as the patrons of the parish, which was formed in 1884. The Crown alternated with the bishop in appointing to nine livings and had in its sole gift the important benefice of Halifax Parish Church.

Bishop How's commissioners, reporting in 1890 on the spiritual needs of the diocese, anticipated that new livings would normally come under the patronage of the bishop and hoped that other advowsons might be transferred to him too. They suggested specifically that it would not 'materially affect' the position of the Vicar of Halifax if some of the livings in his gift were transferred to the bishop. They were particularly concerned that the bishop had no rural livings to bestow as it was held that he might have wished to present 'semi-retired' clergy to these.

Not all new livings came to the bishop, however. While St Barnabas's, Crosland Moor (1897), St Andrew's, Purlwell (1912), and St John's, Staincross (1928) came directly into the gift of the bishop, the advowson of St Michael and All Angels, Cornholme (1901), was held by the Reverend Arthur Master-Whitaker and his wife, Mary Charlotte, who had built it, and Edward Lancaster retained the advowson of his 1902 Barnsley church, St Edward's.

A gift from 'a liberal layman' of £500 in 1897 enabled the purchase of five of the advowsons held by the Vicar of Halifax: St Martin's, Brighouse, St John's, Bradshaw, St Mary's, Luddenden, Christ Church, Mount Pellon, and St Bartholomew's, Ripponden. Another anonymous gift of £5,000 in 1908 brought to the bishop exclusively eight of the advowsons held jointly with the Crown: St John's, Barnsley, St Mary's, Gomersal, St Paul's, King Cross, St Michael's, Mytholmroyd, Christ Church, South Ossett, St Peter's, Sowerby, St John's, Upperthong, and St Mary's, Wyke.

The first decades of the twentieth century saw the beginning of the transfer of advowsons from landowning families to the bishops or, from 1921, to the new Diocesan Board of Patronage. In 1909, Lord Allendale gave St Nicholas, Cumberworth to the bishop. The patronage of Wrenthorpe was transferred to the bishop in 1908 by William Brooke. Christ Church, Helme was given in 1910 by Charles Brook.

The creation of the Diocesan Board of Patronage in 1920 was a necessary condition of the sale to the diocese of the advowsons previously held by Sir John Ramsden. The original moves for their sale provoked a flurry of activity and had even an element of drama! When Sir John determined to sell his estates in the Huddersfield area, his initial intention was to give the advowsons that went with them, those of All Hallows', Almondbury, and the two Hudderfield parishes of St Peter and St John, to the bishop. Assuming them to have real value, the intermediary who bought the estate with the intention of reselling it to Huddersfield Corporation, insisted that, unless the advowsons were included, he would drop the offer price by some £50,000. Thus it seemed that the local authority would become the patron of three parishes. Acts of Parliament of 1835 and 1888 had implied that municipal corporations should not hold advowsons but there was no law actually banning their acquiring them. Since the expenditure by Huddersfield itself required an Act of Parliament, Bishop Eden retained a solicitor, engaged a Parliamentary agent, got up a petition in Huddersfield, and ensured that the Huddersfield Corporation (Lands) Bill was opposed in the House of Lords. The subsequent Act required the Corporation to sell the advowsons for £4,000. Eden persuaded Sir John Ramsden to pay the sum himself. The Corporation in turn insisted that the sale must be to a Board of Patronage, hence the formation of the Board in 1920. The first appointment made by the Board was that of Richard Piers Whittington to the benefice of Almondbury in 1923.

In the same year, Sir Alexander Wentworth Macdonald-Bosville, Macdonald of the Isles, relinquished the advowson of Midhope, thus facilitating the union of the benefices of Midhope and Penistone.

In 1930, Bishop Seaton purchased the advowson of the Anglo-Catholic Grimethorpe from the Hon. E. W. S. Foljambe since there had been a pos-

St Luke's, Grimethorpe

sibility, or so it appeared, that it would be bought by some trust 'that had no particular interest in the diocese but wanted it for its own ends'.

The extension of the diocese in 1926 brought further parishes where the advowsons were held by Oxbridge colleges including All Saints, Featherstone (the Dean and Chapter of Christ Church, Oxford), All Saints, Normanton (Trinity College, Cambridge), and St Edmund's, Kellington (the Master and Fellows of Trinity College, Cambridge). Members of the aristocracy or landed gentry held St Mary's, Badsworth (Lord Derby), St Martin's, Womersley (Lord Rosse), St Helen's, Hemsworth (Robert Battie-Wrightson of Cusworth Hall) and St Michael and Our Lady, Wragby (Lord St Oswald). St Peter's, Warmfield, was held by the Oley Trustees, and administered by Clare College, Cambridge.

Shortly after Hone became bishop in 1938, the patronage of Kellington with Whitley was transferred by the Master and Fellows of Trinity College, Cambridge, to the Diocesan Board of Patronage.

The Sanderson Bequest

By far the greatest benefaction the diocese has ever had was the legacy from the Wakefield maltster, Michael Edwin Sanderson. Sanderson was the second son of the founder of the family business of Michael Sanderson and Sons, and was the brother of Thomas Kemp Sanderson who, as Wakefield's Member of Parliament, had played a leading part in bringing the see to Wakefield but who predeceased him. Both brothers had lived from 1893 at Kettlethorpe Hall. Michael Sanderson was the chairman of the firm and made a name for himself regionally for his shrewd knowledge of barley. He was one of the first members of the West Riding County Council, created under the Act of 1888, and was credited with ensuring that Wakefield retained its status as the county town, by pressing for the building of the County Hall there. He was strongly attached to the parish church long before it was elevated to cathedral status, and sang in the church choir as both a boy and a man. In the years before his death, he gave money as well as property to the cathedral, including a house in Leeds Road as a residence for its curates. At his death in 1908, he had other houses in Wakefield, four in particular in South Parade, the Kettlethorpe Hall estate, and large estates in Sutherland. Apart from a few minor bequests, Sanderson left everything to the Church. To the bishop for a trust fund went £60,000, which could, if the bishop wished, be used to endow one or more residentiary canonries. A further £10,000 was left to the Bishop and the Vicar of Wakefield jointly to provide pensions for women. However, Sanderson also left the residue of his estate, estimated at the time probate was granted as some £145,000, to his executors as trustees for the benefit of the diocese. This might be used, he suggested, to augment the incomes of poor clergy.

Bishop Eden set up a small committee to advise him on the detail of its application, including Walter Frere, then the Superior of the Community of the Resurrection. Frere suggested the scheme, which was subsequently adopted, to use the greater part of the £60,000 legacy to found three new canonries, each of them to be residentiary. Two would go to the archdeacons, provided that they resigned their benefices. and a third would be available for the Vicar of Wakefield. A chapter was to be constituted with the vicar in the position of sub-dean. A further canonry would provide the diocese with a canon missioner. Much of Sanderson's property was sold at auction but 5 and 5a South Parade did not find a buyer and both houses were conveyed to the Wakefield Church Extension Society in April 1911.

Sanderson's bequest meant that Wakefield could now have a Chapter, including the bishop, the Vicar of Wakefield, and the residentiary canons. The interim chapter was inaugurated on 1 July 1909 having been constituted by deed. Canon Thompson, who lived in another of Sanderson's houses at 6 South Parade, was appointed as the Missioner. A sum of £2,000 was allocated from the residuary estate to provide a new parsonage house for the cathedral.

The bequest meant that William Donne, who had been both Vicar of Wakefield and Archdeacon of Huddersfield could relinquish his place at the cathedral in 1909 to serve as the archdeacon full time. The Archdeacon of Halifax, Foxley Norris, ceased to be the Vicar of Barnsley and moved to live in rather grander style at Ovenden Hall, Halifax. Donne moved to Carr Lodge, Horbury.

The Golden Jubilee and the Death of Bishop James Seaton

The fiftieth anniversary of its founding was celebrated in May and June 1938 across the diocese, with a galaxy of bishops taking part. Bishop Seaton made an appeal for £5,000 for the jubilee thanksgiving with the intention of giving some of this to the Diocese of Gambia. But Seaton himself was too ill to be present at any of the events and the Bishop of Pontefract, Campbell Richard Hone, took his place. The date 25 May was chosen for the climax of the celebrations, with receptions, services, processions and lunches.

Events began with a service in the cathedral on Saturday 7 May for Girl Guides and Members of the Girls' Friendly Society, at which the Bishop of Blackburn preached. This was followed by one on 14 May for Scouts and members of the Church Lads' Brigade with the address given by the Bishop of Jarrow. On 21 May, the service was for youth, with the Bishop of Burnley preaching. The teachers of both the day and Sunday schools had their special service on 28 May, with the Bishop of Hull. On 16 June, the Bishop of Peterborough preached to members of the Mothers' Union.

Each rural deanery had its own service: on 9 May the Bishop of Liverpool came to Halifax Parish Church; on 27 May it was the turn of the Bishop of Durham at Wakefield Cathedral. There followed, on 1 June, the Bishop of Newcastle (Birstall Parish Church), on 3 June, Canon Harvey (Huddersfield Parish Church), on 7 June, the Bishop of Sheffield (Pontefract Parish Church), on 8 June, the Bishop of Manchester (Barnsley Parish Church), and on 14 June, the Bishop of Chester (Dewsbury Parish Church).

The principal events, on 25 May, brought the Bishop of Ripon, Geoffrey Lunt, to the morning service, and the Archbishop of York, William Temple, to preach in the afternoon. The most distinguished visitors were entertained to lunch at the County Hall by the chairman of the West Riding County Council, Sir William Cartwright, while the lesser dignitaries, including mayors and mayoresses from the principal towns in the diocese, had lunch at Unity Hall.

Sir William Cartwright, Chairman of the County Council, and his lunch guests, 25 May 1938

There were processions of county and civic heads from the Town Hall to the cathedral, and of 400 clergy from the Cathedral School in Brook Street. The recently appointed Bishop of Gambia, John Daly, and Bishop Eden returned for the event to join the two diocesan archdeacons, the Dean of York, the Provost of Sheffield and Bishop Nash (from the Community of the Resurrection).

Both the Archbishop and Bishop Eden visited James Seaton at Bishopgarth during the day. He died the same evening. After cremation his ashes were interred in the chancel of the cathedral.

PART II

The Diocese between 1938 and 1967

Introduction

The diocese escaped with little serious damage during the Second World War but the post-war world brought cultural change, a loss of certainties, and a realization that neither the Established Church, not indeed the practice of Christianity, was as significant to the general population as it had seemed in the past. There was a shortage of clergy as fewer men came forward for ordination. Post-war redevelopment led to the closure of some urban churches and the opening of others, or the creation of dual-purpose church buildings, in the new residential suburbs. Parsonage houses, built when priests had adequate incomes and servants were the norm, were too large and costly to heat and maintain. As the value of endowments declined, live giving became increasingly vital not only to ensure that parishes could support their own ministry and buildings but also to meet increasing demands from the wider Church.

The two archbishops identified Trinity Sunday 1950 as a day on which all parishes should be asked to contribute towards the national fund for clergy training. In the few years since the war, most of the men seeking ordination in the Church had been ex-servicemen, and government support had been available for their training, but that was coming to an end. It was estimated that it cost £1,200 to train a man. In 1900 there were 20,000 Anglican clergy for a population of 32 million. By 1949 there were only 15,000 yet the population had risen to 45 million. Each parish was asked to contribute £5 to the national pool so that a figure of £50,000 or £60,000 could be achieved. An editorial in *The Times* remarked that 'the days of a ministry chiefly sustained by the benefactions of the past ages have gone. The Church must now depend on the generosity of its congregations.' To keep pace with the population it was estimated that the Church needed an intake of 600 men a year. It was thought unlikely that it could recruit more than 400. The causes of the decline was attributed to the condition of church and society, materialistic tendencies, the lack of home religion, financial considerations, and the disturbances of the minds of young men caused by science and the disillusionment of two world wars.

Congregations were called on increasingly in the 1950s to enhance the stipends of their incumbents. Diocesan Conference determined in 1947 that beneficed clergy should have a minimum of £500 a year, regardless of the endowment income. In 1950, an article in the *Wakefield Diocesan News* urged parochial church councils to raise more for their own minister if the stipend fell short of the £500 and to contribute what they could to the diocesan pool, from which stipends were supplemented, if the stipend were already above it. By 1955 the income for most of the benefices in the diocese had risen to £600.

In September 1946, in the light of the shortage of clergy, rising costs and declining church attendance, Bishop McGowan initiated a survey of mission churches and mission rooms, their staffing and maintenance and future use.

National concern that many parishes would be increasingly unable to afford to keep their churches in good repair led to the launch in December 1952 of the Historic Churches Preservation Trust, with the Queen as its patron and the Duke of Edinburgh as its President. In recognition that churches were of significance to the general community, its original twenty-three trustees included people who were not necessarily members of the Church of England. The first major donation, of £100,000, came from the Pilgrim Trust. The Trust was founded in 1930 by an American philanthropist, Edward Harkness, for the benefit of Great Britain, and was given its name by him as an allusion to the Pilgrim Fathers; the preservation of buildings has always been one of its central objectives.

It was national – even international – rather than local issues which concerned the diocese during John Ramsbotham's years as its bishop, although the growing ecumenical movement in particular had local impact. Both Ramsbotham and the Provost, Philip Pare, attended the great Anglican Congress in Toronto in 1963. This was the third of its kind in the history of the Anglican Communion. Its theme was the Church's mission to the world. Among the principles emerging from this was that of a commitment to work in the future far more closely with fellow Christians of other communions. The 1960s saw the inquiries which led to the publication of the Paul Report on *The Deployment and Payment of the Clergy* (1964), and the Morley Report, *Partners in Ministry* (1967). The far-reaching Pastoral Measure of 1968 which facilitated the reorganization of parishes and the making redundant of churches was under discussion from 1964. In the face of a decline in church attendance and the growing materialism within society, Christian Stewardship became national policy, with

THE DIOCESE BETWEEN 1938 AND 1967

stewardship advisers being appointed at a diocesan level. The changes in church government, with the move from a national Church Assembly and a local Diocesan Conference, to synodical rule at both local and national levels, were on the horizon and were discussed at meetings of parochial church councils.

A fundamental anxiety was the general turning away from religious faith and belief. In his address to the Wakefield Diocesan Conference in September 1952, the Archbishop of York, Cyril Garbett, said that the mass of the population looked upon religion 'as something irrelevant to their daily lives'. One of the causes, he thought, was the decline in house-to-house visiting. But in the 1950s and 1960s, society had new secular attractions. Television began to dominate home life, and increased car ownership brought the possibility of family trips at weekends. Rugby League matches were played on Sundays by amateurs from 1956 and by professional teams from 1967. The 1945 Diocesan Conference noted that 5 million went to a place of worship each week whereas 45 million went to the cinema.

Evangelizing was to become ever more essential.

The Bishops

Campbell Richard Hone, who followed Seaton and was enthroned on 14 October 1938, had already had a long association with the diocese and had been the Suffragan Bishop of Pontefract since 1931. He came to Wakefield first in 1902 as Bishop Eden's domestic chaplain before going on in 1905 to be the vice-principal of Leeds Clergy School where he had trained in 1898 and where, at the time, James Seaton had been the vice-principal. Born in Manchester in 1873, Hone was the son of the Reverend Evelyn Hone, Warden of Hulme Hall and Rector of Esher. He went to Blackheath Proprietory School. Writing of

Bishop Hone

his confirmation during this period he noted that he 'owed much to Dr Walsham How's book on the Holy Communion for some apprehension of the deeper spiritual significance of the service'. He went up to Oxford as an exhibitioner at Wadham College in 1892, where he played rugby for the University, was active in the College Literary Society, attended many Union debates, and took a degree in Classics in 1896. After a short period as a teacher, he returned to Oxford to read Theology in 1897. In his unpublished Memoir he admits that he 'came to realize that I certainly needed more help and discipline on the spiritual side as well as training and direction for the work of the ministry', and consequently he moved after a term to Leeds Clergy School. After ordination in 1898, he served as a curate at Holy Trinity, Habergham Eaves, in 1898–1902. In 1909, he returned for a substantial period to the Wakefield Diocese, first as the incumbent of Mount Pellon and subsequently, in 1916–20, as Vicar of Brighouse. From 1920, he was the Rector of Whitby and Rural Dean. His return to Wakefield in 1930 was initially as the Archdeacon of Pontefract, but within a year he had been installed as the first suffragan bishop. He proved to be the administrator that the diocese needed during the Second World War. Realism and optimism marked his career. Noel Hopkins, Provost of Wakefield, noted that he had many times heard him say, 'We must face the facts', but equally his exhortation had been 'to have faith and courage'. In the recollection of his grandson he was 'a striking looking man, like an eagle. Immensely spare, not to say gaunt, with his long face, high cheekbones, strong mouth, and skull-like head.' Hone took a keen interest in religious education and enjoyed committee work. While at Whitby he had worked with Bishop Eden on the revision of the West Riding concordat which formed the policy of the West Riding Education Committee until the 1944 Education Act. He served as Chairman of the National Society and steered the progress of the measure dealing with the relations of the National Society and the Church Assembly's Council of Education. He was also active in shaping the Church's policy in regard to the 1944 Education Bill and, as a member of the House of Lords from May 1944, took part in the debates in regard to its proposals for religious instruction. He was largely responsible for a successful amendment requiring Local Education Authorities to set up a standing Religious Advisory Committee. He retired in 1945.

Henry McGowan, the fifth bishop, had been called the diocese's 'only tragedy'. Always an immensely hard worker, he had seriously over-taxed his strength for years before coming to Wakefield, so developing a serious heart condition. He was consecrated in York Minster on 2 February 1946 and enthroned at Wakefield on 16 February 1946. In the short time that he was bishop, he spent periods in hospital in Birmingham and London and, between November 1947 and Easter 1948, was unable to undertake any work. Nonetheless, his ready friendliness swiftly earned the regard of his clergy. McGowan was born in Bristol in 1891. He attended Bristol Grammar School and went on to St Catharine's College, Cambridge. He graduated in 1913, taking second-class honours in the Classical Tripos. He trained for the ministry at Ridley Hall, Cambridge, and served as a curate in Cheltenham in 1914–16, and at St Michael and All Angels, Bournemouth, in 1916–23 with a break as chaplain to the 4th Division of the British Expeditionary Force in 1918–19. A man of liberal evangelistic views, his first living was at St Mark's, Birmingham, in 1923–25. From there he went to Emmanuel Church, Southport. During his time in Liverpool his contribution to church life expanded considerably. He was an able musician and in 1927–31 he was the organist and choirmaster of the College of Cantors, Liverpool Cathedral. He was also a lecturer at St Aidan's College, Birkenhead. He became Director of Music of the Cromer Convention in 1928, retaining the role after he moved back to Birmingham until 1938. In 1931, McGowan became Vicar of Aston, one of the largest parishes in England, combining that from 1938 with the role of Archdeacon of Aston, one of the youngest archdeacons in the country at the time. He was a member of the Anglican Evangelical Group movement and was its chairman in 1937–38. During the Second World War, when he showed energy and foresight in facing the difficulties caused by the bombing of the city, he added to a heavy schedule by taking lunchtime services in industrial plants. He found something of a recreation in Freemasonry and in Wakefield he joined Richard Linnecar Lodge. His major contribution to the diocese lay in pursuing the 1945 appeal set up by his predecessor, with an energy and unsparing commitment that was perhaps greater than his waning strength could bear. He was admitted to

Bishop McGowan

the Brotherton Wing of Leeds General Infirmary in August 1948 and died on 8 September.

Roger Plumpton Wilson, who oversaw the post-war reorganization, was still only forty-four when he was consecrated on 25 April 1949 and enthroned on 30 May, slightly younger even than Bishop Eden had been. He had the youth and the vigour for the work. He also had a young family – three children between the ages of two-and-a-half and eleven. Wilson's nine years in Wakefield were said to have been some of the happiest of his life. Inclined to a liberal Catholicism with gifts that were primarily pastoral, he promoted ecumenism. He has been described as one of the Church of England's 'most elegant bishops'. However, he was also homely and tolerant. He showed a particular understanding of the divorced. Born in 1905, he came from a clerical family. His father was a vicar in Bristol and his cousin, Michael Ramsey, rose to be Archbishop of Canterbury. He was educated with Ramsey at Sandroyd Preparatory School in Surrey, at Winchester School, and at Keble College, Oxford, obtaining his degree in Classics in 1928. Rather than going directly into the Church, as was something of a norm at that time, he went on to teach at Shrewsbury School and at St Andrew's College, Grahamstown, South Africa. He trained at Westcott House, Cambridge in 1934–35. Once he took orders, he progressed quite swiftly through positions as a curate in a Liverpool slum parish and in London, where he and his vicar helped to bring in Jewish refugees escaping from Hitler, and as a vicar at South Shore, Blackpool, to become Archdeacon of Nottingham, within ten years, in 1945. Education was always one of his central interests and in 1957–71 he chaired the Church of England Schools Council. In 1958 he became Bishop of Chichester. Some years after leaving Wakefield, in 1963, he was appointed Clerk of the Closet to the Queen, which

Bishop Wilson

meant that he advised Her Majesty on the appointment of her honorary canons and examined theological books and articles that she had been asked to read. He retired in 1970 and was invested with the KCVO. After his retirement, he served as an assistant bishop in the Diocese of Bath and Wells until growing blindness made the work too difficult. He died at Stanton Drew, Somerset, in 2002.

John Alexander Ramsbotham had been the Suffragan Bishop of Jarrow for eight years before he was enthroned as the Bishop of Wakefield on 28 June 1958. Born in 1906, the son of a clergyman, he was educated at Haileybury, and Corpus Christi College, Cambridge where he was a choral scholar and took a first in Theology as well as a second in History. He trained for the ministry at Wells Theological College and served as a curate at All Hallows, Lombard Street, London, but gave much of his time to working as the Chaplain to the Student Christian Movement. He returned to Wells as chaplain and vice-principal before becoming Warden of the College of the Ascension, Selly Oak, where much of the work lay in training missionaries. In 1942, he moved to become Rector of Ordsall, Nottingham, then Vicar of St George's, Jesmond. He was a leading figure in the Parish and People Movement and, in his enthronement address, he spoke of the need to recognize the relationship between the clergy and the laity in a shared extended pastorate. He was a supporter of the Fellowship of St Sergius and St Alban, a movement, advocated too by men from the College of the Resurrection, seeking closer relations between Anglo-Catholics and the Eastern Orthodox Churches. He was essentially a pastor and spiritual guide rather than an administrator. His love of singing and music underlay his concern for public worship at the parish level. He gave a new emphasis to the importance of the service of women to the Church. In Wakefield his concern was primarily to further the church's role in the civil, cultural and industrial life of the community. He was the first President of Wakefield Civic Society when it was formed in 1964. During his last two years in the diocese he suffered from ill-health, and a stroke in the summer of 1967 led to his resignation that October. However, after his retirement he was able to serve in the Diocese of Newcastle as an assistant bishop.

There were four bishops of Pontefract in 1939–68. The longest serving, Tom Longworth, had been Rector of Guisborough in 1927–35 and would very probably have known Hone during his time at Whitby. He held the additional role of Archdeacon of Pontefract. Following Longworth's translation to Hereford in 1949, 51-year-old Arthur Harold Morris was consecrated in York Minster on 1 November. During the war Morris had served as a chaplain in the Royal Air Force. He had come to the diocese in 1946 as Archdeacon of Halifax and, as an economic measure since the Sanderson bequest was no longer sufficient to cover as many posts, held the position of Archdeacon of Pontefract as well as that of Bishop. Morris left the diocese in 1954 to be Bishop of St Edmundsbury and Ipswich. He was succeeded in November 1954 by George William Clarkson, formerly Vicar of Newark. He moved in 1961 to be Dean of the new Cathedral of Guildford which was consecrated that May and where he was installed on 9 September 1961. Of the fourth suffragan bishop of the period, Eric Treacy, much more will be said in later pages.

New Churches and an Old Chapel

One of Hone's first acts as bishop, on 29 October 1938, was the consecration of St Paul's, Old Town, Barnsley, which had been designed by C. F. Moxon and is the only Byzantine church in the diocese. Its origins lay in a mission 'planted' by St Mary's in 1887 with services in a room in a cottage; the old building had been bought in 1890 and dedicated by Bishop How in 1894. St Paul's occupied a new site. Bishop Wilson later described it as the 'loveliest little church in the diocese'.

St Paul's, Old Town, Barnsley

THE DIOCESE BETWEEN 1938 AND 1967

Work on the new front for the Chantry Chapel on Wakefield Bridge, 1939

A second new church, Holy Trinity, Denby Dale, a daughter church of the parish of Cumberworth, was consecrated on 15 June 1939.

One of Hone's roles as Bishop of Pontefract had been to chair the committee appealing for funds for major restoration work on the Chantry Chapel of St Mary the Virgin, Wakefield Bridge. The scheme was warranted after the erection of the new bridge across the River Calder in 1933 took traffic away from the medieval bridge and its chapel. The venture was rather a civic than ecclesiastical one and was supported by the Chantry Lodge of Freemasons with little reference to the parish authorities. A new front, designed by Sir Charles Nicholson, the diocesan architect, was dedicated in July 1940 but the six stone figures which had been created to fill its niches were kept in store until the end of the war.

The restoration was not done without the friction which marked clear differences in churchmanship. Albert Chatfield, the vicar of the parish of St Mary which included the Chantry, and who had been appointed by the Peache Trustees, was staunchly evangelical and asserted that he would have no statues on 'his' building. The figures were put in place only after Chatfield left.

Bishop Hone's Primary Visitation

In 1940, Hone revived the ancient practice of the Bishop's Visitation, sending a form with a substantial number of printed questions to each incumbent. These related, *inter alia*, to the staffing of the parish, confirmation candidates, the times of the Sunday and weekday services, the extent to which the 1928 Service Book was replacing the 1662 one (evidently very extensively), the numbers on the electoral roll, the Sunday and day schools (if any), and the existence of regular groups such as the Mothers' Union, Girls' Friendly Society, and the Scouts. Incumbents were asked to quantify the numbers of their congregation who were then on active service and to state whether they had written about them to the men's military chaplains. Figures requested for the number of baptisms in 1910, 1920, 1930 and 1939 showed a progressive decline except in parishes where there were new housing estates.

The 226 completed forms, which provide a fascinating snapshot of the diocese of the time, included ones from every parish, the conventional districts of Lundwood and of Wrangbrook with North Elmsall, the chapelry at Stainborough, and Holgate Hospital. Their evidence shows the very wide variety of attitudes, churchmanship, practices and activities across the diocese. Some few returns show problems where old and failing incumbents could no longer fulfil their role: Frederick Egerton had been at Knottingley since 1885; the incumbent of East Knottingley, Walter Musgrove, who had served as Curate in Charge since 1938, completed the return for both parishes.

The returns show that Wakefield Cathedral and St Martin's, Brighouse, had three curates. There were two curates at All Hallows, Almondbury, St Mary's, Barnsley, All Saints, Castleford, St Mary's, Elland, St James's, Heckmondwike, St Peter's Huddersfield, St Paul's, King Cross, All Saints', Normanton, St Mary's, South Elmsall, St John's, Penistone, St Stephen's, Rashcliffe, and St Helen's, Sandal. A further 64 parishes had one curate but by far the great majority of incumbents were without any ordained assistance. Church Army captains served as stipendiary Readers at St Cuthbert's, Ackworth, St John's, Carlton, All Souls, Haley Hill, All Saints', Normanton, St Giles's, Pontefract, St Luke's, Sharlston, and St Mary's, Todmorden. The diocese had one ordained stipendiary deaconess, Alison Dale, at Halifax Parish Church. Very little use was made of lay workers although in some parishes members of youth clubs and other laity helped with visiting. St Helen's, Hemsworth, continued to rely on the old tradition of District Visitors.

Tensions over the reservation of the sacrament were still quite marked.

Hone asked for information about the practice. The Rector of All Saints', Castleford, waxed enthusiastic about it. Elland had never had reservation but Morris Maddocks thought 'the time was now ripe to do so'. Charles Welsh at St Barnabas's, Crosland Moor, remarked that in the past it had been badly needed and an aumbry was about to be dedicated. But the very great majority of respondents commented that their customary practice was simply to take the consecrated sacrament to the sick and housebound directly from the church Eucharist. Indeed George Savery at St Saviour's, Ravensthorpe, thought that the alleged need for reservation was an exaggerated one.

Hone asked specifically about Sung Eucharist. At St Michael's, Wrangbrook, Sung Eucharist at 9.30am had become the principal service and was followed by a parish breakfast. At St Saviour's, Ravensthorpe, it was a 'well-established tradition' and the people were 'used to nothing else'. But at Emmanuel, Shelley, John Broadhurst held it only at Easter, Whitsuntide and Christmas as his people 'do not welcome this service and education is difficult'. At Emmanuel, Lockwood, William Littlewood had introduced it as recently as Advent 1939 but felt that it seemed to be welcomed and it drew on average twenty-four communicants, twice as many as at the earlier celebration.

In some parishes there were daily weekday services of both Matins and Evensong. In some there were services only on two or three weekdays. In some there were none. What was, however, almost uniform was the near total absence of any laity from any weekday service anywhere. Where some attendance was noted, it was never more than two or three people.

In general, clergy thought that children should be confirmed between the ages of twelve and fourteen. Some were prepared to go as low as ten. Frank Lee at St John's, Wakefield, wanted to follow a practice advocated by the Bishop of Liverpool that children be admitted to Holy Communion as soon as they were old enough to understand the service but only be confirmed later. Many clergy thought that the adolescent period between fourteen and eighteen was inappropriate. A good number of clergy kept an eye on the recently confirmed through Communicants' Guilds.

Where parishes had their own church schools, these might be regarded as a great joy – in particular where the clergy were welcomed and a senior member of staff served on the PCC or as a churchwarden – or as simply a drain on financial resources and of little value to the church itself. In many schools the preponderance of children were from Nonconformist families. Indeed at Ravensthorpe they were 'some of the nicest'. Clergy in some parishes grumbled that the Church of England children went to the school nearest to their home regardless of whether it was a church one or a secular council one. Many also complained that teaching staff lived outside the parish and had no interest in the church. At St Botolph's, Knottingley, Walter Musgrove remarked, 'The school cannot be considered a valuable asset because of the failure of the old-time church teacher. Of our present staff of ten, only four have any real interest in the church, most live away from the parish, all their energies are devoted to educational efficiency. Either the church has failed the church training colleges or the church training colleges have failed the church.'

Beyond Bible classes in some, but by no means all, parishes, the returns showed little evidence of adult education. A handful of parishes had study courses in Lent and, of these few, some were devoted to lantern lectures on work in the mission fields. However, at Whitechapel, William Black had made use of lantern lectures on the history of the Church of England during the preceding Lent.

While the existence of uniformed organizations such as the Scouts and Guides was sporadic, 200 of the parishes had branches of the Mothers' Union. In some that did not, there was instead a Women's Fellowship, Women's Guild, or Fellowship of Marriage. At St Mary's, Woodkirk, there was 'a splendid non-sectarian women's Bible Class' with forty or fifty women who were described by George Reynolds as 'the very backbone of the church'.

As with virtually every other aspect of church life, parishes varied widely in their interest in supporting missionary work. In the majority, missionary collecting boxes were available and there was at least an annual sermon, often at St Andrew's tide. In some there was far more enthusiasm. The Youth Club at St Luke's, Milnsbridge, had just put on a 'Chinese missionary play' in an attempt to stimulate interest. The congregation at Todmorden was supporting a small school in the Madras Presidency. All Saints', South Kirkby, it was claimed, had 'adopted Gambia' (*sic*) and sent about £39 a year. At Christ Church, South Ossett, the Boys' Brigade and the Guides supported hospital cots in Korea. The Sunday School at Milnsbridge had 'adopted' a girl in Zanzibar. Treleaven Sweeting at Holy Trinity, South Crosland, who had served at Medicine Hat, Canada, remarked that there was 'some support' there for his 'old prairie mission'. The Youth Club at Trinity Church, Ossett, was supporting an African medical student.

The clergy were asked to give some indication of the percentage of their population who were members of other denominations. Many commented that support for Nonconformity seemed to be declining but many, too, commented that a good proportion had no church affiliation at all. Two Barnsley incumbents referred to the sporadic flaring up of 'fancy' religions such as the Calvary Holiness Church and the Four Square Gospellers. George Reynolds at Woodkirk commented that Mazdashan (*sic*) in Leeds attracted 'a few cranks'.

Hone invited his clergy to add to their responses by writing about any particular concerns they had. Most chose not to. A number highlighted what they saw as increasing immorality. The Vicar of St Michael's, Carleton, noted that he needed 'a lay man or woman evangelical to help but there is no money to pay. The moral problem of youth has completely changed in the last ten years and needs trained men to deal with it both collectively and individually. The increased immorality in the best of youth is the despair of the older priests of today.' On a brighter note the Vicar of St Luke's, Sharlston, referred to the value of a recent production of a Passion play adding, 'I think the way is now open for some missionary plays.' His frustration was apparent in another comment, 'How does one get miners to come to church instead of sending their wives?' A handful of clergy referred to the desirability of the union of some town-centre benefices, among them Joseph Butterworth at Holy Trinity, Halifax; Arthur Cooper at St Paul's, Halifax, questioned whether his parish was any longer required as most of his congregation lived outside it. James Gray, the Rector of All Saints', Castleford, thought that the church had wrong priorities: he wanted 'a greater use of the union of benefices in large areas and a sparing policy as to new buildings at the expense of living agents'. Moves towards church unity were mentioned by a few incumbents: George Dawson at St John's, Kirkheaton, said he 'would welcome a keener lead towards unity, firstly with free churchmen then with Romans if possible'. He also thought that another evangelical revival was long overdue 'rather than a ritualistic revival by ceremonial etc inside the church which does not touch the man in the street'.

The Impact of the Second World War

Churches in the diocese suffered comparatively little from enemy attack during the Second World War. The one serious casualty was St Andrew's, Purlwell, which was bombed shortly before Christmas in 1940. Choir practice was in progress when the air-raid warning sounded but members were safely home before the bombs fell. The church was rendered largely unusable. The great East window was pitted with splinters, every door except that at the main entrance was blown out, and one wall leaned badly outward. Services continued, however, in the Lady Chapel. The War Damage Commission gave £90,000 for its restoration and the church was rededicated in 1949. During the war an incendiary bomb landed on the roof of the Lady Chapel at St Hilda's, Halifax, but did no serious damage.

Church crypts, including those of the cathedral and Holy Trinity, Huddersfield, were taken over as public air-raid shelters. The Home Guard used the Quarry at the Community of the Resurrection for exercises. The cellars at the Community were taken over by the West Riding County Council as a shelter for Christ Church Infants School. Among other church buildings which were requisitioned was Lees Moor Church School, Thornhill, which had been closed because of the lack of any air-raid shelter and which became a Municipal Kitchen. Elsewhere parochial halls and Sunday School buildings were requisitioned for use as first-aid posts or bases for the army or the ARP.

At the Community of the Resurrection, the brothers tried to grow more food themselves; in 1943 they took a number of prizes at the Dig for Victory show at Battyeford. Students at the College dug up the lawn in 1940 to grow potatoes. The Mirfield Chronicler recorded that rogation processions 'had more than usual reality'.

Volunteers (often women) were sought from congregations to join rotas for fire-watching. Incumbents were expected to play a part in Civil Defence activities; they could enrol in the local defence volunteer force but were advised that they should not bear arms. One of the brethren at Mirfield became the captain in the local Fire Guards.

Across the diocese, evening services were brought forward to the afternoon to avoid lighting churches at night and to allow the congregation to return home by daylight. Confirmations, too, were in the afternoon. Men who took part in the training activities of the ARP missed services and there were complaints that some missed weekday meetings of their parish branch of the Church of England Men's Society. A men's group at Cudworth closed down because of the demands of the ARP and of additional shift work in the coal mine. The numbers of pupils in church schools (and, of course, state ones) decreased slightly as children under five were excluded.

Some incumbents reported in the Visitation returns that troops stationed locally were a threat to the moral welfare of young women, but at St Michael's, Thornhill, the men staffing a small searchlight battery were welcomed and made honorary members of the Men's Institute.

Issues of the *Wakefield Diocesan News* carried a variety of war-related information and injunctions: church towers were not to be used for guns or searchlights or any military purpose except observation and communication, and there was a warning that the lead on the roofs could be easily damaged; bells were not to be rung except for alarm purposes; place names on church notice boards should be painted over; editors were to take care that their parish magazines did not convey the whereabouts of troops or any other information that might help the enemy.

The annual diocesan conferences were scheduled for one day rather than the previous two. Central among the concerns of the 1941 Conference, held in the Jubilee Hall of Wakefield Girls' High School, seems to have been a report from the Diocesan Dilapidations Board about local authorities surveying iron and steel railings with a view to requisitioning them. Provost Hopkins urged the necessity of keeping the railings round the cathedral in order to 'control' the churchyard.

At the beginning of the war, the diocese dispensed with its Sunday School organizer. The number of candidates for ordination declined. By 1940 nine clergy from the diocese had been called up to serve as chaplains in the armed forces. By the autumn of 1941, when twenty-two clergy had gone for this purpose, including six from the Community of the Resurrection, Hone's concern lay with staffing his parishes. In his Memoir, Hone recalled the extra problems of work involved by the presence of troops stationed in the diocese and his own additional work in taking confirmations for service personnel, usually girls, quartered in the barracks at Pontefract.

New emergency hospitals had also to be served. Pinderfields Hospital, Wakefield, created in the grounds of the West Riding Pauper Lunatic Asylum and making use of its acute block, took its first trainload of sick and wounded soldiers on 18 February 1940.

Emergency wards which were provided for wartime casualties at Pinderfields Hospital and remained in use for a further sixty years

The war found Britain facing the problem of refugees, in particular from mass evacuation of the Channel Islands. Diocesan clergy served on local committees for dealing with their welfare.

As in the First World War, the diocese raised money towards facilities for chaplains to the Armed Services. The five Yorkshire dioceses together gave £5,400 to help the Church Army provide three huts for forces in the Middle East.

Civic authorities organized week-long fund-raising campaigns, such as Warship Week, to provide money for the war effort. In the principal towns, services were held in the parish church to mark the event.

The Call to Worship and Witness

Bishop Hone, who had appointed Patrick Carnegy as the Canon Missioner in 1940, promoted a Call to Worship and Witness with the aim of strengthening and revivifying church life and worship. In November 1941, the *Diocesan Gazette* reported that sixty parishes had embarked on the scheme and that most had received a Bishop's Messenger. Three months later another ten parishes had joined the scheme. Individual parishes in the diocese had over the decades seen numerous ad hoc missions, but this was different in two ways: the initiative had come from the bishop, seeking to engage the diocese as a whole, and instead of recruiting visiting missioners, the Bishop's Messenger prepared the parish priest to be the missioner himself. Each parish was free to pursue the Call in its own way. Some formed prayer and study groups or created a band of lay people to act as 'godparents' to the newly confirmed. The diocese established a Fellowship of Worship and Witness to create a group of evangelists with members in each parish. Hone recalls that ultimately about ninety of the 220 parishes took part. In each of these either he or the Bishop of Pontefract held services at which people publicly renewed their baptism vows and were invited to join the Fellowship, promising to worship each Sunday in church, to be faithful communicants, to pray for themselves and others each day, and to bring at least one person every year to Christ and the Church. In June 1942, for example, 130 communicants at All Saints', Crofton, renewed their vows. Hone particularly recalled a service at St Peter's, Felkirk, where 'some miners and colliery officials made together their profession of loyalty to Christ and His Church'.

The End of the War, the Diocesan Appeal for £250,000, the Renewal of the Cathedral Bells, and Bishop Hone's Retirement

Under a Measure passed by the Church Assembly in 1941, each diocese was expected to establish a Diocesan Reorganization Committee to deal especially with the consequences of war damage. By 1943, discussions, in some part way ahead of their time, had considered the amalgamation of parishes, the redrawing of parish boundaries, the suppression of redundant churches, the abolition of the parson's freehold to make it easier to remove clergy from their benefices and so accelerate amalgamations, the cutting down of higher incomes and the levelling up of smaller ones, the reformation of the system of patronage, and the disposal of large parsonage houses.

As war seemed to be nearing its close, the Ministry of Works (the government department formed initially in 1943 which preceded the Ministry of Public Buildings and Works and which was in some respects the ancestor of the Department of the Environment) asked each diocese for plans identifying what building they hoped to undertake in the next ten years. Taking into account the requirements of the 1944 Education Act, under which each diocese had to indicate which schools it would maintain, the Diocesan Reorganization Committee asked the bishop to form an appeal committee, recommending a target of £150,000 which was subsequently raised to £250,000. Every other diocese in England mounted a similar appeal. Bishop Hone launched the appeal formally in May 1945. It was to be seen as a thanksgiving for the end of the war, and as a means of providing for future need in terms of preserving as many church schools as possible, providing churches in new areas, training clergy (including many men returning from the armed forces who were said to be seeking ordination) and teachers, helping the churches in Europe and helping the missionary work of the church overseas, and was to run for three years. It was to raise £84,000 for new churches and mission rooms, £50,000 for schools, £10,000 for the Church of England's central needs, £3,000 for the training college at Ripon, and £3,000 for churches in Europe. Deanery sub-committees were formed and each parish was asked to raise a sum equal to twenty-five times its annual quota. Raising the money was a struggle; the country was still feeling the financial constraints of the war years. Many parishes found difficulty in raising even their quota let alone a much more sizeable sum. Moreover Hone, having launched the appeal earlier in the month, held a synod of clergy on 29 May at which he announced his intention to retire later that year. He was seventy-two. He retired officially on 15 September and moved to Oxford where he was for a time engaged in writing a biography of the Wakefield-born court physician and philanthropist; *The Life of Dr John Radcliffe* was published in 1950.

It had not been possible to mark the end of the war by ringing the cathedral bells. They had been silent since 1936 as their frames were held to be dangerous. Given the struggle to raise money for the Diocesan Appeal it was scarcely politic to turn to the parish churches for support for their renewal. Instead an appeal was launched by the Mayor of Wakefield, Councillor Effie Crowe, in 1946 for £4,000. Due to its success, the tower was strengthened, a new clock and chime was provided at the time of the re-hanging of the bells, and the peal, with a new bell added, was dedicated by Bishop McGowan on 18 October 1947. He struck one ten times to symbolize the ten centuries of Christian worship on the site. Teams of campanologists from across the north of England spent the next few hours happily ringing changes.

A week later there was a service in the cathedral for parishes to bring their latest donations to the Diocesan Appeal. Representatives of 197 of the 220 parishes attended, bringing £35,000 in all. Despite his failing health, Bishop McGowan was present on 4 May 1948 when parishes from the Wakefield Deanery brought £346 for the Appeal to a gathering in Unity House. He spoke of the need for financial support for men seeking ordination, few now being able to afford to pay for themselves.

The Appeal was wound up in January 1949. The events organized by individual parishes included bazaars, concerts, play readings and whist drives. In April 1946, and for the first time, St Michael's, Emley, put on a Passion Play, *For our Salvation*, in the church hall. Subsequently, the vicar, Harold Pobjoy, referred to his parish's 'woefully small'

In the cathedral bell chamber, Liz Preston

contribution. The total raised from all sources was only £140,000. A service of thanksgiving was held in the cathedral on 8 January when Bishop Longworth, whose work had been much increased by the ill-health of McGowan, received the final donations but the event was further clouded when illness prevented the Bishop of Ripon from attending. The Provost, Noel Hopkins, gave the address in his place. The appeal committee then became an appeal continuation committee.

Another grand diocesan event followed shortly afterwards. Prior to the Lambeth Conference (the first since 1930), teams of colonial bishops visited each diocese. Five came to Wakefield, including Bishop Gwyer of Georgia, South Africa, who had been the incumbent of St John's, Wakefield, and Bishop Daly of Gambia and Rio Pongas, who had been the first Vicar of Airedale. There were two services in the cathedral on 12 June, the one in the morning for children. In the evening, children from thirty-two parishes mounted a pageant, *The World Wide Church*, in St John's Church.

Tom Longworth, the Bishop of Pontefract, became the Bishop of Hereford in 1949.

More New Churches, Dual-Purpose Buildings, and Mission Halls

As Britain's economy recovered after the war, local authorities resumed their activity in clearing urban slums and building housing estates, often on virgin ground on the outskirts of the towns. Private developers, too, created new residential areas. This presented the problem for the diocese of on the one hand churches which had lost their local population and on the other substantial areas where people had no nearby church. In 1952, Bishop Wilson wrote in the *Diocesan News*, 'A new England is arising in our midst, on the outskirts of our towns. Will it be pagan or Christian?' Providing new churches for this 'new England' was regarded as vital. Accepting that some urban churches were redundant was also essential.

A total of £47,000 from Bishop Hone's appeal had been made available for buildings other than church schools and this was allocated to assist twenty-nine schemes, including three new churches, five church halls and three parsonage houses. In the case of the new churches, both economy and practicality suggested the idea of dual-purpose buildings which would provide worship space but which were flexible enough to serve other purposes.

The first new church since the war was a replacement for an old mission room, St Peter's at Hunsworth in the parish of Birkenshaw. The new St

Peter's, which was designed with a hall and meeting rooms, was financed in part by a donation of £2,000 from the Bishop's Appeal Fund, in part by donations of £500 or so from a small number of local industries, and in part by loans which were guaranteed, rather bravely, by individual members of the congregation, each offering to assure a modest sum towards the total. It was dedicated by Bishop Wilson on 29 June 1951. The architect was a Mr Conrad. Birkenshaw further enhanced its mission-church provision in 1958 when it replaced its original church at East Bierley, St Luke's, by buying East Bierley Memorial Hall and converting it into a church and church centre.

A church presence at Fixby, in a developing area on the outskirts of Huddersfield, was envisaged as early as 1944. In 1947, John Lister, then Vicar of St John the Evangelist, Huddersfield, asked a group of women from his church to hold monthly house meetings in the area. A Fixby Ladies' Fellowship was formed a year later. The scheme for a church-cum-hall was launched in 1951. The foundation stone for St Francis was laid on 27 May 1953 and the building was dedicated on 10 February 1954.

The parish of St John's, Carlton, was responsible for the formation of St Helen's, Athersley, just on the north side of Barnsley, to serve Barnsley Corporation's New Lodge and Athersley estates. The project began before the war when a wooden hut was set up in what was then Carlton Lane, and was dedicated by Bishop Seaton on 17 January 1937. Seaton

St Francis's Church, Fixby

blessed its altar, dedicated to St Helen. The new building was designed by Robert G. Easdale. Its foundation stone was laid on 30 October 1954 in the presence of Bishop Wilson. Recognizing the role of Barnsley Corporation in providing new housing, Wilson observed on the occasion, 'No Public Authority can cater for the spiritual needs of the people whatever their resources.' The church was consecrated by Wilson a year later. It had cost £11,000, £4,000 of which came from the Appeal Fund and £1,000 from the Church Commissioners. Within a few years St Helen's became a conventional district with its own Priest in Charge, although it was not until 24 October 1973 that it became a separate parish.

The problem of a moving population was solved at Almondbury by the closure of the two mission churches of St Helen and St Michael and the building of a new church at Quarry Hill to serve the Fearnside Council Estate. The church, dedicated appropriately to St Michael and St Helen, cost £10,000 but some of the money came from the sale of the old St Michael's to the Roman Catholic Church. It was dedicated in May 1955.

The sale of a mission church to Roman Catholics provoked some public criticism. As a consequence, when the closure of one of Thornhill's mission churches, St John the Baptist, Thornhill Lees, was decided by the parochial church council in 1956, with the possibility of offering that, too, to the Roman Catholics, Bishop Wilson suggested the need for a cautious approach. The sale of St Michael's had been made palatable, he wrote, only because it had been replaced by a splendid new church. There were no such plans at Thornhill. The parish could make it known that the building was for sale but it must be for the Catholics to make the first overture in regard to any purchase. Wilson was anxious, too, that the loss should not be seen 'as a retreat'; the money from the sale must be set aside for constructive purposes, perhaps for a house for a curate. The mission church was, in fact, sold to the Roman Catholics in 1957. It had been recognized as 'at a low ebb' in 1947 when a scheme had been mooted – long before reordering became the vogue – to develop the building for social use by converting it into a parish hall and turning the vestries into a kitchen and cloakrooms.

In January 1956, Bishop Wilson launched an appeal for a further £75,000. (John Ramsbotham, his successor, was to comment that it should have been for £200,000.)

Meanwhile Lord Savile had laid the foundation stone of a new church at Mixenden in the parish of Illingworth in July 1954. Again serving a corporation housing estate, Holy Nativity was, like St Francis at Fixby, built for mixed use. The church was opened in 1956. Mixenden became a conventional district in 1958.

St Giles's, Pontefract, had had an iron mission church at Tanshelf, dedicated to St Mary, since 1903. In 1952, it was decided to build a new St Mary's to serve the Chequerfield estate. The parochial church council bought land offered by Pontefract Corporation, and plans for a dual-purpose building were drawn up by the local architects Tennant and Smith in 1954. At the east end were a chancel and an apse-like sanctuary. At the west were a kitchen, two school rooms, a store-room and generously sized cloakroom/lavatories. In between was a hall, with a stage at the further end from the chancel, which could provide the seating for the congregation or be available for other functions including concerts and dramatic performances. Open-air services began on the site in June 1954. St Giles's formed an Evangelistic Committee with members visiting every house on the estate. Sunday Schools and a Young Wives group were started in three of the houses so that the church, when it came, should have a ready-made congregation. The building was dedicated by Bishop Wilson on 8 May 1957. It had cost £12,000. Of this, £5,000 came from the diocesan appeal funds, £5,000 was lent free of charge by the Church Commissioners, and £2,000 had to be found locally. Some of the fittings of the new church came from the original St Mary's.

Before the war there were plans for a church at Lundwood in the parish of Monk Bretton to serve another large Barnsley housing estate. For some years services were held in a temporary building. In 1957, Lundwood was constituted as the new district of St Mary Magdalene, with the provision that it would become an independent parish upon the consecration of a new church. In fact, and after a change of view by the Church Commissioners, the old hall-church was simply adapted as a parish church.

The parish of St Andrew, Wakefield, undertook the provision of a hall-church to serve the Eastmoor Council Estate. The foundation stone of St Swithun's was laid on 13 April 1957 and the building was opened on 20 December 1958.

A number of new parochial halls were supported by the Appeal funds. A hall for St Paul's, Barnsley, for which £3,000 came from the fund, was dedicated by Wilson on 11 May 1957. Like St Helen's at Athersley it was designed by Robert Geoffrey Easdale, the Diocesan Surveyor. Fitzwilliam, in the parish of Kinsley, was in the 1950s effectively a new community. Here, as a war memorial, a hall-church was built to replace a mission hut and was first brought into use on 5 March 1958.

It had been realized by 1937 that a new church would be needed to serve the developing housing estate at Rawthorpe but this was for a time a casualty of the shortfall in Bishop Wilson's appeal fund. A conventional district was formed from a part of Moldgreen and a part of Kirkheaton in

1955 but the church of St James was not completed until 1960. Becoming a parish in 1963, it was the last to be created until the formation of group and team ministries, which began in 1975, saw chapels of ease become parish churches.

In 1956, the Church Commissioners undertook the construction of a new chapel for Bishop's Lodge by converting the coach house. It was designed to hold 40–50 people. The altar, panelling and pews of the old chapel at Bishopgarth were brought back into use.

Bishop Ramsbotham dedicated the chapel of St Raphael at Pinderfields Hospital, Wakefield, on 30 March 1963. Built from stone taken from mill cottages in Nortonthorpe and given by T. Waddington and Sons, it had fittings by the 'mouse man', Robert Thompson. On 1 June 1963, Ramsbotham, who was a frequent visitor there, also dedicated a Calvary in the grounds of St Peter's Convent, which had been erected in memory of Mother Dora, the Superior from 1939 until her death in 1962.

From Fire and Flood

Among Bishop Wilson's acts was the reconsecration of churches which had been in one case removed, because of its proneness to flooding, and in two other cases rebuilt because of fires. St Peter's at Walsden had been consecrated originally in August 1848. As it approached its centenary it was destroyed by fire on 25 May 1948. Fund-raising to rebuild it began immediately and within eight years the work was done. Wilson carried out the reconsecration on 10 March 1956.

St James's, Chapelthorpe, was gutted by fire on 20 June 1951. Despite the attendance of fire engines from eight towns, it took a long time to bring the blaze under control: water pressure was low and hoses were run to Woolley Colliery Dam. Miners from the colliery helped to clear the debris and to lay rose beds around the ruined church; they erected a cross from some of the charred beams. The rebuilt church was reconsecrated on 26 July 1952.

It was flooding rather than fire that led to the rebuilding of St Andrew's, Ferry Fryston. Built at the beginning of the twelfth century, the church stood on the edge of the marshes bordering the River Aire. In recent years it had been out of use in wintertime when water rose to a height of two feet within the church itself. The doggedness of its vicar, Clarence Branch, who had come to the parish only in 1949, led to its being closed in April 1952 and moved stone by stone to a new site in the centre of Ferrybridge next to the vicarage. Wilson consecrated it on 12 September 1953.

St Andrew's after its removal from Ferry Fryston to Ferrybridge

Reordering at St Thomas the Apostle, Heptonstall

The widespread reordering of churches was still some years away but at Heptonstall a reordering of the 'new' (1854) church of St Thomas the Apostle, standing close to the ruins of the medieval church of St Thomas a Becket, was undertaken in 1964. It was financed by a legacy from Abraham Gibson (d. 1956), the last member of a family of cotton spinners who had lived at Greenwood Lee since the mid eighteenth century and had a long association with both the original and the Victorian church. The scheme, which was 'driven' by the vicar, Oliver Forshaw, was a radical one, designed to provide 'a twentieth-century adaptation of a traditional medieval style'. In fact it resulted in a light and open worship space. The Faculty refers to 'the removal from the ... church of all old furnishings'. These included the chancel screen, the pews, the altar, the pulpit and the lectern. The chancel floor was lowered to the level of the nave and a nave altar was installed. The gallery was removed and a new organ loft provided. The Lady Chapel was moved to the original vestry under the east end of the church and a new vestry was created. The old octagonal font

The reordered St Thomas's, Heptonstall, Phil White

from the earlier church was restored and the Victorian font repositioned. In place of the fixed pews, five-seat portable bench pews were provided.

The Union of Parishes, and Redundant Churches

The resumption of slum clearance led to the unions of a number of urban parishes in the 1950s and 1960s. The 1949 Pastoral Reorganization Measure facilitated such steps. Within weeks of his coming to the diocese in 1949, Bishop Wilson acknowledged that some churches in the centre of the larger towns were likely to go. In 1950 he took advantage of the vacancy at Christ Church, Thornes, to appoint the vicar of the neighbouring St James to hold the living in plurality as a first step towards union. (Similar strategies were to become common in later decades.)

In 1951, the Diocesan Pastoral Committee established an inquiry into the 'present and future status' of parishes within the Halifax Deanery. It recognized the eagerness for church building of earlier generations, when 'daughter' churches were founded 'in days when church or chapel, and their concerns, provided one of the few interests for a hard-driven people, and when there was no shortage of clergy'. Now these were difficult to maintain and rendered somewhat superfluous by demographic change. The first scheme, confirmed in February 1953, was for the union of the benefices of the two Halifax parishes of St James and St Mary. The order provided for St Mary's to remain as the parish church of the new benefice and for St James to be taken down. Described rather cruelly as 'pseudo-Gothic', St James had been built in 1832 to the design of John Oates. It was financed, like so many other churches in the diocese, with government money from the 'million' fund. Its parish was formed in 1843. It had been closed since the summer of 1952 when diseased timbers led to the structure being deemed dangerous.

In February 1956, the union of the beneficcs and parishes of St Paul's, Huddersfield, and St Peter's, Huddersfield's original parish church, was determined. There was no question here of demolition. St Paul's, a handsome building in a prominent position, built in the Early English style in 1829–30, was originally to be retained as a chapel of ease, but in 1958 it was leased to Huddersfield Corporation for use by Huddersfield Technical College. In 1975, it was sold to what had by then developed into Huddersfield Polytechnic.

The two further schemes for the merging of parishes during Wilson's bishopric were both in Wakefield and brought the demolition of Christ Church and of Holy Trinity. In the former case the parish was united in 1956 with Thornes, with St James's becoming the sole church for the combined areas. Christ Church had had a comparatively short life. It had been promoted in the 1870s by members of the Holy Trinity congregation, perhaps because of a growing Nonconformist cause near the waterside, and had been financed very largely by the widowed Mrs Rebecca Disney Robinson. The possibility of its redundancy had been mooted, by the Ecclesiastical Commissioners, as early as 1935 when the Lupset Estate was taking people from the Thornes Lane Wharf area. There was concern that small parishes lying close together were overstaffed and that large parishes were understaffed. A Public Inquiry at the time proved hostile but Bishop Seaton forecast that the loss of its population would mean taking a further look at the issue. In 1945, Bishop Hone had thought of uniting Christ Church with St Mary's after both parishes had been in the care of the Vicar of St Mary's during the war. An obvious problem was that St Mary's was also losing its population.

There was clearly reluctance to suppress the parish of Holy Trinity, with its very handsome church, and there was a suggestion that, as there would be little parochial work for a vicar, it would be appropriate for an incumbent who had some other diocesan appointment, but this came to nothing.

THE DIOCESE BETWEEN 1938 AND 1967

The interior of Holy Trinity, Wakefield in the 1890s

The possibility of redundancy had been forecast at least as early as 1939. In 1956, Holy Trinity was united with the cathedral, the original Wakefield parish church. There was some irony in this. Holy Trinity had been built in 1838–39 by people of an evangelical persuasion, very possibly to provide an alternative to the catholic tendencies of the parish church. Holy Trinity was demolished in 1957. Its bell was taken to the cathedral. Some of its fittings were sold to the new church at Mixenden, including a kneeling rail from the Lady Chapel, two short single kneeling rails and two prayer desks, all for £3. The Patrons of Holy Trinity agreed that all rights should pass to the bishop. The cathedral gained Holy Trinity Vicarage with the intention (never fulfilled) of turning it into flats for cathedral staff.

By far the most controversial scheme was the closure of St Mary's, Wakefield, and the union of the benefice and parish with that of St Andrew. Under the Church Extension Act of 1843, the two parishes had been carved at the same time in 1844 from the vast parish of Wakefield. It would be fair to say that St Mary's had been doomed for many years when the majority of properties in the parish were demolished in the 1950s. When Bishop Ramsbotham suspended the patronage in 1960 to facilitate its closure, and gave its care to the Vicar of St Andrew's to hold in plurality, George Clarkson, the then Bishop of Pontefract, warned him of 'a very tough fundamentalist-revivalist-interdenominationalist core' at St Mary's who would oppose any move to make the church redundant. St Mary's parochial church council campaigned vigorously against the proposal, citing its unusually marked evangelicalism as being rare in the diocese and as attracting worshippers from well beyond its parish boundary. In October 1963, the bishop told the protesters that there were two choices before them: the better option was to eliminate the parish, pull down the church, sell the vicarage and let St Andrew's absorb it; less good was the possibility of unscrambling the plurality and requiring St Mary's itself to find the money for its upkeep. It would, he said, be 'a retrograde step ... it encourages a sectarian mind in a small group of supporters'. It was more important, he felt, to set free both money and men to serve the Church overseas. The Peache Trustees, patrons of both St Andrew's and St Mary's, could find no one who would accept the living. The church closed on Easter Sunday 1964 but remained standing for some years, a prey to vandals and a constant anxiety to the Vicar of St Andrew's, who pressed for its demolition.

The first church to be lost in Dewsbury was that of St John the Baptist in Boothroyd Lane, Daw Green, which had been built in 1884 and given parochial status in 1885. The benefice and parish were united with St Matthew's, West Town in 1965, and St John's was demolished. St Philip's, in Leeds Road, Dewsbury (1878) closed at the end of October 1966, although the order for the union with All Saints (Dewsbury Parish Church) was not made until after Bishop Ramsbotham had retired.

The growing shortage of clergy and the poor state of some of the diocese's nineteenth-century churches were reflected in a conference at St Peter's Convent guest house, Horbury, in May 1967. The catalyst was the suspension of the patronage of Middlestown, where scaffolding had been erected over the porch of St Luke's Church to protect people from falling masonry. With Father Christopher Lowe of the Community of the Resurrection in the chair, the purpose was to explore how the churches in Horbury, Middlestown and Netherton could work more closely together. It was said to be probably the first conference of its kind in the district. It was attended by the clergy and by six lay people from each parish. Strategies identified at the time included having some joint services, holding group meetings for Bible study and instruction in the Christian faith, a joint training scheme for lay parish visitors, and taking part in Christian social service. A working group was set up to bring forward proposals for the future.

New Parsonage Houses

Many of the rectories and vicarages across the diocese were, in the post-war world where the real value of stipends was low and where there was no longer any likelihood of resident domestic staff, too large and far too uneconomic. While it was to be some decades before there was a major programme of replacement (after responsibility for the houses was transferred from the individual parish to the diocese), some houses were replaced and new ones built for new parishes. As was the case with new churches, the individual parish was expected to raise the bulk of the money required, but the appeal funds provided some assistance.

The first parsonage house to be built since the war was the new rectory at Thornhill. Here the vast Elizabethan residence and its 26-acre park were acquired by Dewsbury Corporation in order to use the house as a home for elderly men. Its estate became a public park. The new house was hallowed by Bishop Wilson on 26 February 1950.

The Diamond Jubilee

Bearing in mind the overriding needs of supporting the Diocesan Appeal it was determined to have only a very modest celebration of the Jubilee in 1948. It was marked during the weekend of 22 May 1948 in a much quieter way than the Jubilee of 1938 – just one major service, in the cathedral, with the Archbishop of York, Cyril F. Garbett, making his first visit to Wakefield and giving the address. Ten mayors with their mace-bearers walked in procession from the Town Hall after a civic lunch at County Hall. The procession included some 200 clergy from across the diocese together with Readers. Members of the Horbury and Mirfield religious communities were seated in the Lady Chapel. Both Bishop McGowan and Bishop Longworth were present. Bishop Hone returned for the event. Garbett spoke about the role of bishops, noting that although their legal powers were limited, the possibilities they had for moral and spiritual influence were almost unlimited. A collection was taken for the Appeal. Music was provided by the Brighouse and Rastrick Band.

Other Festivals and a Celebration of Television

Pageants were still popular in the 1950s. To mark the 1951 Festival of Britain the Huddersfield Deanery put on a pageant, *The Church and the Nation*, in June in Huddersfield Town Hall. A year later there was a pageant in the Old Rectory Park, Thornhill, on eleven centuries of the history of Thornhill, written by Harold Pobjoy, Rector of Emley, and produced by Canon Harold Coney, the Rector of Thornhill. The cast was drawn from the church, chapels and a social centre, and music was provided by the colliery band. The venture was a financial success, with audiences totalling 13,000. This was a time when Emley itself enjoyed the presence of a talented family at the rectory. The rector's wife, Marion Pobjoy, wrote the words and music for a number of light operas, performed to tremendous acclaim by the parishioners. Pobjoy wrote further pageants. The two daughters, Lorna and Nada were on the stage, the former working in various repertory companies.

The 1951 Festival of Britain was celebrated at St David's, Holmbridge, with a service on 14 October, shortly after the opening of the Holme Moss TV station. Television was integrated into the service. It was attended by the BBC Chief Engineer, a Mr Buckle, and also by the chairmen of Waterworks Committees and Water Engineers from both Batley and Huddersfield Corporations, on account of their water undertakings in the area.

After the end of the war, the annual Commemoration Day at the Community of the Resurrection was revived after a six-year break. The Anglican Players, founded in Leeds by Philip Lamb, Vicar of St Aidan's, gave a performance in the Quarry of *Go Down Moses*, written by Lamb himself. The play became one of the most popular religious dramas of the post-war period. The Mirfield Chronicler described it as 'a superb drama of Christian apologetic and tragedy of the soul of everyman'. 'One thanks God', he added, 'for the development of this new genus of drama by the Christian church proclaiming to a faithless generation the gospel of God.' The diamond jubilee of the Community was celebrated in July 1952, when it was estimated that over 5,000 people attended the service in the Quarry. Giving the address, Archbishop Cyril Garbett spoke of the blessing brought to the church by the revival of the religious life in the past hundred years. The medieval religious drama *Everyman*, directed by a member of the Community, was performed in the Quarry on 12 July.

The 250th Anniversary of the Society for the Propagation of the Gospel

Individual parishes, and in some cases deaneries, had always, to a greater or lesser extent, supported one or other of the missionary societies which had been formed in the eighteenth and nineteenth centuries to take Christianity to the British colonies and beyond. Some churches had their own particular missionary project: in the 1950s Holy Trinity, Wakefield, for example, supported a child at St Margaret's School, Ranchi and, when the church closed, the cathedral accepted this responsibility.

A degree of enthusiasm for the work of missionary societies was renewed after the war. It was, perhaps, the last time that they were given major attention before support gradually waned: £3,000 from Bishop Hone's appeal was given, divided equally, to the Society for the Propagation of the Gospel and the Church Missionary Society. The appeal fund also gave £500 towards the endowment of the new Diocese of Basutoland which was founded on 1 July 1950. It was said at the time that Wakefield was the only English diocese to contribute.

In May 1950, the Halifax Deanery Missionary Committee mounted a five-day missionary exhibition, *The Church Advancing*, featuring the work of the Society for the Propagation of the Gospel, the Church Missionary Society, the Society for Promoting Christian Knowledge, the Church of England Zenana Missionary Society, the British and Foreign Bible Society, the University Mission to Central Africa, the Mission to Seamen, and the Jerusalem and the East Mission.

A year later, the 250th anniversary of the founding of the Society for the Propagation of the Gospel provided an extended festival. The Society had been founded in 1701 to enhance the work of the Church of England among the American colonists. It expanded to evangelize native Americans and slaves. By the end of the century it was providing missionaries in Canada, Australia, New Zealand and West Africa. The diocese-wide celebrations began with a service in the cathedral on 16 June 1951. During the year, bishops from Jamaica, Pretoria and Rangoon toured the diocese. Bishop Coote, the new Bishop of Gambia, came to the diocese in September attending engagements at Christ Church, Staincliffe, St Michael's, Thornhill, Christ Church, Livesedge, St Paul's, Halifax, St Barnabas, Crosland Moor, All Saints', South Kirkby, and Huddersfield Parish Church. Finally, Bishop Wilson led a mass pilgrimage (there were 1,500 participants) by rail to Goole on 4 October 1952 to see HMS Centurion, a life-size replica of the ship which took the first missionary to the American colonies. There was a civic reception in Goole, then services in the parish church, where Wilson gave the address, and at St Paul's Church, where the Bishop of Pontefract spoke. The party was welcomed at Centurion by a team of Missioners led by the Bishop of Accra.

In January 1956, there was a four-day missionary exhibition in the recently built Sandal Parochial Hall, Wakefield. Entitled *Adventures by Land and Sea*, it embraced the Melanesian Mission, the Colonial and Continental Church Society, the United Society for Christian Literature, the Church of England Zenana Missionary Society, the Jerusalem and the East Mission, the Oxford Mission to Calcutta, the South American Missionary Society, and the Mission to Seamen. It was visited by some 1,800 schoolchildren and their teachers.

The subsequent decline in support for the missionary societies had a number of causes. Looking back, a paper of 1992 set out some of the reasons: Christian relief and development work had become separated from the rest of world mission, provided by, for example, Christian Aid, the Tear Fund, and the Oxford Committee for Famine Relief. Decolonization had its religious side and the traditional missionary era came to an end. There was a shift in giving, individually and from the parishes – publicity afforded to disasters led to giving to development and relief agencies. The political and social climate in the United Kingdom led to the perception that charity begins at home with donations given to anything from hospices to school equipment, and television spectaculars raising millions of pounds but none of it for the traditional missionary societies. It was said, too, that the success of the Church Urban Fund had an adverse effect on giving for overseas. Then there was the fundamental issue of whether missionary societies were seeking to convert when they had no right to do so.

The Industrial Christian Fellowship

In 1950, the diocese gained for the first time a figure whose role was to forge links with local industries and their workpeople. William Simpson came from similar positions in Bristol and Lichfield to be the Industrial Christian Fellowship Missioner, representing a body which had been founded shortly after the First World War as a result of the Archbishop's Report on Christianity and Industrial Problems. His appointment led to a conference of clergy, works managers, and trades union leaders in April 1951 at which a Diocesan Industrial Christian Fellowship was formed. This was to take a stand against 'atheistic materialism, apathy and indifference and to offer in the name of the Church some solutions to the problems of society'. In the next few years there were hundreds of visits to factories. Simpson retired in 1957.

Other Evangelizing Efforts

The youth of the diocese were the target of a missionary campaign in 1952. It was run rather along the lines of the Call to Worship and Witness of a decade earlier. For this project, however, it was young people who were commissioned to act as Bishop's Messengers. Their task was to visit youth groups and to challenger their peers to more vigorous work and service. A Fellowship of Vocation was formed in June 1953 for young men who might feel that they had a calling to the priesthood. Members were expected to do definite work in their own parish, to pray each morning and evening, to attend a communion service each Sunday, and also every Sunday to say the Collect for St Andrew's Day which reflects on the readiness of St Andrew to obey the call of Jesus. Members of the Fellowship had a Quiet Weekend at Hickleton Hall the following September.

There were renewed efforts to promote lay leadership, including the perennial quest for more Readers and for trained Women Workers who might make visiting a priority, especially in the new housing estates. An article in the *Wakefield Diocesan News* in February 1952 reminded of the opportunities for women to work in the field of moral welfare. In February 1958, Bishop Wilson wrote in the *Wakefield Diocesan News*, 'I could wish that Church Councils and others gave themselves more seriously to thinking out what should be expected of the witness of lay Christians today and thought less about what is expected of the ordained ministry.' However, he referred specifically only to Readers 'ministering on the one spare day so often to small groups of worshippers and all too little recognized'.

The Church Army mobile cinema van toured the diocese in September 1951. In a one-year experiment, Canon Cashmore, the Diocesan Missioner, commissioned a 26-seater motor coach for the parish of Felkirk with Brierley to operate from 1 March 1953 with the simple purpose of getting more people to the church and taking them to parochial functions, decanal and diocesan meetings, and for parochial outings. The vicar and other parishioners were to be the drivers. In 1963, after the bus had been in operation for a decade, a new vehicle was acquired for £450 and 'commissioned' by the Bishop of Pontefract, Eric Treacy.

The Diocesan Education Committee devised a Lent course, The Apostolic Church, for study by both clergy and laity. (It was possibly the first time they had done so.)

The 1950s was the era of Billy Graham, the 'popular' American Christian evangelist with his mammoth public meetings, like that in 1954 in the Harringay Arena, seeking to promote instant conversion with the plea to his audiences to receive Jesus as their personal Saviour and to live for Christ. Writing in the *Wakefield Diocesan News* in July 1954, Bishop Wilson said that the vast crowds attending his meetings 'were a mark of spiritual restlessness' and asked what people got 'after a new religious experience' when they went back to their own church? He sent out a questionnaire to the parochial church councils of each parish asking in particular about worship and the spiritual life of the church and what their church was doing towards fulfilling lay responsibilities and the evangelizing of their parish. Eighteen months later he made a report on the responses. Some PCCs answered very briefly. Some answered with an air of satisfaction as if all were well. The results were discussed by the Evangelistic Committee. Very few of the PCCs responded at all to a question about the lack of unity among Christian people.

There were (as there always had been since the inception of the diocese) individual and sporadic missionary events and activities. Father Mark Tweedy of the Community of the Resurrection led a Parish Convention in Featherstone in the Autumn of 1952. In 1953, St John's, Clifton, planned a three-year evangelistic campaign beginning with a convention in October. Their parish team of twelve missioners studied the diocesan Lent course, The Apostolic Church. From Easter 1954, members were to go out in pairs to visit lapsed communicants, parents and godparents. The plan was to hold house meetings for them.

There was an Evangelistic Crusade in Wakefield in November 1957 which brought together the Established Church and the Free Churches; it was led by Joe Blinco, a Methodist Minister on loan from the Billy Graham Association, who was the author of *Mass Evangelism*. The inaugural service was held in the cathedral.

The Parish and People Movement

'Parish and People' was founded in 1949 as a response to the Liturgical Movement in Europe. Its membership was never large but it succeeded in bringing together people from both the Anglo-Catholic and Evangelical wings of the Church. One of its consequences was the (gradual) shift towards making the parish communion the main act of Sunday worship, replacing Matins and occurring at, perhaps 9.30am or 10am, allowing for people still to fast beforehand, as they had done for an 8am communion service, but late enough to attract a wider range of people. In October 1957, Noel Hopkins, the Provost of Wakefield and a fine musician, wrote about what he styled the Parish Eucharist (a term which 'Parish and People' preferred to avoid because of its Tractarian connotations) becoming increasingly frequent in parishes throughout the country.

It was, he suggested, usually sung but he urged that care was needed to ensure that the musical setting and the singing 'are made as worthy as possible of their high purpose'. 'Parish and People', while having its conferences and producing a regular paper which was given the Movement's name, was somewhat amorphous and its achievements have never been quantified. As Peter Jagger noted in his history of the Movement, its prime concerns were with the centrality of the parish communion, 'a new emphasis upon the biblical teaching of the Church as the people of God, and ... a new and common understanding concerning the Church's call to evangelistic activity'. In this, it saw the laity as having a significant role. In May 1951, there was a conference on Parish and People at Huddersfield for clergy from the dioceses of Bradford, Ripon and Wakefield. Bishop Wilson was among the speakers.

Noel T. Hopkins

It is impossible to discern how far the thinking among leading figures in the diocese was influenced by the Movement and how far there were new ideas and attitudes which were in any case 'in the air' and which, while giving birth to 'Parish and People', exerted an independent influence. It was perhaps in the light of the Movement that Wilson wrote in the *Wakefield Diocesan News* in May 1950 of the problem of simply having too many services (he termed it a 'running buffet') on Sundays.

Christian Stewardship

Payment of the clergy and the cost of the day-to-day maintenance of churches became pressing matters in the 1960s as congregations began to diminish and live giving in no way kept pace with the increasing costs. Individual churches mounted stewardship campaigns emphasizing the need to give not only money but time and talents to the service of the church. In 1965, a number of parishes pursued a new Lent course, No Small Change, which was led by specially trained lay people. At St Paul's, Alverthorpe, for example, house groups were started to follow the course. St Paul's, King Cross, had its first direct-giving campaign in 1959. St Peter's, Walsden, started a planned giving campaign in 1961. The vicar, Frank Butterworth, wrote in the appeal brochure: 'Christian Stewardship means using God's gifts in the way He intended ... giving ourselves, our talents, our abilities, and our possessions, in His service.' The stewardship scheme was a part of 'a movement of spiritual awakening taking place in the Church of England throughout our country'.

Deaconess Aglen and the Board of Women's Work

The first woman actually to be ordained as a deaconess in the Wakefield Diocese seems to have been Elizabeth Sarah Aglen who was ordained in the cathedral by Bishop Ramsbotham in 1959. At the same time, she was licensed as the Assistant Director of Voluntary Education to work particularly with Sunday Schools. In 1960, she was elected to the House of Laity of the Church Assembly. She remained in the diocese serving its Children's Council and the Board of Women's Work until 1969.

The *Wakefield Diocesan News* of July 1960 reported the setting up 'for the first time' (overlooking the venture during Bishop Eden's day) of a Diocesan Board of Women's Church Work. Deaconess Aglen was its secretary. The article referred to the 'many opportunities' for full-time work in the Church for women – either as deaconesses or lay workers. These were said to be in pastoral, educational and evangelistic work, chiefly on the staffs of parishes. The aims of the Board were to make known the opportunities for service, to recruit suitable candidates and recommend them for election, and to see that there was adequate provision for their training. The 1962 Diocesan Directory listed four women who were attached to parishes; these included a Church Army Sister at Halifax Parish Church and three others (at All Saints', Castleford, St James's, Rawthorpe, and St Stephen's, Rashcliffe). The modest numbers listed in subsequent Diocesan Directories suggest that few women were actually recruited.

The Introduction of Further Anglo-Catholic Features and Practices

A growing acceptance of items which would in the past have been denounced by some as 'Popish' continued in the 1950s and 1960s. In 1950, new figures were placed above the rood screen in the cathedral. Writing in the *Cathedral Magazine*, in January 1961, Provost Hopkins referred to his own 'strong desire' to see them 'restored to their place in that unsightly gap' which had been 'a mute reminder of the prejudice and intolerance of a past age'. The figures were designed by Sir Ninian Comper and the work was financed by Alfred Ernest Greaves, Clerk to the Governors of the Wakefield Charities, in memory of his wife, Eva. In subsequent issues of the magazine there was a series of articles on 'Signs and Ceremonies', focusing on Anglo-Catholic practices such as making the sign of the Cross while saying the Creed, genuflecting, and the use of incense.

The Lady Chapels were restored at Felkirk in 1951 and at Batley parish church in 1952. Purston with South Featherstone was granted a faculty for a Lady Chapel in 1943. St Giles's, Pontefract, gained a Lady Chapel in 1954 as did St David's, Holmbridge, in 1955. Aumbries were installed at St Peter's, Felkirk, and at St Hilda's, Halifax, in 1951, at St Paul's, Glasshoughton, in 1953, and at St Peter's, Birstall, in 1954. Faculties were granted for the installation of images representing the Stations of the Cross at St John's, Dodworth, in 1944, and at St John's, Carlinghow, in 1952. Further churches, including Holy Innocents, Thornhill Lees (1953), obtained faculties for statues of the Virgin and Child.

What may well have been the first pilgrimage made by a Wakefield parish to the Shrine of Our Lady of Walsingham took place from St John the Baptist's, Cudworth, in 1957.

New Secondary Schools

The extensive history of church schools in the diocese is beyond the scope of the present book but two achievements of the 1960s are distinct enough to notice. The majority of the church schools in the diocese, originating generally as National Schools in the nineteenth century, were at first elementary schools and subsequently schools (whether infant or junior or both) catering for the primary stages of education. Secondary education developed nationally following the First World War although the school-leaving age was then only fourteen. Municipal authorities built their own secondary schools, which had no church association. But the Cathedral Boys' School, then housed in the Elizabethan Grammar School building in Brook Street, became a senior Church of England school but continued

Holy Trinity School, Illingworth, about 1976

to cater solely for boys. However, close co-operation between Wakefield City Council and the Church led to the opening of Wakefield's first post Second World War secondary school, in Thornes Road, as the co-educational controlled Cathedral School, with the Provost, Noel T. Hopkins, as the Chairman of the Governors. The building was designed by the City Engineer, J. N. Sedgewick. Its first intake of pupils was in 1959 and it was formally opened on 1 May 1960 when it was dedicated by Bishop Ramsbotham. The new Holy Trinity School, Illingworth, which like the Cathedral School can trace its origins back to the early nineteenth century, was formally opened in May 1962 as the only voluntary aided secondary school in the diocese. (In January 2012 both it and the Cathedral School became Academies.)

Some Other Post-War Changes

There were changes at the two long-standing residential homes for girls and young women. St John's Home had become an Approved School in 1937. During the war the House of Mercy too became an Approved School. Up to 1942, girls had come voluntarily, but numbers had dropped off and, as St Peter's Training School, it took delinquent girls at the instigation of the Home Office.

The House of Mercy, Horbury

Most Approved Schools were in this period run by voluntary bodies, albeit subject to Home Office inspection, and most of the institutions were for boys. The Approved School at Horbury was discontinued in 1949. In 1950, the House became a home for maladjusted girls under the aegis of the Department of Education.

Following the nationalization of coal mines in 1945, the National Coal Board discontinued the grants that many coal owners had made to the diocese's mining parishes.

The raising of the school-leaving age necessitated an emergency programme for training more teachers. Bishop McGowan dedicated a training college on Stanley Road, Wakefield, when it was opened by the West Riding County Council in July 1947.

The effects of the 1944 Education Act proved the main issue at the 1947 Diocesan Conference. County Councils and County Borough Councils had been asked by the Ministry of Education to submit their development plans for schools in their area. Those from the four County Boroughs in the diocese, Barnsley, Halifax, Huddersfield and Wakefield, were held to be satisfactory, but the West Riding proposals were 'so drastic' as to have prompted extensive objections from the Diocesan Council of Education: the number of church schools would be reduced from 118 to 53, bringing the number of children attending church schools down from 15,538 to 4,773. The Diocesan Council submitted counter proposals for 76 schools.

The moral welfare of troops stationed in Germany was the other main issue at the conference. Frank White, Vicar of Clayton West, who had been a chaplain in Germany, put forward a motion: 'This Conference deplores the practice of sending immature conscript soldiers to Germany because of the moral difficulties of life there and desires that the practice should cease as soon as possible.' He argued that British soldiers were wealthy compared to the German people: they had luxuries such as soap, chocolate and the 'almighty' cigarettes. Hence they could obtain anything they wanted, in particular the favours of men (*sic*) and women. The statistics for venereal disease among members of the services stationed in Germany were alarming.

The role of the cathedral as a parish church had always meant that its vicar, and subsequently provost, was torn between the claims of his parish and the demands of the diocese. In August 1966, for a three-year experiment, and under the new Cathedrals Measure, Bishop Ramsbotham appointed the first Canon Parochial, Derek Cater, who had since 1962 been the Vicar of St Edward's, Barnsley. He was to concentrate solely on parish work although he was also a member of the new Wakefield Diocesan Committee for Religious Drama.

Ecumenical Moves

There had been movements towards ecumenism before the war. Although its constitution was not ratified until 1948, the World Council of Churches had been initiated in 1937. In the diocese special events, such as Good Friday processions of witness, had been shared with Free Churches long before the war. In Castleford, for example, Good Friday 1939 saw a procession of witness followed by a united service for Anglicans and the Free Churches, with William Temple, the Archbishop of York, and a speaker from Leeds Methodist College. Other clergy wrote in their Visitation Returns of similar Good Friday processions and of participating in ministers' fraternals.

The war itself brought further rapprochement; there were united services, between the Anglicans and some of the Free Churches for various events such as Empire Youth Sunday. This had been prompted by the bringing together of young people from across the British Empire for the coronation of George VI in 1937, but seems to have become an annual event nationally only from 1942.

If one issue dominated the Ramsbotham years it was that of the, ultimately abandoned, reunion of the Anglican and Methodist churches. Following the publication of the second report of the 'conversations' between Methodists and Anglicans, the issue was discussed at the Diocesan Conference in May 1963 when the bishop reported that he had to discern the opinions of the clergy and laity in the diocese by the end of July 1964. Meanwhile, he appealed for discussions within the diocese between members of the two denominations to end the 'unnecessary divisions'. At the Autumn Conference in the same year, Bishop Ramsbotham spoke particularly about the question of Methodists being admitted to the Eucharist; there was no clear statement anywhere, he declared, of a requirement to have been confirmed and he spoke of the 'deep need' to rediscover the meaning of baptism in Christian initiation. He remarked, 'A good strong dose of Wesley's hymns might do us all, from archbishops down, a power of good.' He convened meetings of the diocesan synod on 26–27 June 1964 to focus solely on Anglican–Methodist union.

The new post of Diocesan Ecumenical Officer was created in 1963 and undertaken by Francis House, the recently appointed Vicar of Pontefract who had served as the assistant editor of *The Ecumenical Review* in 1960–62.

There were ad hoc ecumenical ventures. Coventry Cathedral, replacing the building destroyed in the Second World War, was consecrated on 25 May 1962. In April 1963, a group of 123 people from fourteen churches or chapels in the diocese, visited it for a service in its Chapel of Unity, led by Congregational minister J. L. Stevenson. Among the number were Anglicans, Baptists, Christadelphians, Christian Scientists, Congregationalists and Methodists.

The Wakefield Diocesan Committee for Religious Drama

In 1952, the Huddersfield branch of the Religious Drama Society, sponsored by the Huddersfield Council of Churches, gave as its first production, Fry's *The Firstborn*, a play about Moses giving up his privileged life to lead his people out of Egypt.

A drama group was founded at St Francis, Fixby, at much the same time as the church was opened, in 1954.

The Girls' Friendly Society held a Diocesan drama competition at Clayton West in 1955, which the Almondbury branch won with *Footprints* by Violet Methley.

It was at Bishop Ramsbotham's instigation that the Wakefield Diocesan Committee for Religious Drama was formed in 1961 as a branch of the Committee for Religious Drama of the Northern Province. Under his influence the highly talented Pamela Keily came to the diocese, first as a producer of occasional plays and then as the Diocesan Drama Adviser. She saw the purpose of her appointment as 'to raise the level of dramatic production in the diocese and to get away from the image of the nativity play'.

Pamela Keily had trained at RADA and in 1937 joined the cast of Martin Browne's production of *Murder in the Cathedral*. This, it was said, had given her her first feeling for religion on the stage. In the early years of the Second World War, she joined Browne's touring company, the Canterbury Pilgrim Players. In 1943 she was persuaded by the Religious Drama Society (Radius), which had been founded in 1929, to respond to a request from the Association of Christian Communities to explore whether there was scope for drama among the churches in Sheffield. A Sheffield priest, Richard Roseveare, who became chair of the Sheffield Committee for Religious Drama, persuaded her to settle in Sheffield as the Religious Drama Adviser for the City. Her role lay in working with amateurs in individual churches and chapels and subsequently too with students at Sheffield City Training College. While at the College, Keily organized the first nation-wide religious drama summer school. Still working in Sheffield after the war, with groups of amateurs, Keily was asked by the Religious Drama Society to run a tour with a professional company. Her New Pilgrim Players, selected in part from drama students

Bishop Ramsbotham

seeking their first jobs, began the experiment in Sheffield with *The Holy Family* by Richard Ward, and a specially commissioned play, set in an industrial works and called *T'Other Shift*. The company toured for something over three years, performing in churches and chapels, or their halls, until acute shortage of money brought the experiment to an end in 1956. The Bishop of Sheffield's conviction that religious drama should continue led to the founding of the Committee for Religious Drama in the Northern Province. This developed, with the Dioceses of Durham and Manchester joining Sheffield and with John Ramsbotham, then Suffragan Bishop of Jarrow, as its chair.

At much the same time, in the mid 1950s, Keily began what was to be for some years an annual visit to the Community of the Resurrection in Mirfield, when Raymond Raynes was the superior, and where she spent three weeks at a time producing the Commemoration Day plays with a cast from the students at the College and from the Hostel of the Resurrection in Leeds. Her first play there, in 1956, was *Old Man of the Mountains* by Norman Nicholson. The performances, in the quarry, drew some 4,000 people. Father Nicholas Graham composed the music for a later production, *Hopeful Travellers*, in 1962. Keily wrote of the experiment, 'Living in the environment was always a delight that made up for the exhaustion of shouting in the open air and endlessly traipsing up and down the Quarry steps. There is no denying either that the ultimate problems of relaying the voices of the actors to some four thousand people constituted a major headache – when the wind in the trees at the back of the Quarry frequently competed against our endeavours. Yet there were occasions when complete stillness and sunshine made for nothing but sheer bliss, and never did I feel anything but regret when we neared the termination of my sessions in the environment of the Community of the Resurrection.'

When the Diocese of Durham withdrew from the Northern scheme, the Dioceses of Ripon and Wakefield took its place. Ramsbotham, by then Wakefield's bishop, already knew Pamela Keily well and she had sometimes stayed with him and his wife when in the area with her New Pilgrim Players. Coincidentally, Keily had met Wakefield's third bishop, James Seaton, as a child when he stayed with her parents, who were his friends, in County Wicklow.

Keily was described as a 'tall dramatic woman with fine-drawn features'. It was also said that she did not 'quite fit into our modern pattern', she 'had a bearing that belongs to a forgotten aristocracy, a spirituality that could be called old-fashioned, and a feeling for the theatre that is of the boards themselves'. She was also said to be 'a woman of great talent, tremendous devotion, and enormous courage'. One priest who took part in some of her productions for the Wakefield Diocese, including *Murder in the Cathedral*, was later to write, 'Drama in the diocese has been one of the most formative influences in my ministerial life – and if I owe anything to anybody in shaping who I am and what I do (and I owe a lot to many, of course) Pamela has claim to one of the highest spots in my esteem and gratitude. Those years were years I return to again and again. She can never have known how the demands she placed on me changed things for me.'

Keily had clear views about religious drama, insisting that it could 'illumine religious truths in a direct way to different sorts of people on very different levels'; she hoped that the church would 'again realize the use of drama both as liturgical offering and by presenting plays by secular writers so that the communication of religious experience is kept fresh and alive through artistic sensibility and language'.

The Wakefield Committee was Bishop Ramsbotham's personal creation, with its members appointed by him and any recruitment of new members referred directly to him for approval. Its early meetings were held at Bishop's Lodge.

Bishop's Lodge

Its first members, apart from Deaconess Aglen and Pamela Keily, were drawn from the diocesan clergy. In Wakefield, as in Leeds, Ripon and Manchester, Keily, employed by the Northern Province Committee for Religious Drama, worked with volunteers, advertising across the diocese for people willing to audition for a particular play, or, if a name was suggested to her, making direct contact either herself or through Elizabeth Aglen who served as the secretary of the Wakefield Committee for some years. One of Keily's earliest ventures in Wakefield was a production of *The Way of the Cross* by Henri Gheon in 1962–63. The play was taken to churches or church halls across the diocese.

Keily offered to provide advice to any church group planning its own production of a religious play and in March 1963 the Wakefield Committee provided a two-day workshop at the Parish House in Venn Street, Huddersfield, which attracted twenty-nine participants including three parish priests, eight day-school teachers, and three Girls' Friendly Society leaders.

At this time Keily was producing plays under the aegis of the Ripon Committee for Religious Drama as well as for the Manchester Committee. Plays produced from an amateur cast in one diocese were sometimes performed in another. In March 1963, the Ripon cast brought *Birth by Drowning*, by Norman Nicholson, to St Peter's, Morley.

The performance of T. S. Eliot's *Murder in the Cathedral*, in Wakefield Cathedral in April 1965, was described at the time as its first large-scale production in the Wakefield Diocese and the most exciting venture of the Committee so far. Something of an ecumenical venture, the cast was drawn from members of the cathedral, All Saints', Castleford, St Peter's, Huddersfield, St Matthew's, Rastrick, St Botolph's, Knottingley, St Paul's, Cross Stone, St Mary's, Todmorden, St Mark's, Dewsbury, St George's, Lupset, St James's, Chapelthorpe, St Peter's, Morley, St Paul's, Mirfield, the Baptist Church, Normanton, St Austin's Roman Catholic Church, Wakefield, and St Peter and St Paul's Roman Catholic Church, Sandal. The cathedral choir provided the music. The Committee found an able lighting technician in Thomas Briggs, the Vicar of Harley Wood. The performances yielded a profit of £120 allowing for a donation of £60 to be made to the Wakefield Freedom from Hunger appeal.

Both the Northern Province Committee and the Wakefield Committee sometimes commissioned plays, in particular from Philip Turner and John Hunter. Throughout his Wakefield years, Bishop Ramsbotham was a diligent and enthusiastic chair of the Northern Province Committee for Religious Drama. He wrote about 'the power of Religious Drama to open people's minds and stir people's hearts over the great themes of the

Christian life'. According to Keily it was Ramsbotham himself who commissioned R. H. Ward to write a play about the trial of Edith Cavell, the British-born nurse who was tried and executed by the Germans in Belgium in 1915 for helping allied soldiers to evade the German authorities. The play, produced by Keily, was presented in Wakefield in 1966 by the Sheffield Committee for Religious Drama.

Links were forged between the Wakefield Committee and Bretton Hall College of Education which had opened in 1949 and specialized in training teachers of Art, Drama and Music, and in 1966 Keily was invited to tutor student teachers there for a morning a week. The Religious Drama Society (Radius) held its summer school at Bretton Hall in 1967.

It cannot be claimed that the Wakefield Religious Drama Committee made any considerable impact in the diocese during Bishop Ramsbotham's years. Most parish drama groups remained deaf to Keily's offers to act as an adviser. Keily herself was overstretched in working for four dioceses at once, and without her own means of transport. The occasional productions promoted by the Committee within the diocese were sometimes ill-publicized and poorly attended. However, a Religious Drama Group was founded in Spenborough as a consequence of people from the area having seen a production of *Ruth* by John Hunter.

John Ramsbotham had a stroke in the summer of 1967, and in October of that year he announced his retirement, through ill-health. His successor as Bishop of Wakefield, Eric Treacy, lacked his enthusiasm for Religious Drama and, while providing some sponsorship for a young person from Wakefield to attend the annual Radius Summer School, took little other interest in the Committees either of the Northern Province or the Wakefield Diocese.

PART III

Years of Challenge and Change, 1968–2013

Introduction

The last three decades of the twentieth century and the first years of the current one saw major changes. Within the Church there was the administrative change from diocesan conferences and a national Church Assembly, to synodical government. There was a shortage of manpower. Even fewer men were coming forward for ordination and their full-time service was for a shorter period, as they were older than in the past and were for a period able to retire on full pension at sixty-five (at sixty-eight from January 2011) although they could continue if they chose until seventy. There were severe financial pressures. The Church Commissioners even warned in 1974 that clergy might have to seek part-time jobs in order to make ends meet. There was a radical change to the delivery of clergy stipends, with a standard scale introduced after the Central Stipends Authority was established in 1972. Under the Measure of 1976, the endowments and glebe held hitherto by individual parishes were transferred to diocesan pools. From 1978, a central payments system operated with a standard scale. In the period in question, the status of the clergy has moved from being largely independent office-holders, towards a position where, under 'common tenure', they enjoy many of the features of the protection provided for employees. There was also, partly as a consequence, a very substantial rise in the 'parish share' (the quota payment sought from each parish), aggravated by a considerable decrease in the financial support available from the Church Commissioners. The shortage of full-time stipendiary clergy led to the introduction of the 'Sheffield scheme' under which, from 1980, dioceses were 'rationed' in the number of full-time priests that the Church Commissioners would support, and led, too, to new forms of ministry, and to a new emphasis not just on the work of the Reader but on a wider lay participation in pastoral work. The Wakefield Diocese was in the forefront here with Colin James's Shared Ministry scheme which anticipated the recommendations of John Tiller's 1983 Report, *A Strategy for the Church's Ministry*. Women were admitted, by stages, into the priesthood. More benefices were united, the spur of new thinking in the Paul Report, *On the Deployment and Payment of the Clergy*, and the subsequent 1968 Pastoral Measure, led to the introduction of group ministries and team parishes. There was a new emphasis on in-service training for the clergy and on lay training and Christian adult education. More, and very varied, Lent courses were developed in distinction to the traditional Bible-study classes. Then there was the impact of the Charismatic Movement and the revival of some pre-Reformation practices, including the Chrism Eucharist. There was the development of what became known as 'nurture courses' designed for prospective members, the most popular being the Alpha Course which emanated from Holy Trinity, Brompton, a church in the evangelical tradition.

Many more churches across the country, and in the Wakefield Diocese itself, were made redundant. The maintenance of parsonage houses ceased to be the responsibility of the incumbent and from December 1973 was overseen instead by the Parsonage Boards with a subsequent drive to replace many of them either by building new houses or buying – and perhaps extending – properties deemed suitable. (The Wakefield Board included two wives of clergy as co-opted members.) There was growing ecumenical activity, including a strengthening of relationships with the Roman Catholic Church. In the wider society, increased immigration brought a new cultural mix, with a need to foster interfaith relationships. Changing moral and social attitudes led to the closure of the mother and baby homes and to the renaming in 1972 of the Diocesan Moral Welfare Council as the Diocesan Family Welfare Council. In 1974, a new local-authority administration came into being with some considerable impact on the relationships between the Church and the secular authorities. Practising religion became even less significant in most people's lives and the Church sought to counter this with a renewed missionary zeal. The 1990s was designated the Decade of Evangelism. The publication in 2004 of *Mission-shaped Church: Church planting and fresh expressions of church in a changing context* prompted some parishes to seek new contexts for providing faith-based activities. From 2005, churches across the diocese have taken part in the annual Back to Church Sunday. The Wakefield Diocese saw the closure of most of its textile mills, the lengthy miners' strike of 1984–85 and a decade of pit closures. The seminal, if controversial, *Faith in the City* (1985), recognizing the extent of social deprivation in particular in the inner city and in local-authority housing estates, led to extensive action nationally including the founding of the Church Urban

Fund and to many projects within the diocese which drew on its support.

At the time this book was written a further momentous change, to unite the Diocese of Wakefield with the neighbouring Dioceses of Bradford, and Ripon and Leeds (as the Diocese of Ripon was known from 1999), remained under discussion.

The Bishops

The diocese was served by five bishops in the period under review. Eric Treacy, bishop in 1968–77, was already a familiar figure in the diocese before his appointment to the see and, like Hone, he moved to the episcopal throne from being the Suffragan Bishop of Pontefract. He had been in the diocese for almost twenty years, coming first in 1949 as both the Archdeacon and Vicar of Halifax. He was enthroned on 26 March 1968. Although intelligent and witty, Treacy was the least educated, formally, of any Bishop of Wakefield and perhaps his entry into orders came via the least conventional path. His father was a furniture salesman and neither parent had any interest in churchgoing, but he was drawn into the Anglican fold after encountering the Children's Special Service Mission during holidays in Norfolk. Certainly there were those among the Church hierarchy who doubted his suitability for the head of a see. Among lay people he was undoubtedly the best known and perhaps also the most loved. A senior layman once said of him, 'If that man had been Moses, I would have followed him into the Red Sea whether the waters had parted or not.' Initially firmly evangelical, Treacy became increasingly liberal and, while capable of roundly condemning some Anglo-Catholic practices, gradually came to be more comfortable with a degree of ritualism. Provost Lister described him as having a vision too wide to permit him to be identified with any one form of churchmanship. Treacy was something of a self-publicist and certainly

Bishop Treacy

a popular communicator, never apparently refusing to give a comment to the press and proving a ready after-dinner speaker for many and varied organizations. His manner towards his clergy could often be acerbic. His wife, May, was not without influence on his work.

Colin Clement Walter James, bishop in 1977–85, was an Anglo-Catholic and apparently the only one of Wakefield's bishops (so far) to have been seriously considered for the position of Archbishop of Canterbury. He was one of the first clergy to become an expert on broadcasting and spent eight years, in 1959–67, in the BBC religious broadcasting department, for most of that period as the Religious Broadcasting Organizer for the Western Region. He came to Wakefield after serving as the first Bishop Suffragan of Basingstoke, in the Diocese of Winchester. Earlier, as Vicar of Bournemouth, he had established the city-centre team ministry. He was enthroned on 9 February 1977. Something of a patrician figure, he was ready to move the Wakefield Diocese on in terms not only of parochial reorganization and parish development but also in the areas of clergy and lay training, understanding well how best to use the talents of his sector clergy. His was the period when information technology was entering diocesan and church administration, an innovation he was happy to pioneer and in which he was fully supported by the Suffragan Bishop Richard Hare. He sought to maintain close contact with his clergy. As the turn of each parish approached, in the Diocesan Cycle of Prayer, he wrote to the incumbent asking to be told of their anxieties and achievements; he responded to their replies individually, fully, with appreciation and compassion. He visited each new incumbent after the priest's first six months in place. He presided over the diocese at a time of considerable economic stress in the Yorkshire area: the textile industry was in serious decline and in 1984 came the devastating miners' strike, the routine and agonizing clashes with police, and the desperate poverty of miners' families. He was much respected for his graciousness and his

Bishop James

strategic skills. He excelled both in good relationships and shrewd and efficient administration. He returned to Winchester as its bishop in 1985.

In the tenth bishop, later to become the Archbishop of York and the country's foremost Anglo-Catholic, the Diocese of Wakefield got its own man. David Michael Hope, bishop in 1985–92, was born in Thornes, Wakefield, in 1940, the son of a builder running the family firm founded by Hope's grandfather. His mother was a teacher at All Saints School, Pontefract. Fellow pupils at Gaskell's School recall his coming to school with his twin sister Anne riding a two-seater tricycle. Hope returned to his home town after serving as Principal of the theological college, St Stephen's House, Oxford, and as vicar of the magnificent All Saints, Margaret Street, London. He was consecrated on 18 October 1985 and enthroned on 29 October. (The enthronement was attended by Frank Williams who played the part of the priest in the BBC's 'Dad's Army', who was there to represent Hope's London church.) His episcopacy was in every way outstanding. During his years in Wakefield, Hope was committed to making his churches far more outward-looking. His years in Wakefield saw the publication of *Faith in the City*, the ordination of women as deacons (1987), the establishment of the Church Urban Fund (1988) and the diocesan centenary. Hope's major contribution to the work of the diocese lay in his insistence that providing for the community was fundamental to the church's mission and if this meant a radical alteration to church property, including the parish churches themselves, this was entirely appropriate. While in Wakefield he worked to help those in the mining communities devastated by pit closures. Like Wakefield's third bishop, James Seaton, Hope never married. He said of himself that being single was a way of responding to God's will to serve Him and the sacred ministry and of being wholly free for the service of others. Hope ordained Wakefield's first women deacons. He was never in favour of their ordination as priests but his misgivings were tempered by a recognition that there must be constructive debate and that the theological arguments could not easily be foreclosed. Hope became a Guardian of the Shrine of Our Lady of Walsingham in 1978. He led a diocesan pilgrimage there in 1991. Hope initiated the link between the Wakefield Diocese and that of Mara, Tanzania. As a man he had the common touch: he was always available, always fair, and without a shred of pomposity; he grasped the heart of matters very swiftly. When he was created a life peer in 2005, he took his title, Baron Hope of Thornes, from his home area.

Hope's successor, Nigel Simeon McCulloch, bishop in 1992–2002, described as a 'man with a heart for mission', had been Suffragan Bishop of Taunton before the move to Wakefield. He had also had five years' experience as the Norwich Diocesan Missioner. At forty-nine he was at the time the youngest diocesan bishop in the country. He was enthroned on 28 March 1992. Recognizing the degree of alienation from the Church in the Wakefield Diocese, and, at a practical level, that the diocese was running at a very substantial deficit, he set out swiftly to effect spiritual and administrative change. He declared Wakefield a 'Missionary Diocese', set up a Vision and Strategy Group to explore, in particular, what administrative changes were needed, and succeeded in attracting some of the country's most able clergy. It has been remarked that his pace of sharing and bringing about the mission was too fast and that lay people found it difficult to cope at parish level. McCulloch had grown up in Liverpool. His father, an accountant by profession, had served as a bomber pilot in the Second World War and had been killed in action in 1943. McCulloch later wrote, 'Watching the huge liners when I was a boy made me aware of how large God's world is, and yet how close we all are too.' He was an outspoken critic of the harmful effects of the then Tory government on the community and vigorously opposed the programme of pit closures. He used the facilities of Bishop's Lodge for training purposes and sometimes brought the churchwardens there for their swearing in, emphasizing their importance to the mission of their parishes. His book, *A Gospel to Proclaim*, was one of the best explanations of the purpose of the national Decade of Evangelism. Unlike Hope, McCulloch chose to ordain women as priests and ordained the first nineteen from the Wakefield Diocese in June 1994.

Stephen Platten, Wakefield's twelfth bishop, was consecrated on 1 May 2003 and enthroned on 19 July. He had been Dean of Norwich since 1995. Platten, whose father was the advertising manager for Aertex, was born in London in 1947. Although sending him to an evangelical free church with a Baptist theology, his parents had little interest in organized religion and he found his faith only when encouraged in his late teens by friends of the family to attend St John's, Clay Hill. The key and lasting influence of the Franciscans as his vocation developed, began when he first visited Alnmouth Friary in 1966. Later becoming a tertiary member of the Society of St Francis, he was for six years in the 1990s the Minister Provincial for the European Province. After a secondary education at the Stationers' Company's School and three years working for Shell International Petroleum, he took a BEd degree in Natural Science before going on to Cuddesdon Theological College and Trinity College, Oxford. He gained a post-graduate Diploma in Theology (with distinction), following this by undertaking research at Trinity College in New Testament and Christian Ethics (gaining an Oxford BD in 2003). He remained in the Diocese of Oxford, where he was ordained deacon in 1975 and priest in 1976, serving as a curate at St Andrew's, Headington. In 1978–82 he was the chaplain and tutor in Ethics at Lincoln Theological College and in 1983–90 was the Director of Ordinands for the Diocese of Portsmouth. In 1990, he moved to Lambeth Palace as the Archbishop of Canterbury's secretary for Ecumenical Affairs. He has described his churchmanship as radical catholic. The author noted in 2012 that as Bishop of Wakefield he has placed particular emphasis on consultation, on supporting clergy and encouraging continuing learning and training. Aiming to promote good community relations, he initiated monthly Bishop's Breakfasts, held at 8am in Barnsley, Halifax, Huddersfield and Wakefield, bringing together people from many walks of life beyond the Church. Something of his focus has lain beyond the diocese in fostering links not only with Mara but also with Adelaide, Faisalabad, Georgia, Herne (Ruhrgebiet) and Skara, and in his role in the House of Lords, to which he was introduced in 2009 with a brief on Defence, Foreign Affairs, Rural Issues and Universities. As chair of the Church of England Liturgical Commission, he introduced a new form of service, published in 2009, which incorporated the baptism of children into the occasion of a marriage. While Theology remains a central concern, he has a strong interest in Art, Literature and Music. He is a trustee of the Hepworth Wakefield, has sung in choirs, operatic societies, and choral societies, and enjoys giving lectures on aspects of literature. Huddersfield University conferred a doctorate on him in 2012.

Five men served the diocese during these years as Bishops of Pontefract. Uniquely, William Gordon Fallows, who was appointed in 1968, was consecrated (on 11 June) in the cathedral, York Minster being under restoration at the time. Fallows was formerly the Principal of Ripon Hall, Oxford. He went on to become Bishop of Sheffield in 1971. It was from this position that he chaired the Clergy Deployment Working Group which was set up by the House of Bishops in 1972 and which proposed what became known as the 'Sheffield scheme'.

Richard Hare, then Archdeacon of Westmorland and Vicar of Winster, followed Fallows. He had previously been the domestic chaplain to the Bishop of Manchester and then Vicar of St Luke's, Barrow in Furness. He was consecrated in York Minster on 21 September 1971 and instituted on 2 December 1971. He became associated nationally with the charismatic movement and had an immense influence in the diocese itself on evangelism, on innovative styles of worship and on the reordering of churches to facilitate these. Inclined to informality, Hare was once reproved by Eric Treacy for attending synod in casual clothes. Hare gained a positive response from all branches of the Church, his warmth and sincerity and sense of fun overcoming most people's suspicions of things charismatic. He retired in 1992.

With the idea of the Missionary Diocese firmly in mind, Nigel McCulloch secured the appointment of John Thornley Finney, then the Church of England Officer for the Decade of Evangelism, as Hare's successor. Finney, like David Hope, had been to school in Wakefield, albeit to Silcoates rather than the Grammar School. He was a broadly based churchman with sympathy for all traditions. He moved from being against the ordination of women to being in favour. He was consecrated in York on 14 May 1993 and immediately headed Nigel McCulloch's Vision and Strategy Group. Finney retired in 1998.

In David James, Bishop of Pontefract from 1998, McCulloch gained another enthusiastic and successful evangelist to his 'missionary diocese' team. Prior to coming to Wakefield, James had run the very large and active parish of Christ Church, Portswood. He was consecrated on 25 September 1998. He became Bishop of Bradford four years later in 2002. A trained scientist, he had a particular ability to talk to sceptical teenagers and sought to establish 'youth cells' across the diocese. He undertook a number of visits to secondary schools with teams of clergy and lay people where they spent a full day at a time taking part in lessons on a variety of subjects rather than just Religious Education.

The year 2002 heralded further changes in the diocesan hierarchy within eight weeks of James's move, McCulloch himself translated to Manchester and Richard Inwood, the Archdeacon of Halifax, appointed as the Bishop of Bedford. An element of continuity was maintained with the consecration of Anthony Robinson, who had been Archdeacon of Pontefract from 1997, as the Bishop of Pontefract on 6 December 2002. From the moment of his consecration, he took over all episcopal responsibilities for the diocese until the consecration of Stephen Platten. Robinson was born and educated in Bedford. He trained to be a teacher and taught mathematics and computer studies for two years at a comprehensive school in Chelmsford. He trained for the priesthood at Sarum and Wells Theological College. Before his move to Wakefield he served from 1985 first as Team Vicar and then as Team Rector at the Parish of the Resurrection, Leicester; the parish included three urban priority areas with associated social problems. During his time there he helped to establish four community projects including an innovative scheme working with men who had committed domestic violence, and secured £1.5m to employ a number of community workers. Firmly against the ordination of women as priests, Bishop Robinson was brought to the diocese by Bishop McCulloch with the aim of maintaining a balance between the 'two integrities'. Among his many significant contributions has been his work with other faith communities throughout the diocese and supporting the Asian Christians from the diocese in developing links with the Church in Pakistan and particularly the Diocese of Faisalabad.

Bishop Robinson pledging support for Wakefield City of Sanctuary

Bishop Treacy's Primary Visitation

Perhaps as good a starting place as any for the period in 1968–2013 is Bishop Eric Treacy's Primary Visitation of 1969. At that time comparatively few benefices had been united and the diocese still had 219 parishes or conventional districts. The broad impression created by the 111 extant returns suggests a clergy which was both impoverished and overworked, and even daunted and depressed, and the churches themselves and their congregations in something of a state of stagnation. A good number of writers revealed a sense of isolation and would have welcomed friendly visits from the bishop, their archdeacon, or their rural dean: one complained that in nine years he had never had a personal visit from the rural dean but added that the system made it impossible for rural deans to supplement the bishop's pastoral oversight; they should, he thought, be in small parishes where they were not already overworked; he felt the need to share the joys and sorrows of his ministry but did not like to trespass on his own rural dean's limited time. The Rector of Thornhill expressed the value of the informal association that had been maintained for the past five years between himself, his curate, and the Vicar of Whitley; this had included the latter providing a course for each of their congregations on prayer.

Treacy asked eight direct questions about his parish priests themselves, some of which might well have been expected to prompt something more than the monosyllabic replies most of the clergy gave. Asked whether they were experiencing financial difficulty on their present stipends, some replied 'No' and some replied 'Yes' without further elaboration. More extensive answers emphasized the necessity of a wife in at least part-time employment or the dependence on additional income from teaching commitments, a hospital chaplaincy or private means. One family had to delay going to the dentist because they did not have the money to pay the charge. Another incumbent reported that he and his wife had to take in lodgers.

Some respondents wrote rather more extensively in answer to a question about whether there were problems that prevented them fulfilling their ministry. The most usual comments were about the apathy in the community in relation to church attendance or the inertia within their congregations; one writer observed, 'People are not hostile but they will not come to church. Many people live good lives but feel they can be Christian without coming to church.' One priest, remarking on the passivity of his congregation and the absence of any young people, was 'bewildered by a congregation that worships the status quo, that refuses to engage in any evangelism or in social service, and that basically doesn't want to know what it means to be the Body of Christ ... so long as they can pursue their individual ways'. For one there was 'a prevailing attitude of congregationalism', showing in reluctance to pay the diocesan quota or take any interest in neighbouring churches or the church overseas. One referred to the instability created by uncertainties in the mining industry. One said that 'all energy and enthusiasm have been spent in raising money to preserve the fabric without much thought as to the purpose of the fabric apart from a quaint sort of entertainment on Sundays'. There was a unique remark about the difficulty of ministering to the sick because of 'a lack of provision for reserving the blessed sacrament'.

Questions about parsonage houses brought two fairly frequent answers: they needed central heating, or the lack of any downstairs lavatory was keenly felt because of the use of the house for meetings, or interviews with parishioners.

Treacy asked whether there were matters that the priests might wish to bring to his attention. The fullest response came from a writer who referred to 'these anguished days in the matter of vocation ... The uncertainties regarding the future, especially in the realms of theological upheaval, administrative re-organization, ecumenical developments, and liturgical reform are at once heady wine, stiff medicine, and unnerving insecurity and when one seeks to plan for the overall future in a parish it is almost impossible to do so.'

The first question on the Visitation form enquired whether the daily offices were said regularly 'in the church'. Almost all priests answered in the affirmative but, not infrequently, referred to the absence, except on Sundays, of anyone else. One priest, anticipating the loss of his curate, said that once he was faced with saying the office alone, he would choose rather to join a fellow minister in a neighbouring church. One said that as it was too expensive to heat the church on weekdays, he preferred to encourage family prayers at home. In his subsequent Visitation Address, Treacy referred to this sternly, commenting, 'My experience has been that the Daily Offices are the anchor upon which our prayer discipline rests. Once they go, we begin to drift into a flabby kind of subjective prayer which has little to do with the worship of the whole church.'

There was a question about the links forged between the incumbent and the congregation, with the wider community. Where there were any detailed answers, these noted the incumbent's role as mayor's chaplain, or as chaplain to a local firm, a hospital, a care home, their branch of the British Legion, or the local fire service. They noted their seat on various committees, the use of their church for services by a range of institutions, including in some cases the Freemasons, and their visits to collieries, factories, mills, and working men's clubs, or their membership of Rotary. Many were governors of schools, including some non-church ones. One priest observed, 'My own opinion is that one can dissipate a lot of one's time in this way without any real result but I try to keep in touch as much as possible and encourage my flock to do likewise.' One would have liked to bring the church and community closer together by offering the use of the church hall for local activities but saw the question of raffles as a barrier. None revealed any outward-looking activity by the congregation as a body, but some noted the voluntary work undertaken independently of the church, by some public-spirited individuals.

Answers to the questionnaire provided little evidence of innovation but there were some few signs of the developments that were to become more widespread. At St Luke's, Grimethorpe, a children's eucharist had been introduced as part of the Sunday School provision. At St Botolph's, Knottingley, older children were being encouraged to attend the parish communion rather than the Sunday School. A 'pram service' had been introduced at Hanging Heaton's mission church, St Luke's, Soothill. The Vicar of St Andrew's, Wakefield, hoped to start a 'pram club' to introduce mothers to members of the congregation. The Vicar of St John's, Wakefield, was starting a play group. Both a major hospital and the West Riding Police Training School were within his parish and he had established evening gatherings for visiting police, nurses, and flat-dwellers. Lent house-groups had been started at St Saviour's, Ravensthorpe, to train people in baptism preparation. There were few references to supporting the missionary associations, but the congregation at St John's, Horbury Bridge, had pledged to raise £25 a year for three years to support the theological college at Ranchi in the Diocese of Chota Nagpur.

Parochial church councils (PCCs) were evidently meeting regularly with a satisfactory attendance. However, in answer to a specific question, most incumbents had little to report of the wider interest of their councils in matters other than routine parish business except in so far as they discussed the issues of Anglo-Methodist unity, Synodical Government, and the Morley and Paul Reports. But some PCCs had engaged with wider concerns. Among those mentioned were ways of improving worship, fostering community spirit in the local community, the shortage of clergy, putting life into the electoral roll, the liturgy and liturgical reform, foreign missions, parish evangelism, work with young people, immigrants – their education and integration, youth service developments, contacting newcomers to the parish, comprehensive education, moral welfare, the work of Shelter and Christian Aid, the problems of Biafra, ecumenical house-prayer meetings, Christian witness by lay visitation within the parish, laity training, holding a Festival of the Arts, a new approach to missions overseas, cancer relief, the participation of bishops in politics, the impact of changing social patterns on worship and the life of the church, the task of restoring the church building, and a different approach to Harvest with money, to be used both for home and abroad, rather than vegetables and fruits.

Answers to questions about Bible classes and wider teaching revealed that in most parishes little was being attempted beyond Bible study and in many cases there was no provision even for that; the low numbers attending was a frequent complaint. At St Thomas's, Gawber, the course, No Small Change, had been introduced but the response numerically and financially had been disappointing. At St Peter's, Stanley, there had been a discussion group during Lent 1969 on 'The Christian Faith in the World Today', with an average attendance of nine people, all of whom were women. But there were a few more positive reports: there were house groups at Christ the King, Battyeford, discussing the Christian Faith and its Implications; at Horbury Bridge there had been a twelve-week course for house groups on doctrine; at Christ Church, South Ossett, study groups had considered doctrine, the sacraments, moral problems, and prayer; there was a class at St Paul's, Hanging Heaton, on Anglo-Methodist unity. The incumbent of St Giles's, Pontefract, wrote with some evident pride of having eight house-groups some of which were interdenominational, each numbering ten to twelve members, studying the Bible and the Christian faith. In Wrangbrook there was a combined Anglican–Methodist group which met fortnightly for Bible study or discussion of the Christian faith.

No doubt with possible closures in mind, Treacy asked specifically about the existence of mission churches and mission rooms and the extent to which these met the needs of the parish. About a third of the parishes for which responses exist still had one or more mission churches or mission rooms. Gawber had sold its two mission rooms and provided a parish coach instead to bring people to the church. St Michael's mission church at Hemsworth, had been closed for the past three years and could be disposed of. All Saints, Castleford, would soon have no need for St John's, Lock Lane. Canon Brumpton at St Mary's, Barnsley, thought that one of their two missions might be closed without any real loss. One incumbent thought that church life was weakened by having a second congregation, although admitting that his mission church still had some active life. Cedric Harris at St James', Thornes, implied the value of concentrating activity in one place when he wrote, 'We sold a parish room, pulled down a church, and let off a parochial hall. Now we use one building to good effect.' Another incumbent thought that having a mission church did not meet the pastoral needs of his parish but hoped to justify its retention by making it available for meetings of old-age pensioners and play-groups. Thornhill Lees' daughter church at St Mary's, Saviletown, had been closed two years earlier and the incumbent hoped that it would be the subject of 'one of the first' redundancy schemes (under the 1968 Measure). George Lawrence, who had only recently moved to become Rector of Crofton, wrote an appended letter about the problems of the mission church in the mining village of New Crofton: this was on land owned by the National Coal Board; there had been good work in the past when it was under the care of a Church Army captain but numbers for the weekly communion were now as low as four to six, and fell sometimes to two; there were meetings there of the Mothers' Union and it had its own Sunday School but people did not like going to the rough area where it stood; he had the impression that his parochial church council would like to close it, and he knew that the NCB was ready to take the site back.

Geoffrey Willett at St Andrew's, Wakefield, also wrote at considerable length, in this case about St Mark's mission church in Pinderfields' Road, the ten-year-old St Swithun's on Eastmoor Estate, and the Chantry Chapel of St Mary the Virgin on Wakefield Bridge. Although lacking any real enthusiasm for it, he saw 'no real hardship' in retaining the Chantry providing the restoration appeal committee could raise sufficient money to cover the expenses incurred in keeping it open to sightseers and insured against vandalism. At St Mark's, evening services had been discontinued in 1965 and the Sunday School had closed some years before that; however, there was still an attendance of fifteen at the weekly morning services and the congregation was both loyal and generous, one member giving sufficient to cover all expenses; he suggested that the matter of closure should be considered in five years' time. From what Willett revealed, however, St Swithun's was proving a major problem: it was in the middle of a housing estate 'where neither loyalty nor service towards institutions abound'; years of uphill struggle had taken the place of enthusiasm, it had become more and more isolated from the parish church, membership was less than fifty with fewer than six men; what had started as a large Sunday School had dwindled; the style of the building did not seem like a church to many so that a large proportion of people wanting their children baptized preferred to bring them to St Andrew's; moreover the building had been changed so as to fail in its role as a dual-purpose church/hall when dark pews from the demolished St Mary's had been introduced.

Treacy was very conscious of the problems of recruiting men for the ministry. Incumbents were inclined to take a defeatist view of how they were encouraging, or might encourage, vocations. William Jubb at St Paul's, Monk Bretton, said bluntly that the problems of recruitment were 'far greater than the compass of the diocese'. The low level of stipends was seen by many respondents as a major barrier. 'In spite of the Ministry calling for sacrifice, parents and teachers are bound to show the advantage of other professions,' John Cowperthwaite at St James', Ryhill, observed. Direct contact was seen by some as the best way to inspire others to enter the Church: one priest suggested there could be value in ordinands spending two weeks of their vacation in an unfamiliar parish; George Nesham, at St Mary's, Woodkirk, reported that during the two years he had taught in a secondary school, some pupils had come forward for confirmation and some has shown interest in the ministry.

While there was no specific question directed at the issue of group ministries or team parishes, some few respondents saw these as the way forward: at Horbury, where there were the three separate parishes of St Peter's, St Mary's, Horbury Junction, and St John's, Horbury Bridge,

Ronald Bullivant at St Peter's advocating group ministry, said, 'Three parochial set-ups for a population of 9,000 is a waste of money and manpower and is reducing clergy and people to caretakers of buildings.' Harold Ingamells, coping with both St Mary's and St John's, said, 'If group and shared ministries are to be the thing of the future may I be bold enough to suggest that (with the addition of a curate) this little group of the Bridge and the Junction could provide an initial training ground for a man believing that this sort of ministry is his particular vocation.'

Many clergy would have liked a curate but said that they recognized it was financially out of the question. Quite a number said that they would like a lay worker and not a few remarked that a woman worker would be particularly welcome.

There was no direct question about ecumenical activity, but a little more than has so far been noted can be garnered from responses to other questions. At St John's, Cudworth, special services for school leavers were arranged in conjunction with the Methodists. Royston Christian Council had ecumenical Bible Study Groups. At St Anne's, Wrenthorpe, Allan Lancashire referred to using the Methodist chapel at Kirkhamgate for a monthly communion service and a bi-monthly joint evening service.

Treacy asked directly whether there were ways in which he, as their bishop, might help his priests. Where there was any positive answer, it reflected the sense of isolation that has already been noted and was described, too, in the Paul Report. A routine visit by the bishop was the most frequent request. One incumbent said that an annual communication between the bishop and the individual priest 'would help to get at the root of much frustration'. Another suggested that the bishop should 'send a spot-check letter asking what clergy have been up to in the last six months'. One said that the bishop should give his clergy thirty minutes each every two years. One wanted more visits to the parish 'to break down the narrow parochialism' and his congregation's 'resentment of "them" at Wakefield'. Perhaps recognizing the two bishops' lack of time, one writer suggested that the archdeacons should be available at Church House on a regular basis for clergy with the need of someone to talk to.

In his rather abrasive Visitation Address (judging it by the extant written draft), Bishop Treacy described at some length his idea of the 'man of God' whom he sought to have in his parishes. He expressed concern that when a vacancy was to be filled, parishes did not ask for this man of God; rather they asked for a good preacher, someone good with youth, someone who had a wife that would help with the women's organizations, and someone who was under fifty. The essence of this man of God lay in his 'Christian Assurance, in that he speaks with certainty and conviction of what he knows to be true, and testifies to what he has seen. He is sure of God and His power and he communicates his own certainty to others.'

In 1970, very probably reflecting on what the Visitation had revealed, Treacy wrote in the *Wakefield Diocesan News* of the problems faced by clergy. 'The work of the parish priest these days is not easy,' he said. 'So many of his securities have gone: it is a heartbreaking business to battle with the indifference of the community, to minister to a decreasing congregation, to have to maintain, very frequently, a large house on a totally inadequate stipend, to see, as is often the case, his parish pulled down around him to fulfil the dream of some remote planner.' He urged parochial church councils to support their clergy rather than being in a critical mood 'jumping on' their ideas.

The Change to Synodical Government

Like every other Church of England diocese, Wakefield saw the introduction of synodical government in 1970 with the formation of deanery synods, the new-style diocesan synod and the General Synod. For the first time, through the Houses of Laity, lay people played a full part in the governing of the church. More weight was given to deanery gatherings: hitherto it was the Diocesan Conference that elected representatives to the Church Assembly. From now on deanery synods elected their representatives to both the diocesan and national synods. It was perhaps in anticipation of this that the rural deaneries of Almondbury, Blackmoorfoot, and Kirkburton were created in 1968. A further Deanery of Chevet was created in 1973. Treacy wrote in the *Wakefield Diocesan News* in January 1970 of the care parochial church councils should take in electing 'men and women of intelligence and proven devotion to the Church' to the deanery synods.

The last meeting of the Wakefield Diocesan Conference took place on 9 May 1970. Elections to the new synods were held in September with candidates offered the chance to speak at preliminary meetings. The first new-style diocesan synod was held on 24 October 1970 at the Cathedral School in Wakefield and was attended by some 200 clergy and laity. Treacy focused on the occasion on the need for much more generous giving – in terms of money – from church members, referring to the expensive cars parked outside churches contrasted with the meagre offerings on the collection plate. He also referred to the low stipends that most clergy had to bear. The diocesan synods have normally met three times a year, with regular changes of venue.

The heads of the two religious communities became ex-officio members of the diocesan synod. Since 1973, all lay people holding a bishop's licence under seal have been ex-officio members of the House of Laity of their deanery synod.

The principal issues on which the synods have been asked to vote in the decades under consideration were Anglo-Methodist unity, the ordination of women as deacons, and then as priests, the Anglo-Methodist Covenant, the Anglican Covenant which the Diocesan Synod was, on 12 March 2011, the first in the country to oppose, proposals in 2011 for the amalgamation of the Dioceses of Bradford, Ripon and Leeds, and Wakefield, and, later in 2011, the proposal to consecrate women as bishops.

Bishop Platten, Harriet Evans

Bishop Platten set out to coax a more enthusiastic attendance at diocesan synods by giving less time to the presentation of papers and by promoting debate, especially on matters of national significance, such as the ethics of using human embryos in research, or how far forgiveness and punishment should be related within the criminal justice system.

It has been said that a welcome by-product of the synod system has been the bringing together of clergy who in the past never met. The isolation reported in the responses to Eric Treacy's Primary Visitation has also been mitigated by triennial diocesan clergy residentials, that held in Swanwick in 1982 as part of the 'Church in the Eighties' programme being especially valued.

Local Government Reorganization

In 1974, local government reorganization led to the abolition of the municipal councils and of the great West Riding County Council with which, in terms of many of its church schools, the diocese had had a strong relationship. Much of the diocese now lay in the new West Yorkshire but a part of it fell into South Yorkshire, with all the attendant administrative complexity. Parishes came within the monolithic metropolitan district councils of Barnsley, Calderdale, Kirklees, Leeds, and Wakefield. While the new district of Calderdale was more or less co-terminous with the original parish of Halifax, other boundaries were dissimilar. Relationships which had been built up with municipal councils across the diocese over more than ninety years came to an end and it would be fair to say that the Established Church lost something of its status in the local government arena, although new links were gradually formed. In anticipation of the change, Bishop Treacy questioned whether the three local Dioceses of Bradford, Sheffield and Wakefield, should become two, serving South and West Yorkshire. The end of Wakefield as a corporation, the West Riding as a county council, and of the West Riding Constabulary was marked by events in the cathedral in March and April 1974.

The Changing Position of Women: Readers, Deaconesses, Deacons and Priests, and other Appointments

The last three decades of the twentieth century saw a momentous change in both the roles and status of women in the Church.

Women were not admitted even as Readers in the Church of England until 1969. The first to be admitted in the Wakefield Diocese, in 1972, were Pauline Freda Millward and Evelyn Mary Selwood, the latter being ordained as a deaconess four years later. Pauline Millward was ordained as a deacon in 1992 and was among the first group of women to be ordained as priests in Wakefield Cathedral in 1994. She served as Priest in Charge of St Hilda's, Halifax, from 1995 until her early death in 2010.

Once admitted as Readers, women were authorized to administer the chalice at communion services, a practice which did not always win immediate approval. Eric Treacy told an Anglo-Catholic critic in 1975 that the admission of women to the office of Reader meant that they had his permission to assist with the chalice but he advised his correspondent that he 'should see it is a separate issue from ordination to the priesthood' although he agreed that it could be construed as the 'thin end of wedge'. In 1998, the Lay Education and Training Committee observed that women Readers in the diocese 'greatly outnumbered men' and it was considering how to have a more male-friendly church.

Under the Deaconesses and Lay Ministers Measure 1972, deaconesses, Readers and licensed workers gained new powers (given the consent of their bishop and the relevant incumbent) to church women, to conduct baptisms, and to bury the dead or read the burial service before or after cremations. In 1976, Bishop Treacy published regulations for deaconesses and licensed Women Workers in the diocese: deaconesses or licensed lay workers might assist with the chalice at communion and might take the reserved sacrament to the sick; deaconesses but not licensed lay workers might distribute the reserved sacrament at the discretion of the vicar.

In an unusual venture in 1980, a woman lay worker, Betty Humphrey, was licensed to the parish of Kellington with Whitley on the understanding that she would fulfil all weekday pastoral work in the parish. Her husband, George, was ordained as a priest but working as a school teacher. He had taken many services at Kellington during an interregnum and was licensed as Priest in Charge in 1980; he was to continue teaching while Betty, who was licensed on the same occasion, would look after the parish. It seems that the arrangement worked well but it came to an end when Mrs Humphrey was needed at home to care for an invalid mother.

The diocese gained its second ordained deaconess (Elizabeth Aglen had been the first) when Margaret Bradnum, who had been ordained in the Diocese of York, was licensed to the parish of Illingworth in 1969. Much later, in 1994, she was to become Wakefield's first female Canon, five months after being ordained as a priest.

Margaret Bradnum

In fact – but not in practice – the diocese gained a woman deacon in 1972 when Anne Barnett, who had been ordained as a deacon in Nairobi in 1969 came to serve, effectively as a curate, at Halifax Parish Church. Barnett's responsibility in Nairobi had been to organize and develop women's contribution to the life of the church, home and society on behalf of the Christian Council of Kenya. Bishop Treacy ruled that, as the provinces of York and Canterbury did not recognize women deacons, she had to rate as a deaconess. At the same time, he wrote to her vicar, 'It would follow from this that legally speaking her rightful place is with the House of Laity. However, as the House of Clergy (in the Halifax Deanery) wish to give her a welcome, I, personally, would raise no objection to this but I think it has to be faced that any other deaconess who came to work in the Deanery of Halifax could expect a similar invitation.' He concluded by remarking, 'If the matter was left to my ruling I would say that a deacon or deaconess should be a member of the House of Clergy.' Treacy said that he had no objection to her being styled 'Reverend' and in official documents such as the Diocesan Year Book, that is how she appeared. Anne Barnett became secretary to the Board of Women's Work in September 1973.

For the first time in the diocese, in June 1976, in the closing period of Treacy's bishopric, two women (Evelyn Mary Selwood and Shirley Goldthorpe) were ordained as deaconesses at the cathedral on the same occasion as the ordination of men as deacons or priests.

The 1970s and early 1980s saw a further, but modest, number of women ordained as deaconesses, or coming to the diocese to serve in that capacity. Several of them were the wives of clergy and in the main served in their husband's parish. While deaconesses might already run an ecumenical fellowship, prepare parents for their children's baptism, train Sunday School teachers, take the reserved sacrament to the sick, and exercise other pastoral care, an interregnum might leave them virtually in the role of the parish priest, coping with all demands except the consecration of the elements or conducting weddings: in the early 1980s Angela (Kit) Gray served the parish of Rawthorpe for eighteen months in the absence of any clergyman.

The order of deaconesses was continued after it became possible for women to be ordained as deacons. In 1993, for example, Marlene Wilkinson was licensed as a deaconess at St John the Baptist's, Wakefield.

The ordination of women as deacons, and later as priests, on the same terms as men, was a long time in its gestation. The issue was first promoted with some strength in 1930 when a 'A Group of Oxford University Women' wrote to *The Times,* after having held a series of discussions on women in holy orders and come to the conclusion that 'definite steps should be taken by the Church to further consideration of the matter'. A prolonged correspondence which followed throughout the remainder of April and May covered every point, for and against women's ordination, that was brought to bear again in the 1970s. The Anglican Group for the Ordination of Women was founded in the same year.

Following the Church Assembly's consideration of the report *Gender and Ministry* in 1962 a commission was set up to consider the reasons for excluding women from the priesthood. Its report, *Women and Holy Orders*, was completed in 1966. A consultative document was debated at the General Synod in 1972 and was then to be discussed at parish, deanery and diocesan levels. The main opposition to women's ordination came from two different groups. Some Evangelicals insisted that it was against the teaching, especially of St Paul, in his New Testament letters, on the role of women in the church, 'Man is head of the woman'. Anglo-Catholics argued that the Church of England did not have the authority to make such a fundamental change to the Church's doctrine on its own. It had always claimed to share its Orders with the historic churches of Rome and the Orthodox Communions and so could not alter them unilaterally. But there were also some, clinging to the notion of separate spheres, who based their hostility on the assumption that women were innately different from men in some way which simply disqualified them from the priesthood. In October 1974, the Wakefield Diocesan Synod debated the motion: 'That this Synod considers that there are no fundamental objections to the ordination of women to the priesthood.' It was proposed by the Vicar of Huddersfield, Theo Weatherall, and the principal speaker against it was Milton Lindley, the Vicar of South Kirkby, who had trained at the College of the Resurrection, Mirfield. Weatherall based his argument on the cultural changes between Jesus's time and the present. 'Jesus could not have chosen women as apostles in His day,' he said, 'but He most certainly would have done now.' Lindley spoke of such ordination as 'a severe break with tradition' that would bring about 'a subtle change in the pronouncement of the Gospel'. It would set back the cause of unity with the Roman Catholic Church. It was, he said, quite simply not necessary. The motion was carried in both the House of Clergy and the House of Laity but with, in each case, almost one third of the members opposing it. The ensuing motion, 'That this Synod considers that the Church of England should now proceed to remove the legal and other barriers to the ordination of women', was also carried although with a greater strength of opposition in both Houses.

Colin James took a very cautious approach to women's ordination. In

1977, when he had just been at a meeting of the House of Bishops which had decided to ask the General Synod whether there should be women priests, he argued that it would lead to 'division and anomalies' within the Church and would threaten the unity the Church of England has with the Roman Catholic and Orthodox Churches throughout the world. He was unsure whether he would himself ordain women but would probably take the view of the Church as a whole. He thought the resistance to women priests would be psychological rather than intellectual.

Bishop Richard Hare, who in 1979 attended the inaugural meeting of the diocesan branch of the Movement for the Ordination of Women, made it clear that he was a supporter. However, because of his bishop's view, he was not willing to line up as a campaigner, declaring, 'I am not above doing some back-stage intrigue from time to time but I will not stump the countryside whipping up support. I will not conceal what I think but my views will be those of a private individual, I will not use even such minimal leverage as a suffragan bishop can apply to further the cause.'

The lack of any further move nationally led on 29 June 1980, during an ordination service, to a protest within St Paul's Cathedral by members of the Christian Parity Group, and protests on the same day by members of the Movement for the Ordination of Women outside the cathedrals in Birmingham, Durham and Newcastle.

Until 1980, arguments about whether women should be ordained had centred on the priesthood, with ordination as a deacon being simply a preliminary to ordination as a priest, giving women the same status as men and thus most importantly having the authority to consecrate the communion bread and wine. The shift in focus to their ordination solely as deacons was critical. In November 1981, the Church of England bishops decided to propose to General Synod that 'in principle the order of deacons is an order within the threefold ministry open to women'.

The Deacons (Ordination of Women) Measure of 1986 provided that those who were already deaconesses could progress to ordination as deacons without further examination. Eight women, all of whom were serving in the diocese as deaconesses, were ordained as deacons by Bishop David Hope on 29 March 1987. Less than a year later, Barbara Lydon, one of the ordinands at the time, was licensed as 'minister in charge' of Kellington with Whitley. By 1990, three women deacons were in charge of parishes in the diocese.

The ordination of women as deacons, and their new role as ministers-in-charge, led to the anomalous situation where male priests were still required to consecrate the bread and wine for the Eucharist. One retired priest wrote to Bishop Hope in 1988, 'At the beginning of this year, I was twice invited to officiate at St Matthew's, Northowram, where Deacon Jean Hoggard was in charge. I found there a church humming with vitality where Jean, with a lot of enthusiastic lay help, was exercising a very effective ministry. On each occasion she preached – it being evident that she could speak to that congregation as a known and loved pastor much more relevantly than I could. I did little more than say the Eucharistic prayer, the Absolution, and the Blessing. I felt how unnecessary it must seem to that congregation to bring in a stranger to take the most essential part of the service when Jean was so obviously the focal part of their fellowship and the natural "president" of their worship. What was it, they might well ask, that disqualified her from completing the job?'

Following the ordination of women as deacons, Bishop Hope set up a working party to compile a booklet giving the arguments for and against their ordination to the priesthood. After its completion and distribution he held open meetings across the diocese during October and November 1989. He observed at the time that it was 'important that people listen to each other no matter how firmly they believe their own point of view'.

In 1994, after substantial further controversy, it became possible for women to be ordained as priests. Prior to this there was again extensive formal (and informal) debate. The Diocesan Synod of 9 March 1991 debated the proposals embodied in the draft Priests (Ordination of Women) Measure and in the draft Canon C 4B (of women priests) and the draft Amended Canon 13. A motion approving the proposals was moved by Christine Bullimore, with Timothy Slater opposing it. Mrs Bullimore pointed out that Wakefield was already affirming women's ministry and that there were women in charge of parishes and now the first woman in charge of a prison chaplaincy team. It was 'difficult for women to cope with the idea that they cannot be called by God'. Mr Slater argued that the proposed legislation did not address the issue of women bishops and that it would be wholly divisive. Women would be ordained to a second-class priesthood which could be openly disowned and rejected by any parochial church council or cathedral chapter. The subsequent vote showed a very divided synod. Neither bishop voted in favour. Forty-three members of the House of Clergy voted for and thirty-eight voted against the motion. Forty-nine of the House of Laity voted in favour and twenty-three against.

At his first meeting of the diocesan synod in June 1992, Bishop McCulloch made it clear that he was in favour of the ordination of women and said that he was pleased to have appointed a woman deacon as minister in charge of a parish as one of his first acts. Prior to the vote in General Synod in 1992, he asked each church to pray that it might be guided by God. St George's, Barnsley, for example, had a 24 hour vigil on 6–7 November

1992. There was a vigil in the cathedral at the same time, with Nigel McCulloch celebrating Eucharist on the morning of the 7th. McCulloch wrote personally to each priest in the diocese whom he understood would be hurt by the vote.

The decision to admit women to the priesthood created considerable unhappiness. A letter from an Anglo-Catholic incumbent in the diocese expressed it plainly. 'The result of the vote came as such a shock that it was like going through a bereavement after someone dear to you has been murdered. All that I have ever held true and dear about the Church of England, not least her Catholicity and Apostolicity, has been as it were killed off by those who voted for this measure ... that the Church could vote itself into a Protestant sect is beyond my comprehension.' Four incumbents in the Wakefield Diocese resigned their livings. One priest withdrew his acceptance of the post of a team rector, explaining that he had planned to take his woman deacon with him but felt that the possibility of her being ordained as a priest could cause unrest.

Under the Priests (Ordination of Women) Measure 1993 (no. 2), which provided for women to progress from the status of deacon to that of priest, nineteen women, all of whom were already serving as deacons in the diocese, were ordained as priests by Bishop McCulloch at the cathedral on 25 June 1994. Two already held diocesan posts: Margaret Bradnum was the Warden of Readers and Eileen Turner was the Diocesan Family Life and Marriage Education Officer. Four already held appointments as ministers-in-charge. Four were ordained as non-stipendiary ministers.

Cathedral worshippers, where Anne Jennings became the chaplain, were promised that they would be given notice of when the celebrant was a woman and might choose either to stay away or treat the bread and wine as if it were simply food and not a sacrament. They were also told that, in the event of their being unable to get to the Eucharist, they could be confident that the reserved sacrament would always have been consecrated by a male priest.

Within the diocese, the first woman to be appointed as an incumbent was Gillian Swallow, who became Vicar of Ripponden with Rishworth and Barkisland in 1994. The first woman rural dean in the diocese was Dorothy (Dhoe) Craig-Wild who was the Priest in Charge at St Andrew's, Bruntcliffe, when in October 1996 she was appointed to the Deanery of Birstall. She had become a deaconess in 1981, serving at Middleton St Mary in the Ripon Diocese. Following ordination she had served in the Diocese of Sheffield. The first team rector was Margaret Dye, licensed to the Morley Team Ministry in January 2008. The cathedral gained a woman precentor when Andrea (Andi) Hofbauer, who had come to

Britain in 1998 to work for the Missions to Seamen (now the Mission to Seafarers), was appointed in May 2009. Anne Dawtry, formerly the Rector of St Werburgh's, Chorlton-cum-Hardy, became the diocese's first female archdeacon in December 2011.

The 1993 Measure allowed for parishes who could not accept the ordination of women as priests for theological reasons to decline to be served by them. Seventeen Wakefield parishes took advantage of this at the time. Fewer parishes opted for the further provision, under Resolution C, to have alternative oversight from a bishop other than one who had ordained women. There were arrangements nationally for three Provincial Episcopal Visitors, known as 'flying bishops', two for the province of Canterbury, the Bishop of Ebbsfleet and Richborough, and once for the province of York, the Bishop of Beverley, who could be called upon where necessary. Successive Bishops of Beverley (John Gaisford until 2000 and Martyn Jarrett thereafter) gave some service to the Wakefield Diocese. Under legislation which allowed diocesan bishops to appoint an additional suffragan for this role, Bishop McCulloch invited Anselm Genders of the Community of the Resurrection, formerly the Bishop of Bermuda, to become an assistant bishop. When Tony Robinson became the Bishop of Pontefract in 2002, he took over the oversight of parishes signing resolution C.

There were men who refused to be ordained as priests in the same ceremony as women. For these, separate ordination services were arranged and were carried out by the successive Bishops of Beverley or Tony Robinson. Jarrett's last ordination for the diocese was in 2003; thereafter Tony Robinson has undertaken ordinations where the issue of women priests has rendered it necessary.

Before the ordination of women as priests, a number of Wakefield parishes forged links with Forward in Faith, an Anglo-Catholic movement for those resisting the priesthood of women. In 1993, fifty-eight of the clergy in the diocese had joined three alternative chapters in the movement.

Since some parishes in the diocese continued to exclude women priests, Betty Pedley, the diocesan's Parish Education Adviser and Chaplain for Youth and Children, chose to remain a deacon when other women were priested in 1994, as she was working to encourage parishes to be more child friendly and felt she would be disbarred from working with some of them. She was ordained as a priest only in 2003. Mindful of their years working together, Bishop McCulloch, invited by Bishop Tony Robinson, returned to ordain her.

There could be difficulties where a part-time sector position was to be combined with the ministry of a parish which refused to have a woman incumbent. At a diocesan synod, Anne Jennings raised the question of the appointment of a parish priest to St Anne's Southowram which was to be combined with the new post of Urban Community Adviser. Bishop McCulloch's rather ambiguous response was that the diocese supported both the letter and the spirit of legislation introduced to reflect the 'two integrities'. Thus it followed that in the matter of diocesan posts linked to parishes, appointments would be made both to parishes which accepted the ministry of women and to those which did not.

While Anglo-Catholic opposition remained, other male priests accepted women colleagues happily, even in some cases finding themselves rather surprised to do so! One referred to attending the first mass taken at Brotherton by Marion Bamford: 'It was the first time I had been present at a celebration by a woman priest and I'm bound to say that it did not seem in the least out of the ordinary – totally appropriate and natural.'

For the first time, in 1995, at the July ordination of deacons, the number of women (four) outnumbered the men (two). In 2012, there were some 70 ordained women serving the parishes in the diocese out of a total of 215 clergy.

Sister Mary Clare of the Community of St Peter's, Horbury, was ordained in June 1996 and served as the curate at St Michael's, Wakefield. The College of the Resurrection admitted women to train for the priesthood only in 2005.

Voting at the synod in October 2011, on the issue of the consecration of women as bishops, reflected the continuing divisions in the diocese in regard to women's place in the Church and drew passionate speeches from conflicting points of view. The motion to approve the proposals in the draft Bishops and Priests (Consecration and Ordination of Women) Measure divided the bishops, was supported by the House of Clergy by twenty-four votes to fourteen and was more strongly supported by the House of Laity by twenty-three votes to ten. The Measure made provision for each diocese to make a scheme providing for a parish that requested it to have a male bishop to provide sacramental and pastoral care. However, the authority of that male bishop was to come by way of delegation from the diocesan bishop who almost by definition would himself (or indeed herself) be in favour of women in the episcopacy. Such delegation would in some eyes, and certainly if the diocesan were a woman, come from a tainted source, or from a source which was seen as having no authority to delegate. Jonathan Greener, Dean of the Cathedral, proposed a following motion. He said that he believed that women had added immeasurably to the priestly ministry but, as was the case in 1994 when provision had been made for parishes to have care from bishops who had not ordained women as priests, now a similar provision should be made for those who wished to have care only from male bishops. The General Synod should be asked to reconsider a defeated amendment by the Archbishops to the text of the Measure which would provide for the authority of the male bishop to come from the Measure itelf. While the motion was passed, showing the support for the continuing formal recognition of the 'two integrities', it was favoured only narrowly in the House of Clergy, who voted by twenty votes to nineteen.

The distinctive diaconate

The ordination of women as deacons led the Church of England to look closely at the nature of the diaconate at a time when a distinctive diaconate was being rediscovered in the Church of Rome. The National Diaconal Association was formed in 1988 by bringing together the Deaconess Committee and Anglican Accredited Lay Workers Federation. Since then, and in particular since the ordination of women as priests, it has developed as a body for members of a distinctive diaconate, both male and female. While the task of the deacon is understood as, in part, one of assisting a priest in the liturgical role, it is regarded very much more as a specific means of proclaiming the gospel beyond the Church. Deacons are 'mission minded'. They are focused primarily on the community, working as go-betweens, and may find a particular purpose in working as chaplains in, for example, hospices. The role, grounded in the appointment of Stephen and six others as recorded in The Acts of the Apostles, 'encapsulates the servant nature of all Christian ministry'. As Anthea Shackleton, who was ordained in 2007 as the third distinctive deacon in the diocese, remarked, 'We're called to serve; not to positions of authority or to be in charge.' The role of the diaconate is the focus of a chapter in Stephen Platten's book, *Vocation: Singing the Lord's Song*, where he suggests that deacons 'should be out working in the community in any number of different ways' and cites the example of Gill Butterworth who, as the Ministry Development Officer, was working with those parishes which had core group-ministry teams and who was also the chaplain to a hospice. By 2011, Wakefield Diocese had nine distinctive deacons, more than in any other Church of England diocese. The number included a woman catholic traditionalist who was opposed to the ordination of women as priests and who was ordained as a deacon by the Episcopal Visitor, Martin Jarrett, in 2001.

Women in other positions in the diocese

Outside the priesthood it was again only slowly that women rose to senior positions. In what was a very bold step for the time, David Hope appointed Felicity Lawson, a lay woman, in 1987 as the Director of Ministerial Training. Lawson was a lecturer in Pastoral Studies at St John's College, Nottingham, and had visited the diocese previously to hold training courses. Subsequently she took orders and in 2000 was instituted to St Peter's, Gildersome. She became a canon of the cathedral in 2001.

The first woman to hold the post of Diocesan Registrar was Linda Mary Box, who had served as the Deputy Registrar since 1979, and was appointed in 1993. In 2005 she became the Chancellor of the Diocese of Southwell. In 1994, the Diocesan Board of Finance sought new and younger members and, in particular, women. Despite her having had no other position on any diocesan committee, the Board invited Pamela Green, a chartered accountant with Price Waterhouse, to join it. A year later, she became the first woman in the country to chair a Diocesan Board of Finance. It was a period when finances were very seriously strained and she brought a marked rigour to diocesan budgeting and readily and robustly tackled parochial church councils which failed to pay the parish quota in full (or even at all!). The first woman to hold the post of Diocesan Director of Education was Anne Young who had started working for the diocese in 1993 as Education Adviser and was appointed as the Director of Education in 1999. She was the first lay person to hold the post. She left in 2001 to begin training for ordination.

New Forms of Ministry

Non-stipendiary ministry

The shortage of stipendiary clergy and lack of the money to pay them, changing attitudes towards the role and status of the laity, changing notions of a clerical 'class', and no doubt, too, the commitment and calibre of many, largely unpaid, Readers, led the Church to a positive quest for new forms of ministry in the 1960s and 1970s. Taken together they brought about a cultural shift within the diocese from parishes being heavily dependent on stipendiary clergy to a much greater – and positive – degree of self-reliance on home-grown leadership.

Writing in the *Wakefield Diocesan News* in March 1971, Bishop Treacy commented on the need to take advantage of opportunities like that, newly given episcopal approval, for the Auxiliary Pastoral Ministry, although rather curiously, he was reported in Patrick Vaughan's unpublished thesis of 1987 on the non-stipendiary ministry as signalling to an Advisory Council for the Church's Ministry working party in 1972 his opposition to its development in the Wakefield Diocese! Prompted by the General Synod, the diocesan synod held a debate in December 1972 on recruitment to the ministry 'with particular attention to the establishment of a local ordained ministry'. The Archdeacon of Halifax presented a paper in which, referring to an experiment in Stepney, he observed that the 'hard core of the industrial classes can be penetrated by a local church community by men *thrown up by the community itself*'. It was said that the 1944 Education Act had led to the education of lay people who were well equipped to play a leading role in the life of the Church. A new self-supporting and part-time ministry could develop drawing in men over thirty who would be trained in their own free time. The North West Ordination Course was pioneering such training. Synod then simply referred the issue to parochial church councils and deanery synods.

In 1974, the Diocesan Board of Ministry was established and promptly set up four sub-committees to consider recruitment and training, stipend policy and caring, accredited lay ministry, and the Readers' Committee.

The Auxiliary Pastoral Ministry, as it was termed originally, brought into the priesthood men who had other income – either because they were working or had a retirement pension – who could serve the Church on a part-time basis and without a stipend. As Patrick Vaughan pointed out, it was 'an institutional change of major proportions'. It can be seen as a response to pressure for each parish to be self-sufficient in providing for ministry and the sacraments, pressure to provide a ministry which would resonate with an industrial working-class, the lessening of the divide between the laity and the ordained ministry, and would have the value of providing professional Christian witness in the world of work. One of the most vigorous, and in his lifetime entirely thwarted, advocates of a voluntary priesthood, was Roland Allen (1868–1947) who from 1902 until his death campaigned via publications, for example *The Case for Voluntary Clergy* (1930), and correspondence, for a non-stipendiary ministry. His thinking was a substantial influence on the ultimate decisions of the Lambeth Conference of 1968 to recommend it. Two leading members of the Community of the Resurrection, Walter Frere and Neville Talbot, were in favour of the idea long before it finally gained acceptance. The 1930 report of the Church Assembly Commission on the Staffing of Parishes (of which Bishop James Seaton was a member) suggested for an experimental period the ordination of a few men engaged in other forms of work. In 1955, Bernard Pawley, then Rector of Elland, told Convocation that he knew of two men, one a bank manager and one a foreman in a mill, who were also ordained priests.

Why, when both colonial dioceses and the Church in England itself, were short of professional clergy, did it take so long for the Church formally to adopt the non-stipendiary principle? At the root of the opposition seems to have been a fear of a break with tradition and the conventional model of the full-time parish priest. There were other concerns: a non-stipendiary ministry might become so desirable (and cheap) that the need to pay a professional incumbent might be seriously questioned; there could not be adequate training for a man who was in full-time employment; educational standards would be lowered; the voluntary priest would, because of his employment, be geographically constrained and, when his incumbent left, the new one might not care to have him in the parish; lay people would reject such 'second-class' priests, even the ordination of hitherto lay people would run counter to the growing emphasis on the roles and value of the laity itself. Arguments in favour of the idea saw a pool of untapped ability; men with daily contact with the world of work would form a bridge between a somewhat isolated profession and ordinary working people; they could exercise a priestly role in a secular field; the career priesthood did not engage with social realities; the ministry still tended to attract young men fresh from university and with little experience of 'life' while a voluntary priesthood would counter this. Always, importantly, the early Church had depended on the drawing of priests from among local working people.

The idea of an auxiliary priesthood was firmly rejected by the Lambeth Conferences of 1930 and 1948, but in 1960, acting unilaterally, Mervyn Stockwood, then Bishop of Southwark, and the Suffragan Bishop, John Robinson, established the Southwark Ordination Course, a wholly new approach to part-time training and designed for men fully engaged in employment. The report, published in 1968 for the Advisory Council for the Church's Ministry and edited by Canon Paul Welsby, was fundamental to the recommendation of the Lambeth Conference of that year that an Auxiliary ministry be pursued. The Report, *Selection and Training for the Auxiliary Pastoral Ministry*, looked for mature laymen, aged 30–50, who were well established in their job and who would pursue a three-year training course based largely on evening classes and weekend residentials. Two years later the bishops' regulations for their selection and training established the voluntary ministry officially. By 1985 non-stipendiary candidates accounted for twenty-five per cent of all ordinands nationally.

Among the other advantages of the recruitment of Auxiliary Pastoral Ministers was that they were not included in the 'rationing' of priests which occurred when the 'Sheffield' formula was implemented in 1980.

The first person to be ordained to the auxiliary pastoral ministry in the diocese was John Bryan Calvert Robin who was on the staff of Rishworth School and was ordained as a deacon in the school chapel in June 1977 by Richard Hare. The first auxiliary pastoral ministers to be accepted as curates were ordained as deacons in September 1977. They had been trained on the North-West Ordination Course at Manchester alongside candidates for the stipendiary ministry. Barry Firth was licensed to St Martin's, Brighouse, and Gordon Fisher, the Head of Religious Studies at Airedale High School, was licensed to Airedale with Fryston, a parish of 25,000 people where there was rampant vandalism, a lack of social amenities and, it was said at the time, a substantial immigrant population. Fisher played a particular part in educational work in the parish, for example in preparation for baptism, confirmation and marriage. He felt that his being a priest also helped in his work in school; he and his vicar together addressed the problems faced by his pupils and their home relationships.

The title of Non-Stipendiary Minister (or NSM) was adopted nationally, only later to be followed much more recently by Self-Supporting Minister (SSM) as a means of embracing both the Non-Stipendiary Ministry and the Ordained Local Ministry.

The North West Ordination Course, formed in 1970, was renamed the Northern Ordination Course in 1980 when the Dioceses of Bradford, Ripon, Sheffield, Wakefield, and York joined the original sponsors, the Dioceses of Blackburn, Chester, Liverpool, and Manchester. From 1996 it provided training based at the College of the Resurrection. This was relaunched as the Yorkshire Ministry Course in 2008.

The Shared Ministry project

Prior to the 1970s, the basic contribution of the laity to the work of their church was as members of their parochial church council or in positions such as churchwardens or Readers, and, in some fewer parishes as deaconesses or Women Workers. Church Army captains assisted in some parishes, effectively serving as curates. Many lay people were also involved in the basic work of distributing parish magazines. From the 1970s, lay people besides Readers and deaconesses – usually no more than four in any one parish – were authorized to administer the communion chalice. But the notion that they could have a more extensive role, in teaching, counselling and visiting, for example, which would require training, developed with Colin James's Shared Ministry project. The first step in the diocese towards collaborative ministry, it reflected a national perception of the pastoral contribution which could be made by the laity. Bishop James regarded it as one means of compensating for the forced loss of stipendiary clergy under the Sheffield scheme.

Bishop James's address to the synod in May 1978 was a preliminary to the project. He quoted an observation from the House of Bishops: 'We welcome the opportunities for more effective pastoral care and for mission offered by the development of a variety of ministries – ordained, lay, stipendiary and voluntary – and believe that every diocese should be considering its responsibility for recruiting, training and developing the forms of ministry which the church will need in the next twenty-five years.' He added, 'Today we are recovering the New Testament insight that ministry means that Christ is working things through the whole body and that every church member, by virtue of his baptism, exercises some kind of pastoral ministry – in the home, at work, in the local church and in the community.' He spoke of having recently commissioned fifteen pastoral visitors in one church and recommended the development as one that set the parish priest free to exercise his ministry in depth where his particular experience and training were most needed.

James restructured the Board of Ministry. He recruited Brian Smith, then on the staff of Ripon College, Cuddesdon, and later to be the Bishop of Edinburgh, as its secretary, with a complementary part-time position as the Vicar of Cragg Vale. Deaconess Margaret Bradnum became the Ministry Training Officer and Tutor to Readers. Smith and Bradnum set up a one-year programme involving twenty-six sessions. In three terms this focused on an overview of church life and ministry, an introduction to Christian doctrine, and the study of fundamental aspects of the Christian faith. Students explored the many references to shared ministry in the New Testament, the Ministry of the Word, the Ministry of Worship, and the Ministry of Care and Preparation (baptism, marriage, death, and bereavement). A pilot project began in the Halifax area in 1979. Some parishes pursued the scheme more readily than others. For one non-participating parish which had had a firmly traditionalist incumbent, Richard Hare wrote an item for the magazine urging the laity to seize the opportunity of an interregnum to show what they could do.

Wakefield's first Adviser in Evangelism, Christopher Edmondson, who had been appointed by James, played a part in the training from 1981.

His first engagement was to speak at an open meeting of Ardsley parochial church council which led to the commencement there of baptism visiting.

By October 1982, twenty-one men and women had been trained and commissioned in the Halifax area for a variety of pastoral service in their home parish. By January 1984, some 200 lay men and women had been commissioned or were in training at one of six centres.

Bishop James hoped that the scheme would lead to local ministry teams and in some places it did but, according to Margaret Bradnum, 'The programme could not carry that weight.' No promises could be made to people pursuing the course that they would have a satisfying outcome. There was an absence of agreement by the incumbent to use those who trained, and some trainees experienced considerable frustration. There were incumbents who were reluctant to delegate or who felt that asking others to do what they saw as their job would be regarded as 'putting on them'. Some people went on to become Readers, possibly because for them it was the only option. During his parish visits, James often talked with parochial church councils about the possibilities of shared ministry – sometimes to what he admitted were deaf ears. In some largely working-class parishes members of the councils admitted that the course seemed intellectually above their heads. Another problem lay in the tensions created over courses for Readers and those for the shared ministry, with Readers themselves asking where the difference lay. A different perspective emerged at the diocesan synod in 1985 when it was suggested that too much lay involvement could weaken the spiritual base of a parish!

While success was patchy, it could be impressive: at Gawthorpe with Chickenley Heath, a lay women proved so 'right' that her vicar spoke of her as being as good as a curate and asked the bishop to authorize her to take the reserved sacrament to the sick.

An immediate result of the shared ministry project was the increased number of people coming forward in the diocese for ordination in 1984 and subsequently. In the longer term there has been a renewed demand for courses similar to those it offered.

A special service on 28 September 1991 celebrated ten years of shared ministry in the diocese. Brian Smith returned for the occasion.

Lay Pastoral Ministers

The pursuit of shared ministry continued when David Hope succeeded James as Wakefield's bishop. However, a report by his working group on Urban Priority Areas noted that the shared-ministry courses reached only a restricted number of people most of whom already had confidence in their own ability. Nonetheless it emphasized the continuing importance of lay training. Extending this in 1988, Hope initiated a Certificate in Pastoral Ministry for people who wanted a similar training to Readers but did not want to take services. In preparation for this, Christine Bullimore, a Reader involved in Reader training, was funded to study for an Advanced Diploma in Counselling. After the training was completed she, together with John Marsh and Christopher Sterry, devised, wrote and delivered the course leading to the Certificate. In 2012, training for the Certificate continues. It offers a three-year course in the theology and practice of pastoral ministry and aims at the same standard as the Readers' course. In 1989, there were thirty-two students following the course, the majority of them women. The first certificates were presented in the cathedral in July 1992. Those who complete the course are authorized by the bishop and designated lay pastoral ministers. They work alongside the priest in a parish and also serve in chaplaincies. Students pursuing the course have the option of undertaking work which accumulates credits towards a foundation degree in Ministry and Theology. By 2012 Wakefield had some 135 lay pastoral ministers.

Ordained Local Ministry

Towards the end of Colin James's bishopric, the Diocesan Board of Ministry looked to develop a scheme to foster an Ordained Local (Non-Stipendiary) Ministry. A leaflet, which was never published, pointed out, 'The Church is suffering from a shortage of priests. It is becoming increasingly difficult to maintain a regular Eucharistic ministry in many areas.' It noted that many clergy were grossly overworked which, *inter alia*, made for difficulties in their family life. The underlying thinking was that ministry should emerge from within a local worshipping community. The compelling ideas were that 'in some cases men could be ordained to the priesthood after a different form of training, and that they would be authorized to exercise priesthood only in their local congregation'. The congregation might itself identify a suitable person and encourage him. It accepted that the Church already had two basic patterns of ordained ministry – the full-time paid minister and the non-stipendiary minister, both trained to the same academic level. But the nub of the matter was that vocations for the non-stipendiary ministry did not necessarily arise where they were needed. Before he left, Bishop James had identified some men whom he regarded as eminently suited to the role in their parish of a local minister.

The scheme was not pursued at the time. Subsequently *Faith in the City*, published in 1985, gave strong backing to the idea of the Ordained Local Minister. However, it was not an avenue that David Hope wanted to pursue.

In his first address to the diocesan synod in 1992, Bishop Nigel McCulloch declared that he wanted the Wakefield Diocese to look at Local Ordained Ministry.

The Wakefield Ministry Scheme consequently built on the Shared Ministry Project and on the idea of team and group ministries. Much of the initial thinking was done by Margaret Bradnum, as co-ordinator of Lay Training. It was a response in particular to the recognition that there would not in the foreseeable future be enough full-time stipendiary clergy to serve every parish and yet there was a desire to maintain the local church presence. The first pilot projects began in 1995. Setting them up involved visiting congregations to explain the scheme and then supporting them in establishing a 'Core' of people who would share the parochial work. Fundamental to the scheme was the identification of a member, or members, of some of the Core groups who were willing and suitable to enter the ordained ministry. While the congregations themselves would put candidates forward, it was recognized as vital that those chosen felt a vocation and went through the normal selection procedure, going before a national Advisory Board just as would other ministry candidates. There were concerns, especially among Anglo-Catholics, that the concept of priesthood might be warped by this approach, in particular as some saw it as a means simply of providing someone to consecrate the Eucharist whereas priesthood embraced a far wider role. A major issue was the 'universal' opposition to the idea of a purely local ministry; instead, it was argued, those ordained to the priesthood should have the same status and freedom to move as others entering in the traditional way.

After eighteen months, diocesan synod agreed in October 1996 to support the development of the scheme. From September 1997, Margaret Bradnum took on the additional role as the Principal of the Wakefield Ministry Scheme and John Williams, then the Director of Clergy Training, became also the Wakefield Ministry Scheme Officer.

Four people were ordained deacons as the first local ministers in July 1999, two of them women, Lesley Ennis from St Peter's, Sowerby, and Irene Greenman from St Michael's, Cornholme. David Andrew was from Birkenshaw with Hunsworth, and Geoffrey Bamford from the Upper Holme Valley Team.

Bishop McCulloch wrote very positively about the ordained local ministry in *See Link* in August 2001: 'It has for some time been clear that the rising costs and a reduction nationally in the number of full-time clergy, is already leading us into new and positive patterns of resourcing our missionary task. It is encouraging, for example, that there are now more – not less – clergy in this diocese than there were ten years ago. Indeed, the last two years have seen the largest number of people being ordained in this diocese for several decades. The difference is that many of them are part of unpaid ministry teams trained through the Wakefield Ministry Scheme. In the future this will be the pattern that will continue to provide a Christian presence in each community and parish.'

The new forms of ministry have brought people from a range of professions and occupations into the ranks of the clergy; a number have come from the teaching profession but they include, for example, a beauty therapist, a gardener, a handyman, and a painter and decorator. A former baker, David Wheatley, became the warden of Holgate's Hospital in 2009.

David Wheatley in the chapel of Holgate's Hospital

Malcolm Reed, who had been a director of Swallow Hotels and worked as a hotel and restaurant inspector for the Automobile Association, served in 2011 as the acting Bishop's Chaplain. On his resignation from the Master Innholders, he was appointed as that body's chaplain.

The Wakefield Ministry Scheme has not been without criticism. Some have been sceptical about the selection of candidates who have little academic background and who are not 'intellectuals'. However, it is argued that a priestly person is not necessarily an academic, that the position of an Ordained Local Minister is a vocational one, and that such a person can still moderate the grace of God. There has been some mistrust of the principle of the scheme: one parish, already feeling under threat by proposals for a team ministry, asserted that its congregation saw it as 'a mechanism for preparing us for life without an incumbent'.

It has been most successful where candidates have been able to take early retirement from their other employment.

Churchmanship seems to have played little or no part in the readiness of parishes to participate in the scheme and there has been considerable value in the trainees working together across the spectrum.

The proportion of Non-Stipendiary and Ordained Local Ministers among ordinands has become significant (if not critical). In June 2002, of the twelve people ordained as deacons, seven were either NSMs or OLMs. Of the eight deacons ordained in 2010 (five men and three women), five were local ministers and three were stipendiary ones. In December 2011, the diocese was served by some 133 stipendiary clergy and seventy-one self-supporting ones.

In the absence of any incumbent, Local Ministers have been licensed to parishes to serve under the direction of the Rural Dean as at Kirkburton and Meltham in 2008.

Initially the local ministers were ordained as priests at the same service as other stipendiary or non-stipendiary ministers but an innovation by Stephen Platten led in 2005 to each being ordained as priest in their own parish church, with something of a relay of ordinations each June with up to three services in different churches in a single day.

The experience of three parishes may be cited as examples of what the Shared Ministry project could achieve and how it could feed into the Ordained Local Ministry. The neighbouring parishes of St Matthew and St John, Rastrick (which were united as a single benefice in 2008), took part in the Shared Ministry project from the outset. By 1980 St Matthew's had members of the congregation involved in bereavement support; lay people had taken part in worship and had given addresses during Lent. Five people from St John's, Rastrick were commissioned in 1983: two women to be available to visit people in their homes or elsewhere as confidential ears, one man to assist the vicar in parish visiting, one to help people develop leadership skills in Bible, prayer or study groups, and one serving as a baptism visitor and counsellor. Both churches went on to take part in the Wakefield Ministry Scheme. The continuing strength of lay commitment ensured that, when St John's had a four-year period without effective ministerial oversight, it survived because of the ethos of collaborative ministry which gave it a strong lay leadership. In 2012, St John's had a pastoral carers' network and St Matthew's had nominated pastoral visitors. Both had Core Groups which the incumbent of the united benefice described as 'invaluable in discerning and guiding the churches through mission initiatives'. At St Matthew's Stephen Hannam, then the headteacher of a Bradford primary school, was ordained in 2005 and subsequently shared the priestly ministry across the two parishes.

At Birkenshaw with Hunsworth, incumbent David Clarke fostered shared ministry with considerable enthusiasm in the early 1980s. Groups were formed to take responsibility for different aspects of parish life including baptism, social responsibility, and site and finance. As it developed, further groups organized all-age worship, Cafe Church, the parish magazine, and the social life of the parish. Work with children and young families blossomed. Fortnightly meetings of the parish team, including the clergy, Readers, church wardens and group leaders became the norm.

The Wakefield Ministry Scheme made it possible to recognize the vocations to ministry that were latent in the congregation. The parish retained its dynamic of spirituality and vision. In addition to David Andrew, one of the first to be ordained to the Local Ministry, it had gained by 2012, when it was headed by Martin Lowles, two further self-supporting ministers who took part in all aspects of ministry in the parish and helped out elsewhere in the deanery.

Recognizing the future dependence of the Church on non-stipendiary local ministers, Bishop McCulloch set out his vision in 2002 of there being 239 such ministers by 2010, working with 100 full-time stipendiary clergy. But how, he asked, were parishes which took no interest in the scheme to be persuaded? He questioned whether the age for admission to training might be reduced to twenty-three to parallel that for the stipendiary ministry. However, in practice local ministers are rather older, necessarily being already well established in their congregations.

The Wakefield Ministry Scheme came to a natural conclusion in 2008. Somewhere between half and two-thirds of the parishes had participated in the scheme. The ordination training component came to an end as the Yorkshire Ministry Course (formerly the Northern Ordination Course) began to include locally deployable ministers in its cohorts. The diocese kept a firm place in the training, with the newly founded Diocesan School of Ministry, under the direction of Canon John Lawson and based at Mirfield, providing some of the training alongside training for Reader and Lay Pastoral Ministry. Enthusiastic training continued to be a vital and a nationally recognized feature of the diocese. It was felt important that the parish part of the Wakefield Ministry Scheme should be retained in some way and this was replaced by the Wakefield Ministry Consultancy, responding to a small but steady flow of requests for help for a range of things – collaborative working, project advice and shorter teaching courses.

Both Non-Stipendiary Ministers and Ordained Local Ministers were later designated as Self-Supporting Ministers distinguished as 'deployable' or 'local'.

Turnaround teams

Towards the end of Bishop McCulloch's Missionary Diocese years, the first two experiments in forming turnaround teams took place, under the leadership of John Holmes, the Canon Missioner, and his assistant, Simon Foulkes, the Parish Evangelism Adviser. A team was formed to revive St Paul's, Morley, in January 2001. This was led by Anne Wood who had been a non-stipendiary curate at St Thomas's, Batley, while also working as Head of Information and Communications Technology in a school, but who took up a stipendiary post as Priest in Charge at St Paul's. The church itself was open only for special services such as baptisms, with other worship taking place for the small congregation in the church hall. Its one existing organization was Club 2000, founded by Betty Pedley, the Diocesan Children's Adviser. New music, with live performers, was introduced to the services, using an overhead projector rather than books, to provide flexibility. New forms of worship, including a healing service, were provided. Alpha courses and Bible study groups were introduced. A Wednesday Club for children under 18 months, Chatterbox, was formed.

The second team was at St Mark's, Siddal, where Christine Smith was licensed as Priest in Charge on 13 February 2001 with a turnaround team commissioned around her. The purpose was quite simply to revive the church. The 21-strong team included twelve people from All Saints, Halifax, where Smith had been curate, and five from St Mark's itself. Planning and prayer were the foundation stones of their activity. In terms of worship, the strategy involved introducing *Common Worship*, evolving a more modern style, using new as well as traditional music and engaging members of the congregation in reading lessons and leading the intercessions. Outreach brought first a coffee club for people at home in the daytime and a children's club for 5–9 year olds. In the second year a Bible study group was formed. Much of the work of the team lay in first supporting each other and second in knocking on doors, making personal contact with families and others living in the parish, and renewing contact with its schools.

In both cases the influence of the teams during their two-year operation brought modest growth to the congregations.

St Paul's became part of the Morley Team Ministry in 2002.

A third rather different turnaround adventure took place at St Mary Magdalene's, Lundwood, a former mining community, in 2004–06. The congregation had dropped to a dozen or so and the parish was seriously in arrears in contributing its parish share. The impetus for the project came from the television Channel 4 which was looking for a parish that was struggling in order to make a programme about how it might be turned round. Their contact with the Canon Missioner, John Holmes, and discussions with Jonathan Greener, then Archdeacon of Pontefract, and Bishop Stephen Platten, resulted in the scheme for Lundwood. Funding came from the Jerusalem Trust, and a marketing company, Propaganda, was engaged to use modern marketing techniques to rejuvenate the church. Advertisements for a priest to undertake the challenge brought James McCaskill, from Pennsylvania, who had had some of his training at the College of the Resurrection. A team of eight people, seconded from their own parishes, offered him support from February 2005 for two years. Toby Foster, from Radio Sheffield, provided coaching in preaching and communicating. The diocese offered a reduction in the parish share. The three television programmes, *Priest Idol*, screened in the autumn of 2005, showed the enormity of the challenge McCaskill had faced, and the real steps forward using the Propaganda methodology, Church Lite, in engaging with the community, and with young people in particular. For a time there were 70–100 worshippers on Sunday mornings. Sadly, just as the parish was beginning to flourish, the church hall burned down in an accident as it was undergoing roof repairs. Much of the new activity was disrupted and McCaskill was unable to maintain the levels of support and enthusiasm. The church itself was reordered as a community space but McCaskill returned to the States, and St Mary Magdalene's was put in the care of a new priest whom it shared with St Paul's, Monk Bretton. The Channel 4 series has been marketed as a DVD with study notes.

The Net

While 'church planting' has been much advocated, few significant steps were taken until 1998 when, led by David Male, a 'church without walls' was established in Huddersfield as The Net. Providing a new model for church life, it aimed to draw in those who would not otherwise attend a place of worship, and focused particularly on those aged under-18–40. It has met in the McAlpine Stadium, Huddersfield's George Hotel, Brian

Jackson House, the North Light Gallery at Armitage Bridge, Almondbury High School, Greenhead College, Huddersfield, Huddersfield Methodist Mission, and St Paul's, Armitage Bridge. David Male left in 2006. After a three-year period when it was led by Priest Missioner Nicholas Haigh, a lay-leadership team took over in 2009. In 2007, it initiated a youth event, the Battle of the Bands, at Brian Jackson House, with rock bands competing against each other before an audience of non-Christian young people under the supervision of Christian stewards.

Fresh Expressions Evangelists and other ventures

By 2012, a number of parishes, inspired by the Fresh Expressions movement, had experimented with new approaches to evangelism. The pursuit of community mission led in 2007 to two Church Army captains, Mick McTighe and Neil Walpole, being licensed to St John's, Kirkheaton, and other parishes in the local cluster as Fresh Expressions Evangelists. One was to work with young adults and the other to work with children and families. Their initiatives included forming two Rocky Kidz after-school clubs, a 'Streetlight' youth group, a new Sunday evening adult group, and 'Church to Go', a project which involved a bus and house-to-house visiting.

Encouraging children to come to church and providing something that will attract them without alienating adult worshippers is a perennial problem. Individual churches have continued to experiment. Toddler Church, a form of worship for pre-school children, parents and carers, was introduced on Wednesday mornings at St Mary's, Luddenden, in 1999. Inspired by the course, 'Everybody Welcome', by Bob Jackson, which had been discussed in the Autumn of 2010 by home groups and at a parochial church council away day, a weekly 4pm Sunday Service, Praise Party, commenced at Easter 2011. It has proved a means of bringing children in to worship with their families, makes use of video and action, and involves children actively in every part of the service. It has drawn in a number of people who had not previously attended the church.

Messy Church, supported by the Bible Reading Fellowship, originated at St Wilfred's, Portsmouth, in 2004 as a means of providing church contact for families on a day other than Sunday. It has been described as embracing 'chilling, creating, celebrating, and chomping'. Among parishes in the diocese which have begun their own Messy Church groups is St Cuthbert's, Birkby. The first session took place in August 2011 with the theme of Picnic on the Seashore. It brought twelve children and their families to follow a programme which included a welcome, a workshop with a range of craft activities, a short act of worship, and some food.

Campaigns and Celebrations

The Call to the North

It would be fair to say that the diocese (and indeed the wider Church) has been in missionary mode for more than forty years prior to 2012. In 1969, there was a concerted effort across the country to recruit church members. In part this developed as the Call to the North and embraced the dioceses within the northern province under the guidance of Donald Coggan, then Archbishop of York. Earlier missions had sometimes brought Nonconformists and Anglicans together, rather on an ad hoc basis, but the Call to the North was from the outset a joint project, planned in association with the Councils of Churches. The initial impulse had come from a Roman Catholic layman named Todhunter and the Anglican clergyman, Hugh Gillespie Pollock. One of its architects, John Gaunt Hunter, who was the Diocesan Missioner in Liverpool, admitted that he would have preferred it to be a 'purely Anglican effort' because of the complexity of working with Nonconformist bodies whose administrative areas bore little relation to diocesan boundaries, but the spirit of ecumenism was in the air. Evangelism was to be seen as the vocation of the whole Christian Church in the north. It was hoped that civic authorities, the mass media and cultural groups would collaborate. The main endeavour was to come in Holy Week 1973.

The rationale for the Call was summarized as 'a malaise' in a spiritually impoverished Society. Many, it was said, thought that the social goals of the nation were either obscure or simply non-existent beyond the maintenance of economic viability; there was widespread disillusion with the democratic process and consensus politics; young people had become alienated and cynical; there was a 'massive' failure to realize the human potential of vast numbers of individual people in the things of the mind and the spirit; traditional moral standards were declining. As attendance at public worship diminished, the nation was becoming increasingly godless. There was a danger of people becoming dehumanized under the modern economic, political, technical and industrial pressures.

Some blamed the quality of witness in the Church itself. It faced an intellectual and theological task in understanding and explicating the essentials of the Christian faith in terms which were intelligible to, and capable of commanding the consideration of, secular men. There was a need to consider a range of new moral and social questions.

There were dissentient voices. It was pointed out that mission should be an on-going process, not a matter for quick fixes. Then much church energy was directed towards the scheme for Anglican–Methodist unity and should not be diverted into such a campaign. There was a fear of failure. There was concern that different denominations would preach 'different gospels'. There was also anxiety that Christians working together in this way might find their denominational loyalties reduced and come to assume that which body they actually belonged to was of little concern, so that there would be a drift into vagueness. Some of his correspondence suggests that Bishop Treacy was himself unenthusiastic. Writing in the *Wakefield Diocesan News* in April 1973, at the height of the activity, he questioned the outcome. Would more church men and women take part in the voluntary work? Would they work more aggressively for peace and justice? Would those church people who were members of Trades Unions, were involved in political organizations, or who worked in Local Government be prepared to 'confess' that they were Christians?

Treacy established a (perhaps somewhat unbalanced) consultative committee for the Wakefield Diocese, with three representatives from the Roman Catholics, three from the Free Churches as a whole, and three from the Anglicans. In his pastoral letter for Advent Sunday 1971, he hoped that Holy Week 1973 would see a 'United Christian undertaking to stand up for Jesus'. He suggested that parishes might have a campaign of visiting, hold open-air meetings, and hold meetings in schools and factories. He hoped that ecumenical study groups could be established.

Lent study courses were arranged for both 1972 and 1973.

The *Yorkshire Post* provided a supplement about the Call in the spring of 1973.

It was left to individual parishes to determine how they would support the Call. At both Armitage Bridge and Lockwood, for example, where the two parishes were under the care of a single priest under an informal sharing arrangement, there were weekly meetings of a number of house groups studying the 1972 Lent course on St Mark's Gospel. There was a meeting at Lockwood with the Salvation Army following an evening service in January 1973. Volunteers from a range of denominations in Lockwood formed a team to call on every household and to tell them about the different churches. The campaign culminated in an interdenominational service at Lockwood Baptist Church, with the Bishop of Norwich as the speaker and with music provided by the Salvation Army Band.

The impetus continued for a while. In 1974, St Michael and All Angels, Thornhill, ran a lent course on Basics for Christians which, for the first time, was peripatetic and was shared with other denominations. It began at the parish church but then continued at Chapel Lane Methodist Church, the Independent Methodist Chapel, Thornhill Edge, Thornhill Lees Independent Methodist Church, and St Anne's Roman Catholic Church.

But the energy and commitment to the Call waned and it has been said that its most permanent legacy was the improvement in relations with the other Christian churches.

The ninetieth anniversary of the founding of the diocese

There is an understandable tendency to look to anniversaries as a focus for special services, missionary campaigns or fund-raising activities, or perhaps all three together.

The ninetieth anniversary of the diocese was celebrated on Saturday and Sunday 29 and 30 April 1978. Four of Wakefield's bishops took part. The main event was a 'solemn Eucharist' at the cathedral on the Saturday morning at which Colin James, Roger Wilson, John Ramsbotham and Eric Treacy were the concelebrants. Guests of honour included representatives of both the religious communities. There was a festival lunch at Wakefield College of Technology. Choirs from across the diocese provided choral evensong. The following day Bishop Ramsbotham and Bishop Wilson each gave the address at one of the morning services and Bishop Treacy preached in the evening. It was his last formal appearance in the diocese. The anniversary was marked at the same time by a Flower Festival in the cathedral organized by its body of Friends and with each parish that was affiliated to the Friends taking part.

The Church in the Eighties

At the diocesan synod in November 1979, Colin James set out his vision for a diocesan-wide scheme of action under the title, 'The Church in the Eighties'. It was the most ambitious, extensive and thorough exercise to have been carried out in the diocese up to that time. It was given the slogan, 'Not so much a programme, more a way of life'. The Shared Ministry project was a part of his plan but he gave emphasis to the major role he envisaged for all lay people in directing their Christian activity beyond their congregations and fostering the mission of the Church in their area. He developed the theme in the November issue of the *Wakefield Diocesan News*, writing of the Church as a 'Missionary' Church. 'We approach the 1980s with our eyes open,' he said. 'Our Society is very secularized. Yet many people have deep spiritual longings. The desire for God is real. Yet there is much ignorance and confusion about Christianity. The Christian message must be clearly presented and the Church's mission must engage with the problems and the joys that people face in their family life, their neighbourhood, and their jobs. It must penetrate the Yorkshire we know, where we live, where people earn, and where decisions are made. The Mission has to take shape in the life of the local church, in its community setting, and in the lives of individual Christians.' He acknowledged that the Church was weak in equipping lay people to make their contribution. There was a particular need to develop social responsibility and industrial mission. Adult lay training was fundamental.

The Church in the Eighties had its own 'three Rs': the Response to God's Call, Renewal in the parish, and Re-engagement with the world in witness and service. Engagement was to include the development of adult lay training, social responsibility work, and industrial mission.

Working-groups were set up to devise resource material. Two leaflets, *Know Your Church*, and, *Know Your Neighbour*, were distributed before the end of 1979. The latter was to enable congregations to identify the 'unmet needs of their area and to consider how they might be mobilized to meet them'.

The year 1980 itself was to be one of stock-taking, with parishes looking back to what had been achieved since 1970, deaneries looking at their role and their geographical and social character, and the diocese reviewing the policies and effectiveness of its boards and councils. Parishes were asked to look during Lent at the 'five essentials' of life in their local church and for the individual Christian – worship, education, pastoral care and fellowship, witness and evangelism, and service to the community. A Lent study course was devised giving a week to each essential, with Bible readings and between five and eight questions for discussion suggested for each meeting. Some of the questions were searching and surely designed to spark discussion, even controversy. Among those for the Worship week, and probably prompted by the Charismatic movement, was, 'What is best for worship? Is it what has been hallowed by centuries of use or what springs spontaneously from the hearts of the congregation?' Other questions included, 'Would you be prepared to accept the pastoral ministrations of a lay person?' (pastoral care), 'Do adult members of your congregation feel that they have an adequate understanding of the Christian faith?' (education), 'In what ways does the disunity of the Church weaken our proclamation?' (mission), and 'With the present variety of services by the welfare state, is there anything left for the Church to do?' (service).

Between February and May 1980, Bishop James used the *Wakefield Diocesan News* to reinforce his thinking on the essentials. In March, focusing on Education, he asked what use was being made of new learning methods and whether sermons were discussed and the preacher questioned. In April, writing on Witness, or Mission, he said, 'We have to find ways of sharing the life and message of Jesus with the uncommitted – on their ground, not ours.'

James sustained the impetus with circular letters and more articles in the *Wakefield Diocesan News*. He asked each parish to meet near Whitsuntide to pray for guidance, to consider what had been learned from the Lent course and to decide on their priority in terms of the 'essential' they would pursue. Their choices were to be taken forward into 1981 with parishes enriching their worship, improving their pastoral care and fellowship, advancing religious education, undertaking witness and evangelism, or engaging in service to the community. In September he invited everyone to 'come and celebrate our life together' at one of four 'centres of celebration' in the autumn.

The 'centres of celebration', spaced across the diocese, provided events where, on one Sunday afternoon at 4pm–6.30pm, people could look at resources for the pursuit of the 'essentials' and could end their exploration with an act of worship. The first of the 'markets' (in fact the events were referred to by James as a 'circus') was on 12 October 1980 at the Parish House, Venn Street, Huddersfield. Others followed in Halifax, Dewsbury and Hemsworth. At each there were exhibition stands on the 'five essentials'. The Community of the Resurrection and the Community of St Peter showed the life of the two religious houses. For 'Witness' there were materials from the Board of Mission focusing on Christian Unity, Communications (including parish magazines and the diocesan paper, newly renamed *See Link*), and Community Relations . For 'Service to the Community', Stuart Pearson, the Bishop's Adviser for Social Responsibility, provided displays on the reordering of churches (to create flexible space) and designs for new vicarages. Others providing exhibitions or advice represented the Diocesan Board of Education, the Diocesan Worship Group, the Board of Ministry, the Mothers' Union, the Church of England Men's Society, the Additional Curates Society, the Church Army, and the ministry of hospital chaplains. Pamela Keily provided a stand on Religious Drama. There were specialist advisers on hand to promote each of the five essentials, together with the Diocesan Architect and the Stewardship Adviser for the Dioceses of Ripon and Wakefield, Peter Davies. At Halifax some 700–800 attended the service. It was so successful that, after recovering costs of the 'circus', £100 was sent to Calderdale Hospice.

Stewardship emerged as the underpinning of each of the five essentials and came to be as strongly, if not more strongly, promoted.

In November 1980, James wrote to all the clergy inviting them to a service being planned for the new year. He hoped that parishes would pursue Lent courses in 1981 focusing on their chosen essential. He offered help from the Diocesan Education Officer, David Woodhouse, on children's worship and education more broadly, from Bernard Chamberlain of the Community of the Resurrection on community relations and interfaith dialogue, from Brian Smith on in-service training and lay training, from Ian Harrison the Diocesan Ecumenical Officer, from Chris Collison, the Communications Officer and new editor of *See Link*, on communications, photography, and transport, and from Stuart Pearson on social responsibility.

The special service of thanksgiving and commitment, 'His Glory Proclaim', was held on 4 January 1981 in the cathedral, with an estimated 600 people present. James preached on the five essentials, dividing them into the 'Godward' ones (worship, pastoral care and education) and the 'Manward' ones (mission and service). Each parish was given a copy of the Alternative Service Book, which had been published the previous November, and each was asked to bring two pledge cards. One related to stewardship and was to promise the giving of time and talents and to show how much money parishioners were prepared to give their church, aiming at the 'standard' of five per cent of each individual's income. The other was to set out each parish's priority for the coming year, selected from among the five essentials, explaining how it would meet the 'new situation' of the 1980s. Sixty-one parishes made Worship their priority, fifty-eight opted for Fellowship and Pastoral Care, thirty-six for Witness and Evangelism, thirty-five for Education, and ten for Service to the Community. Ten parishes submitted pledge cards on stewardship.

Letters were sent out shortly afterwards offering help and support to the individual parishes in their pursuit of the 'essential' they had chosen. The parishes opting for worship were encouraged to contact each other to share ideas and to draw help from Harold Ingamells, the (charismatically inclined) incumbent of Monk Bretton. Parishes choosing pastoral care and fellowship were also invited to work together. Stuart Pearson was ready to visit parishes hoping to extend their service to the community. David Woodhouse would help those choosing education. A more detailed letter was sent to those committed to undertaking mission: the newly established Mission Working Party of the Diocesan Board of Mission, led by Christopher Edmondson, then the Vicar of St George's, Ovenden, offered resources for shared ministry on, for example, training parish visitors, using individual homes for witness, and baptism preparation using lay members, and was ready to arrange a small team of clergy and laity with practical experience to help people break new ground. Edmondson, who was consecrated in 2008 as the Bishop of Bolton, had already developed a gift in evangelism as a curate in Kirkheaton when he began leading faith-sharing teams which visited parishes both in the diocese and beyond.

Bishop James sought to keep up the pressure. A new course on Worship was provided for Lent 1982: *The Praying Church and the Praying Christian*, with a training day for group leaders at St Peter's Convent, in February. The course was designed by a team led by Ralph Emmerson, the former Bishop of Knaresborough who had retired to Wakefield in 1979, and included Sister Barbara who was one of four nuns from the Community of St Mary the Virgin then working for the cathedral and who led quiet days for the diocese and provided teaching on prayer. Others in the team were Harold Ingamells, Bryan Ellis, the Vicar of St Andrew's, Wakefield, where he provided services of a charismatic character, Peter Dodson (described by James as 'the contemplative prayer guru from Upperthong'), Mrs Elizabeth Lee, headteacher at the Cathedral School, and Judith Weston who was a Reader at St John's, Kirkheaton. The course provided five workshops exploring silence, intercession, using the Bible in prayer and meditation, tools for prayer, and thanksgivings and expectations in prayer. The art work for the five folded-A4 leaflets was done by Richard Shepley, an architect who was a member of the St Andrew's congregation. They were entitled 'Is anyone there? 'It's me, Lord', 'Prayer – the whole of life', 'God with us', and 'Thanksgiving'. Each included prayers.

In March 1982, James sent out a circular letter headed, 'Whatever Happened to the Church in the Eighties?' In this he reported on four 'important' developments: in regard to stewardship, the newly appointed diocesan Stewardship Officer, Robin Brown, had been in touch with seventy-three parishes, twenty-six of which had firm plans for holding a stewardship mission of some kind; the Shared Ministry pilot project in Halifax was well under way, Thorley Roe was welcomed as the Adult Education Officer, and the Swanwick conference in June would focus on Ministry in the Church and the Ministry of the Church.

Although only thirty-six parishes had indicated originally that Mission and Evangelism would be their priority, the work was given considerable emphasis (eight years before the Church nationally adopted its decade of evangelism). James said in 1981, 'Not so long ago we used to think of mission as something we in the west did to others in foreign parts. Then we awoke to the need of mission in de-Christianized England too.' In 1982, Edmondson was appointed as the Diocesan Adviser in Evangelism. For the next four years, assisted by his Reader, he visited clergy and spoke to parochial church councils, encouraging them to make evangelism a priority. He also ran day courses, provided parish weekends and assisted parishes to run their missions. Gaining a curate at St George's, who agreed to live on the Ovenden Estate in 1983, Edmondson set out to 'plant' a church there. Mobile classrooms were made available at Ovenden Secondary School (later known as The Ridings) and for some years the Cabins, as the mission was termed, flourished, with community and youth activities offered during the week in addition to Sunday worship.

A conference on 'Evangelism in the Local Church' was held in November 1983 with John Finney, then the Bishop of Southwell's adviser on evangelism, as the principal speaker.

Two further Lent courses were devised before Bishop James left for Winchester. The one for 1984 was on 'The individual in the Community'. Its aim was to prompt parishes to look at Mission in the light of course discussions. It was written by John Alford, the Archdeacon of Halifax, and Thorley Roe and was edited by the Provost, John Lister, after consultation with the Diocesan Board of Mission. In 1985 the course, 'Christians making a difference', focused on both witness and service – the two 'Manward' essentials.

The implementation of James's 'Church in the Eighties' scheme was heavily dependent on group discussions. In 1980, John Alford confessed to James that he had serious doubts as to whether these would work. 'People', he said, 'are unready to discuss.' He feared that the material was designed for the 'lively and articulate' and asked whether it would be strategic to consider other methods of pressing the issues on people.

Shortly before he left the diocese, Colin James referred in the *Wakefield Diocesan News* to his two major initiatives: he hoped that the Shared Ministry project would lead to a major resource in extending and strengthening the body of Christ. Looking ahead he wrote, 'This Lent some parishes have been considering how Christians can make a Difference (*sic*) in their local community. As the diocese approaches its centenary in 1988, I hope that parishes will engage more confidently in ways of sharing the Christian faith with our neighbours, and in educating and equipping ourselves to bring our Christian faith and judgment to bear more directly on our everyday life and work.'

'Bread, not Stones' and the diocesan centenary

David Hope's enthronement came just a few days before the publication of the immensely influential *Faith in the City*, the report of the Archbishop of Canterbury's Commission on Urban Priority Areas. Of Wakefield's 202 parishes, twenty-five were listed in an appendix as Urban Priority Area ones. It was a strong influence on Hope's thinking as he looked ahead to the diocesan centenary in 1988. The Report included as an appendix an audit for the local church. It offered the opportunity, Hope said, 'to look

Bishop Hope

not just at the problems of the church in the inner city but at the position of each church in each parish in the diocese'. The idea of the parish profile, which he called 'Bread not Stones' became a necessary part of his centenary planning. Each parish was asked to see the project as 'a unique opportunity', and to tackle it with a true sense of mission, in the power of the Holy Spirit. It was designed to lead to a parish development plan for the 1990s.

To foster development, and to raise the diocesan contribution of £300,000 to the Church's Urban Fund, Bishop Hope launched an appeal to raise a centenary fund of £1m. (This later became the Bishop's Development Fund.) The fund-raising was directed initially by Stan Evans with Ron Carbutt as the chairman of the trustees. A particular goal of the appeal was to facilitate further reordering of churches. Hope wrote in the booklet, *Bread, not Stones*, 'Already a number of our churches have taken the exciting initiative in adapting buildings, often so strategically placed within the local community, in order that they might not only more effectively worship and witness, but that they will be in a particular position to serve and foster the ideal and spirit of "community" locally.'

The appeal, perhaps due in part to the affection and respect for Hope himself, proved popular. It reached its £1m target in 1993. Money came from charitable trusts established within the diocese, from churches, from schools, business concerns, and individuals. An elderly member of St John's, Cleckheaton, sent £10 as profit from her marmalade-making. On a pastoral visit to Alverthorpe, Hope called to give communion to three aged and housebound folk and was offered £5 and £10 spontaneously. A small personal donation came from a member of the Church of the Latter Day Saints who lived at Marsh and who said that he had been impressed by the quality and courtesy of the clergy in the diocese and by David Hope's television series that Easter. On Charter Day, 11 July 1988, the anniversary of Wakefield's becoming a city, Wakefield Metropolitan

District Council took the decision to contribute £10,000. The takings from the Christmas Pantomime performance at Wakefield Theatre Royal on 9 December came to the fund.

One critic of the concept of the fund wrote to say that the Church of England seems to be over anxious to destroy its traditions and its heritage. 'Instead of judging a church by the devotion of its services and the spiritual atmosphere of the building – we now judge it by its toilets, its catering facilities and the frequency of its use for recreational purposes.'

By 2003, the fund had made grants totalling £389,734. Among the many projects it has helped has been the Barnsley Exodus Project which was established in 2002 and which provides clubs with a Christian ethos for children aged 8–11 and 11–15. It focuses particularly on the disadvantaged and helps to build their self-esteem and to listen to their concerns. It originated in the Tuesday night Kidz Club, started at St George's in the 1990s following ideas by the American Bill Wilson, the founder of the child-orientated Metro Ministries.

The twentieth anniversary of the fund was celebrated at Dewsbury Minster in June 2008.

John Allen, then the Cathedral Provost, was asked to devise an audit scheme which would be designed to refocus parish activities. There were a number of audit plans already available. Allen said later, 'Most were excellent in their various ways but as a general rule they were too professional and too demanding for the small and often exhausted congregations that predominated in the diocese. In the context of West Yorkshire, they offered *stones* that would weigh down worshippers, rather than *bread* to encourage and feed them.' Allen explained that his audit had been designed to 'earth their mission' in the needs of the particular parish. *Bread, not Stones*, produced on one of the first Amstrad PCs, was, Allen explained, 'deliberately designed to appear amateurish and accessible'. Its pages were suggestions rather than prescriptions. It was rooted in the locality. And it was closely linked into the planning for the centenary. The booklet included a questionnaire which Betty Pedley, then a teacher, who was studying on the Northern Ordination Course, had devised for use at Holy Nativity, Mixenden.

Besides being used by almost all the parishes in the Wakefield Diocese, *Bread, not Stones* was bought and used by parishes in the Dioceses of Blackburn, Bradford, and Ripon. In the autumn of 1986 the idea of the Parish Profile was introduced to the deaneries. Six weeks were to be given in the summer of 1987 to a survey of the parish, in terms of its streets, it inhabitants (including ethnic minorities, single parents, and people with disabilities), its businesses or industries and employment opportunities, and its other organizations. People were invited to gather as much documentary information as possible, including, for example sales brochures from factories, bus timetables and school prospectuses. They were to create, too, a picture of life in the congregation – prayer groups, its overseas mission links, choir and music, Sunday School and other organizations, and courses attended by its members. Six more weeks were to be given to considering what lessons had been learnt and how to respond to the needs which had been identified. They were to ask what the parish was like as a place to live, whether there was a place for a Community Newsletter instead of parish magazine, how to improve liaison with the local authority, and whether to have a speaker from Neighbourhood Watch. They should identify their allies, including other churches and voluntary bodies.

Parishes were then to determine one thing to do immediately for the centenary year, one thing to start doing in a year's time, one thing to campaign for, and one thing to stop doing. Parishes were asked to share their discoveries. The Parish Development Officer, Richard Giles, hoped that the audit would introduce a new sense of realism in regard to the use of buildings and hoped to see the change Hope sought 'from maintenance to mission'. In an innovation for the diocese, Roy Clements, as Diocesan Communications Officer, was asked to make a 'simple and homespun' video about doing the Parish Profile. He ran a pilot scheme in his own parish, Horbury Junction, gaining help in making the video from the Ripon Diocesan Communications Officer, Tony Shepherd. The filming was edited in a suite in the Bishop of Ripon's basement. The experience of doing the profile made Clements realize how few people really know their own area. He found, too, that it could be fun. Everyone could get involved, including young people, lay members could take on leadership, and the congregation could gain a sense of energy.

Many of the ideas for 'What to start immediately' focused on creating community facilities or working in the community. There were also those parishes, following Colin James's earlier lead, which wanted in particular to encourage the laity to share in ministry, for example by sustaining contact with parents after baptisms, and in parish administration. Among specific ideas were having campaigning missions, making a special study on an ecumenical basis of how the town-centre churches could respond to the needs of the lonely, founding an over-60s club jointly with the Methodists, exploring the possibility of sharing the church with a Methodist congregation, putting on a Gang Show with young people, setting up house groups, and improving the social life of the church. Allen commented that the project had produced a 'multitude of small developments and epiphanies', renewing hope in churches and improving the lot of congregations and their neighbours. Among immediate achievements, he noted, had been the reinstatement of a bus route on one estate, the reordering of worship, a change in the times of services to better meet local needs, the discovery of new talents in the congregation, and, above all, discovering that there was always the possibility of change.

At the beginning of the centenary year, in January 1988, the diocesan branches of the Mothers' Union came together for a service in the cathedral when twelve banners, each with the name of a deanery and each based on a hymn by Bishop How, were carried in.

Bishop Hope made a pilgrimage throughout the diocese in what must have been an exhausting week of 16–23 April. In planning it, he said that its main purpose was to emphasize that the bishop is a focus of unity among the people he is called to serve. It would follow the pattern of usual parish visits except covering a much wider area and taking in both the sacred and the secular. 'It is important', he said, 'that the Church takes a keen and lively interest in all aspects of local life – so I find myself in some very unlikely places.' He visited industrial concerns, hospitals, a farm, and such public bodies as the fire service, the police and the probation service. There were acts of worship each evening in one of the deaneries, with the Bishops of Knaresborough, Sheffield, Chester, Middleton, Bradford, and Repton giving the addresses. The pilgrimage culminated in a visit to the diocese by the Archbishop of Canterbury, Robert Runcie, who preached in the cathedral on 23 June, and at St Peter's Morley on the morning of 24 June before going on to lunch at the Community of the Resurrection, and to Heptonstall to celebrate the 800th anniversary of the church of St Thomas a Becket. The Archbishop also went to Grimethorpe and to Rawthorpe, a Huddersfield Urban Priority Parish, for a seminar on the issues raised in *Faith in the City*.

In May and June deanery exhibitions and congresses brought together the results of the parish profiles. Parishes took immense pride in their reports. There was a great service of thanksgiving Eucharist at Huddersfield football ground on 26 June arranged by the archdeacons.

Music came from traditional and modern sources, some of the latter, in particular 'I the Lord of sea and sky', proposed by Richard Hare. Rehearsals were held in churches across the diocese in April and May run by the cathedral organist, Jonathan Bielby, and the Precentor, David Baxter. A special choir was formed directed by Bielby. Almost all other services were cancelled on the day itself. Seating for 6,000 was allocated to the elderly, others were expected to stand but in covered accommodation. Bishop Hope celebrated according to Rite A. Hymns were accompanied

Members of the Mothers' Union carry banners into the football ground for the centenary celebrations, Roy Clements

by the West Yorkshire Police Band or, where they were of a charismatic character, the Normanton Music Group.

A centenary prayer, used in churches across the diocese during the year, was said at the football ground:

> God our Father,
> bless the Diocese of Wakefield
> Grant that we, with all Christ's people,
> may live and work
> in the power of the Spirit.
> May we, through faith in the Son,
> enter into our true heritage
> as your children.
> Grant this through Jesus Christ our Lord.
> Amen

The whole event was recorded on video.

Returning from a visit to Tanzania in 1986 Bishop Hope had suggested that another way of marking the diocesan centenary should be to form a link with a diocese in Africa. The link with Mara was formally inaugurated on 10 July at a service in the cathedral when the Bishop of Mara, Gershom Nyaronga, gave the address. The covenant was witnessed by the Bishop of Egypt, Ghais Abdul Malik.

The centenary was marked, too, by a series of lectures in May on the history of the diocese, and a flower festival in the cathedral in July. On 3 September there was a family fun day at Silcoates School.

Wakefield Council gave the freedom of the city to the Cathedral Chapter to mark its own centenary.

On 8–10 September, 300 people from the diocese, both clergy and laity, met for conference and consultation at Lancaster University with Canon Eric James as the facilitator. James was a former director of Parish and People, and one of the figures who inspired *Faith in the City*. Bishop Hope used two quotations from the 1988 Lambeth Conference: 'We have to break out of being a club for our own members, to break the purely pastoral model to become a movement in mission' and 'The mystery must be communicated ... the Gospel must not say Go out into the world and do theology, but Go – make disciples'. The conference produced statements on Mission and Evangelism, Worship and Spirituality, Education, Social Responsibility, Ministry, and Deanery and Parish structures. Summing it up, Hope said that it demonstrated the sense of urgency for mission and evangelism. It provided evidence, too, of a desire to move away from parochialism and a recognition of the need for more lay people to participate in ministry. Additionally, it was held to have shown the need for flexibility in corporate worship and the need to understand the place of silence. Hope wrote later of the 'different points of view being expressed, divergent theologies being set forth, strongly held convictions being stated'. He added, 'Yet there was an amazing feeling of unity, and a confidence that the church has something to say and offer.' It was subsequently regarded as a 'good exercise in firing people up' but the numbers attending did not create a critical mass and something of the enthusiasm was lost when they returned to their parishes.

African Sanctus was performed in the cathedral on 27–28 October to mark both the diocesan centenary and the link with Mara. It was an ambitious – and very costly at over £7,000 – undertaking bringing together both dance and song with a large cast. It was described by the *Daily Telegraph* as 'a thrilling collision of cultures'. One of the performances was attended by the cultural attaché of the Kenyan High Commission.

The year's programme ended with a centenary Advent carol service on 2

December in the cathedral, for the diocese, the city and the cathedral itself.

People looked back for many years remarking on the manner in which the centenary celebrations had brought the diocese together and of the family feeling it had generated.

The Missionary Diocese, Christ our Light, the millennium and beyond

The 1990s were identified as a Decade of Evangelism to be launched on Epiphany Sunday, 6 January 1991. That March, Rowan Williams, giving the Bishop's Lecture at the cathedral, described the decade as 'a necessary idiocy'. The intention was that parishes should make evangelism part of the ordinary life of the parish.

By this time, statistical evidence showed that Wakefield was among the dioceses suffering most from falling church attendance and had also experienced a substantial drop in young people coming forward for confirmation. Coming to the diocese in 1992, Nigel McCulloch determined to counter the trend and determined too that the diocese should both be, and be known as, 'the Missionary Diocese of Wakefield', cheerfully accepting the 'flak' from other bishops. The initial response in the diocese to the Decade was a Lent course written by Ken Sawyer, 'Send us out'. Bishop McCulloch launched his Vision for Growth at the diocesan synod in June 1993 and spoke of building on the foundations laid by his predecessors to promote spiritual renewal and a zest for mission. He asked for prayers for the Vision to be said in the chapels of the Community of the Resurrection, St Peter's Convent, and Archbishop Holgate's Hospital. Tony Rolfe was appointed as prayer secretary and parishes were invited to send their requests to him for prayers for mission, people and events.

Bishop McCulloch set up a small Vision and Strategy Group, chaired by Baroness Jean MacFarlane, reflecting on the one hand his Vision for Growth and on the other the news of the cuts being made to the grants from the Church Commissioners. Its brief was to look at the central structures of the diocese, the bishops and their staff, the cathedral, the sector ministers, the boards and councils and the deaneries and parishes.

Shortly after McCulloch's appointment but before his enthronement, the 61st Synod, in March 1992, focused on the report, *All God's Children*, which had been published by the General Synod in 1991. It had featured St Martin's, Brighouse, which in 1988 had opened a weekday evening children's 'Cats' club for 4–11-year-olds, informal, with noisy games, but also teaching about the church. (Cats derives from Catechumen, or learners.) One of the churches in the Brighouse–Elland Deanery had a 'pram club'. The synod papers include a summary of the report: it referred to the rapid social changes which had resulted, by 1992, in only fourteen per cent of the nation's children being in touch with a church. In 1955 a survey showed that eighty-three per cent of adults had been to Sunday School. Sunday Schools had had a wide social mix and had made a contribution to social morality. It was now very hard to maintain a ministry among children. The key factors which had led to the change included a rise in car ownership with consequent opportunities for Sunday leisure, the growth of secular organized activities on Sundays, and changes in home life so that parents spent less time with children. A further factor stemmed from broken homes, with Sunday becoming a day for 'seeing Dad' rather than attending a place of worship. The report noted, 'Parents can no longer control the experiential environment of children – which is provided by TV and videos. Parents don't talk to their children about God. Television throws children too soon into an ambiguous world of adult values; it offers a hyperactive fantasy world; commercial bodies target children.' The report referred to the collapse of junior church membership and suggested that the Church needed to think 'mid week' and to build links with other organizations like mother and toddler groups.

Material was provided at the synod for children to celebrate the bishop's enthronement.

In early 1993, the Board for Mission and Unity produced a paper on Church Planting, looking to the formation of new congregations which might be pioneered by a couple of people, by a group of a dozen or so Christians, or by the transplant of a large section of an existing congregation. The congregations might assemble in a school, a public house, a community centre, or a hall. However, it was felt by the Bishop's Council that the paper should be deferred for consideration until the air had cleared over the ordination of women.

As well as enthusing his churches, Bishop McCulloch hoped to attract new clergy to the diocese who were particularly committed to mission. The appointments of 1993 were a start: John Finney came as Bishop of Pontefract; Stephen Cottrell, who had co-authored a nurture course, 'Follow me', and was Priest in Charge of St Wilfred's, Chichester, came as the Diocesan Missioner and Bishop's Chaplain in Evangelism; Steven Croft, then Vicar of Ovenden, who had been developing a course called 'Christians for Life' and had also written *Growing New Christians*, was seconded to work part-time as the Diocesan Mission Consultant. Robert Warren, later the author of *The Healthy Churches Handbook*, who was appointed as the National Officer for Evangelism in 1993 in succession to Finney, came to live in the diocese for a time at McCulloch's instigation.

Felicity Lawson, already serving as Dean of Ministry, who had co-written the nurture course 'Saints Alive' with John Finney in the 1970s when he was Vicar of Apsley, joined the mission team.

Stephen Cottrell, who became the Bishop of Chelmsford in 2010, was appointed in 1998 as the Missioner and Evangelist for Springboard, the Archbishop of Canterbury's and York's initiative for evangelism. The position of Canon Missioner was revived and John Holmes came from the Diocese of Ripon where he had been the Diocesan Missioner since 1993. Immediately after his installation, Holmes was invited to join the bishop's staff, further emphasizing the importance of his role. Simon Foulkes joined the missionary team a year later as the Parish Evangelism Adviser.

Returning to 1993, Finney, Croft, Lawson and Warren set up training days for clergy and parish personnel on different facets of a parish's mission to its community. Some 600 people attended a day conference at Horbury School on Christian nurture led by Warren in January 1994 and many more applications had to be refused.

Bishop McCulloch wanted to generate a mission-oriented culture not just among the clergy but within the wider church community. Personal visits were for him essential. He initiated an unprecedented series of mission visits to each parish, undertaken in 1994 by himself, Finney, or one of the two archdeacons. Visits were repeated in 1998 by these four with the assistance of additional members of McCulloch's staff. The task, as explained by one of the visitors, Roy Clements, was to 'get the church talking in mission terms', and to encourage rather than to criticise. The day's visit usually included a session with members of the parochial church council. The visitors' reports show that the occasions provided for a very detailed exploration of both any recent problems faced by the individual church and its locality, and the range of initiatives – in particular in the form of outreach – which were being undertaken or which could be undertaken. Visitors themselves made suggestions for further action. Each of the twelve deaneries was asked to identify a mission priority area, and individual projects were devised for each of these. At Almondbury, for example, there was to be a mission audit of the Dalton area where parish boundaries converged, to discern what presence and activity was needed there.

In 1995, McCulloch held a rally, Moving Forward Together, in Huddersfield Town Hall, bringing together clergy, churchwardens, and the secretaries and treasurers of parochial church councils from across the diocese for the first time since synodical government had been introduced in 1970.

Individual parishes held their own missions. In 1995 messengers from St Peter's, Morley, visited every house in 200 streets in the parish in preparation for a nine-day visit in April by ten students from Cranmer Hall, Durham. There were events for children, a question-time event at Churwell School, and an evening in St Peter's with both favourite hymns and items from contemporary musicals such as *Jesus Christ, Superstar*.

Wakefield's being proclaimed as a missionary diocese led in 1994 to an invitation to Bishop McCulloch from Dr David Blackmore, lay chair of the Chester Deanery Synod, for him to lead a mission to the Deanery of Chester in 1996. The unique project, Jigsaw, which was co-ordinated by Stephen Cottrell, was seen as an opportunity to foster skills in mission and evangelism within the Wakefield Diocese. In effect there were to be nineteen missions, one to each of the Chester parishes and one to the cathedral. The vision for the missions was to make contact with people outside the worshipping life of the church, to encourage a deeper commitment from those on the fringes of church life, to deepen the faith of regular church attenders, and to enable those already fully committed to share their faith with others. As Stephen Cottrell put it, they would 'turn disciples into apostles'. Mission teams brought together 177 people, drawn from seventy-three parishes and covering every Wakefield deanery. Among them were Mother Robina and three further Sisters from St Peter's Convent. There were preliminary exchange visits between the teams and their allotted parishes, and training days. The mission itself took place over nine days in October 1996 with the visitors working alongside committed local people. At any one time during Jigsaw Week, there were nineteen different evangelistic activities and events. The small ones in people's homes or pubs were especially effective. Larger events gave a sense of unity to the mission. Its achievements lay in fostering development in individuals and in churches, in bringing a fresh confidence in the gospel, and in giving lay people a greater confidence in mission and evangelism.

In 1997, some 2,000 people from the diocese attended a 'Doors of Hope' conference in Harrogate, convened by McCulloch to help lay people in their task of taking the light of Christ into a new millennium.

During the 1998 round of visits, McCulloch asked that the incumbent and PCC should choose an area of church life to concentrate on from among: Mission through evangelism and social action, Mission through worship and spirituality, Mission through pastoral care, or Mission through parish education. Their reports show that the visitors made extensive and precise recommendations for action. One target for mission was the 'adult catechumenate', people who had been baptized but had had little further association with the Church.

A product of the 'missionary diocese' initiative was *Emmaus: the way of faith* (1996–2003), a set of resources for Christian nurture written by

Stephen Cottrell, Stephen Croft (who became Bishop of Sheffield in 2009), John Finney, Felicity Lawson and Robert Warren.

In 1997, the Church in the Community initiative was launched at the October diocesan synod. Its aim was to promote consideration of the ways in which the church could work in the wider community. It had an essentially ecumenical flavour. A brochure, *The Bishop of Wakefield's Church in Community Initiative,* included articles on how the diocese was engaging in contact with families – through holiday clubs, play schemes or in using church premises for mother and toddler groups – in contact with schools, in the role of its hospital, prison and university chaplains, in the wider role of its cathedral in promoting urban regeneration, and providing an accessible and quiet city-centre space, in the simple acts of kindness shown by individuals to those in need of help or support, in working with the local authority and other churches to fund staffing for community projects, and through the Church Urban Fund projects. It provided the example of the Cephas Project at Dalton near Huddersfield, where a full-time co-ordinator was sponsored by the Baptist Church and the three Anglican churches.

In the year before the millennium, Bishop McCulloch held Christ our Light visits to every place where Anglicans worshipped in the diocese, commissioning those attending the services, by the laying on of hands, to take the light of Christ into the new millennium. On each occasion the Christ our Light four-foot-high candle, which was lit from within by oil, was carried into the building. The candle had previously been taken to the Holy Land to the sites most associated with Jesus's ministry. Each person was given a commemorative booklet, a metal badge bearing the symbolic flame which Roy Clements had designed for the diocesan centenary in 1988, and a prayer card. Each church was given a foot-high candle, to be lit on 2 January 2000, and a certificate to show the number who had been commissioned. Afterwards each

Bishop McCulloch bearing the Christ our Light candle

venue received a framed copy of a photograph, taken on the occasion, of the bishop, the churchwardens and the symbolic candle. The pilgrimage began on 10 January 1999 at the most recently built church, St Catherine's, Sandal, where the service was attended by 200 people; it included a baptism by immersion and the confirmation of thirteen people. Wakefield Prison was visited on Christmas Day 1999. The final visit on 1 February 2001 was to Luddenden with Luddenden Foot. The thirteen-month programme concluded on 6 February 2001 with a service in the cathedral. In all, McCulloch visited 241 churches and eleven chapels, including those in prisons and hospitals, and laid hands on and commissioned more than 20,000 people. On 13 October 1999 the commissioning took place for the first time in a Methodist chapel, at Streethouse where the Anglicans from Sharlston had a sharing arrangement for parishioners living in that part of the parish. The numbers commissioned on an individual occasion varied from forty to four hundred. Parishes which had opted for Resolution C, electing not to have Episcopal oversight from a bishop who had ordained women, readily welcomed Bishop McCulloch for the Christ our Light events as they were not deemed sacramental, and none of the parishes took a wholly rigid view anyway.

The Christ our Light visits were followed each day by Church in the Community receptions at a wide range of centres and with guests from the wider community, in particular from industry and other forms of employment.

Early in his episcopacy, McCulloch had taken an assembly in every one of the 103 church schools in the diocese. He had noticed that very few displayed a cross. In the approach to the millennium, he had oak crosses made for each school from wood from discarded pews and, quite separately from the Christ our Light visits, he returned to the schools to take assemblies again and to present the specially inscribed crosses.

Bishop McCulloch was determined that the impetus of the millennium should be taken forward in the first decade of the new century. In 1999, each parish was asked to put forward its plans for the years 2000–05 as part of the Vision Strategy. There was a near hundred per cent response. Most parishes aimed at growth in the number of worshippers and at raising more money, many hoped to draw more young people in, some referred to training for the lay and ordained ministry, a number focused on reordering or other work on the church itself, and one hoped to 'encourage greater involvement of men'. References to ecumenical activity were rare.

Transforming Lives and Investing in our Faith: looking to the 125th anniversary of the diocese

There is always the possibility that parishes and their people succumb to 'initiative fatigue'. Yet in the face of the complex challenges of fewer stipendiary clergy, the need to sustain quality worship, financial constraints, problematic buildings, ever-growing secularization, and the desire for the Church to serve the community, there is a vital need for church groups to maintain positive local plans and to review their development regularly.

Constraints in the first decade or so of the new century increased with the allocation of stipendiary clergy under the Sheffield scheme dropping in 2012 to 136 and the income from the parish share, having peaked in 2005 at ninety-four per cent of the budgeted figure, falling away thereafter. Less than eighty per cent was collected of the 2010 assessment and it was said that no other diocese had fared quite so badly. Countering the negative aspects of decline was a major issue for Bishop Platten and his senior clergy.

As had become apparent with David Hope's centenary event at Huddersfield, little encourages confidence and morale more than diocesan-wide celebrations. Platten oversaw a number of such gatherings in the years leading towards the diocese's 125th anniversary. In 2005, under the slogan 'Arise' more than 1,500 people gathered at Bishopthorpe to walk in pilgrimage to York Minster for a Eucharist. The Archbishop of York, John Sentamu, gave the address at the 'All the Saints' event at Cannon Hall on a hot and sunny day in June 2007 when the centrepiece was a giant bouncy castle in the shape of Noah's Ark. From this (somewhat shaky) platform, the words for gathering were spoken before the procession, led by drummers and dancers, snaked its way down the field to the worship stage. Platten and Malkhaz Songulashvili, the Bishop of Georgia, dressed in identical purple robes and black hats. Thousands of communicants received the bread and wine at the many 'stations'. In June 2010, in a heavy downpour, crowds gathered in the grounds of Nostell Priory for 'Onward!' when the Archbishop of Wales, Barry Morgan, preached, and displays were provided by deaneries, diocesan departments and other bodies such as the Mara committee, to reflect continuing innovation.

Both David Hope and Nigel McCulloch had looked to a significant date (the diocesan centenary and the millennium) as a goal for forward planning. Bishop Platten's emphasis on consultation and collaboration led to the gradual formulation of a five-year strategy to take the diocese towards its 125th anniversary in 2013. A first step came following a residential meeting of the bishop's staff in 2005 for which Platten had suggested they read *Pursuing the Mystery*, written by George Guiver, the Superior of the Community of the Resurrection, when he was the tutor at the College of the Resurrection. Discussion prompted the provision of the Lent course for 2006, Everyday God, encouraging people to take their faith more seriously and to apply it to daily living. Led by Jonathan Greener, then the Archdeacon of Pontefract, it was planned and written by a team including Richard Burge, Angela Byram, Mark Earey, Mary Judkins, John Lawson, Tony Macpherson, Michael Rawson and Wendy Wilby. More than 4,000 copies were sold for study in 2006. There was a demand for it beyond the diocese.

A modest annual grant from the Church Commissioners, providing a Mission Fund, enabled the appointment of Brian Morris as the Diocesan Stewardship Adviser in 2006. He was followed by Jo Beacroft-Mitchell as the Giving and Resources Adviser.

The concept that became the Transforming Lives programme began as a paper on Transformation prepared in the Autumn of 2006 by Robert Freeman, then Archdeacon of Halifax but who in 2011 was consecrated as the Bishop of Penrith, and was part prompted by the Bishop's Council's reading Ann Morisy's *Journeying Out*. Discussion of the paper yielded the slogan, 'Transforming lives, Transforming congregations, Transforming communities'.

The group which had worked on preparing material for Everyday God continued under the leadership of Tony Macpherson, appointed in 2007 in succession to John Holmes as the Canon Missioner, to plan courses for both Lent and Autumn 2008 and for Lent 2009 on Transforming Lives, looking at the Gospel encounters where Jesus transformed people, aspects of God, and how areas of church life might be strengthened. This last focused on worship, care, prayer and spirituality, evangelism and outreach, community involvement and service. It included a very imaginative booklet of daily Bible notes and prayers, drawing a relationship between biblical words and episodes and present-day experiences, study-group material for the five weeks of Lent, and materials for children and young people.

Transforming Lives evolved into a broader and more sustainable mission strategy, Investing in our Faith, focusing on the necessity for ongoing commitment to change and transformation. The phrase was an umbrella term embracing parish mission thinking and planning, deanery thinking and planning, diocesan thinking and planning, and stewardship and discipleship initiative. Bishop Platten emphasized that, looking at the numbers of clergy, Readers, and Lay Pastoral Ministers together, the diocese was more richly resourced than ever before. He put forward a motion to the June synod in 2008: 'This Synod believes that the transformation of *individual lives, congregations and communities* is central to the Gospel message. We therefore call on the whole diocese to engage prayerfully in the next stage of our life together: "Investing in our Faith 2008–13 – Leading the diocese to our 125th Anniversary".'

In a series of meetings, Platten outlined what the diocese would look like in five years' time: it would be leaner, with fewer paid clergy; it would be better organized, working together more efficiently at a local level in deaneries and across parishes; there would be more collaboration between lay, self-supporting and stipendiary ministries; there would be more people in church; the diocese would be marked by the energy and vision of the Christians who worshipped within it; it would be a diocese which was outward-looking – and an outward-looking diocese would be a growing one.

Deaneries and individual parishes were each asked to prepare a Transformational Plan, the former taking into account the likely number of stipendiary clergy who would be in their deanery in 2013, and placing each of their churches in one of four categories: future-healthy, future-sustainable, diocesan mission parish, and not sustainable. Parishes in this last category were to be considered for either radical pastoral reorganization or for closure. Deaneries were also asked to look for better ways of allocating the financial demands of the existing Parish Share.

Parishes were asked to devise action plans, 'owned' by the whole church community, under the headings Worship, Pastoral Care, Prayer and Spirituality, Evangelism, and Community, and were given a 32-page booklet, 'Ideas for your transformational plan', which offered a wealth of practical ideas (including reminding churches to make sure their websites included up-to-date information about activities). The invitation was to 'pray, review, think and plan, and then do'. The goals were to be attainable, relevant, realistic and given a time scale. Writing of Mission Action Planning, Robert Freeman noted the need to couple pragmatism and experience with Christian risk, faith and adventure. Platten's recent book, *Rebuilding Jerusalem* (2007), was suggested as background reading. The plans were to be produced between Easter and November 2009 and then presented to the bishop at the cathedral. Thereafter implementation was expected, with the resources of the diocese offered for training in areas such as stewardship and mission.

Although not all parishes submitted a plan, many of those that were put forward showed how far the culture of congregations had been influenced by the Church in the Eighties, Bread not Stones, and the Christ our Light initiatives. There was, for example, emphasis on the quality of existing collaborative ministry, or a wish to develop this, and on the continuing encouragement of house groups and the provision of study courses and nurture courses. There was a continuing recognition of the need to modernize and reorder church buildings, with priorities, for those still without them, for providing lavatories and kitchens.

Parishes looked for many ways to engage with their community, some new, some already operating elsewhere. These included founding a community café, singing carols and having a harvest supper in public houses, forming a church darts team to compete in public houses, taking a stall at a local show, distributing hot-cross buns in the shopping centre, holding an Ascension Day procession, inviting the wider community to the patronal festival, having an open-air Songs of Praise at a local beauty spot, holding a joint meeting with a local-history group, running a WEA class on Spirituality, running a luncheon club, and catering for children in need of an after-school club. One parish proposed an occasional non-eucharistic service for those unfamiliar with communion. Another proposed a beer-and-hymns service. Ideas for congregational life included a New Year Resolution service, a parish retreat, prayer breakfasts, a short 'Know your faith' course, Taizé-style services, the provision of prayer trees or prayer-request boards, and walking a labyrinth.

The most ambitious suggestion for congregational life was the decision at Trinity Church, Ossett and Gawthorpe, to undertake a pilgrimage to the Holy Land. This took place in 2010. It was led by Paul Maybury and the erstwhile Canon Missioner, John Holmes, with fourteen participants from the parish and fourteen from other churches in the diocese. A more modest proposal for travel lay in taking a group to the annual Greenbelt Festival, held since 1999 at Cheltenham racecourse.

The parish pledges showed, too, the anxieties of ageing congregations, and a shortage of money. One parish had a population that was ninety-eight per cent Muslim. In recognizing the need to be relevant, one minister noted, 'The threat we face in not addressing the needs of our community is that of becoming an irrelevant institution to the people we live among.' There were concerns, too, about the secular society taking over more traditional church roles, and graver worries in some areas about the growing strength of the British National Party.

Transformational plans were followed up by diocesan officers and departments. There was, for example, a year-long course for Almondbury Deanery focusing on training laity in pastoral care and aspects of worship, ending with a celebration with Bishop Tony Robinson of its achievements. A pilot service was provided at St John's, Staincross, for those looking to Taizé-style worship. Parish development days and reviews were run by Tony Macpherson, Jo Beacroft-Mitchell (on stewardship) and Susan Parker (parish development). Other days were devised for clergy working in multi-parish benefices. Priests taking up new appointments were encouraged to meet Macpherson and review their parish plans. The Ministry of Welcome has been regarded as fundamental to the mission strategy. Hence a welcome-training day was organized in July 2010 in Dewsbury Minster. It drew some 135 people. Tips were shared by the former customer-service manager at John Lewis, Mark Hope-Urwin, and Bob Jackson, formerly the Archdeacon of Walsall, spoke about how to make a church more inviting. He emphasized the finding of research that showed that many more people would attend church if they were invited.

A further phase, Building up our Common Life, which would have focused on countering parochialism and underlining the importance of being a united diocese, was planned for 2012–13 but was set to one side following the recommendations of the Dioceses Commission that the dioceses of Bradford, Ripon and Leeds, and Wakefield should be united.

Ecumenical Steps

The last decades of the twentieth century, despite failures by the Church of England then to reach any agreement on unity, saw an increasing rapport with other mainstream Christian denominations. An Act of Parliament in 1969 authorized the sharing of church buildings. In 1972, the General Synod provided for 'eucharistic hospitality' in agreeing that those from other denominations who subscribed to the doctrine of the Holy Trinity could receive the sacraments at Anglican services. The Call to the North of the early 1970s was promoted on a wholly ecumenical basis. While in 1972 the Church again rejected a scheme for reunion with the Methodist Church, the bishops urged co-operation at a local level. Dialogue on relations with the Roman Catholic Church was formalized by the Anglican–Roman Catholic International Commission established in 1967 by the Archbishop of Canterbury, Michael Ramsey, and Pope Paul VI, with its terms of reference set out in the Malta Report a year later. The 1974 Churches Unity Commission, established on the initiative of the United Reformed Church, renewed the search for an acceptable basis for 'visible unity'. Its ten propositions in the quest for a covenant between the Anglican, Roman Catholic and Free Churches, were published in 1976 and were supported at a diocesan synod in 1977 as 'providing an acceptable basis for continuing consultation with the churches which are partners in the Commission'. But the quest stalled in 1980. The first visit to Britain by a Catholic Pontiff since the Reformation, took place in 1982 with the visit of John Paul II. The Commission that produced *Faith in the City* acknowledged that they had 'paid close attention to the ecumenical dimension to the Church of England's ministries in the cities' and had 'received full co-operation' in their researches from the Roman Catholic Church, the Free Churches and the independent Black-led Churches. A fresh initiative by the British Council of Churches in 1984 led to a two-year ecumenical consultative process, 'Not Strangers but Pilgrims', the 1986 interdenominational Lent study materials, 'What on earth is the Church for?', and a conference of church leaders at Swanwick in 1987 which resulted in the declaration, 'It is our conviction that, as a matter of policy at all levels and in all places, our churches must now move on to clear commitment to each other, in search of the unity for which Christ prayed, and in common evangelism and service of the world.' By 1990, the British Council of Churches had evolved into Churches Together in Britain and Ireland, with the Roman Catholic Church among its members and a greater emphasis on 'grassroots' collaboration. Ecumenical chaplaincy teams were formed in prisons, hospitals and universities. However, the Church of England decision to ordain women as priests erected a seemingly insuperable barrier to union with the Church of Rome.

Looking back in 1992 on his twenty-one years as Bishop of Pontefract, Richard Hare wrote about the 'total transformation' he had seen in the relationship with Christians of other traditions.

The Diocesan Missionary Council, already with an ecumenical remit, became the Diocesan Board for Mission and Unity in 1973. Wakefield Diocese continued to have its own ecumenical officer – albeit usually combining the position with another cure – throughout the period. A more unusual appointment was that of the Methodist, Edmund Marshall in 1998. Marshall was confirmed by McCulloch and licensed to preach in the diocese. He left for retirement in the south in 2008. Glenn Coggins, who had come to the diocese as Vicar of East Ardsley in 2006, followed him as the Adviser for Ecumenical Affairs.

The earliest ecumenical move in our period came in 1969 and at Copley with the support of Bishop Eric Treacy. A Methodist deaconess, Sister Alice Hodgkin, worked with the Vicar of Copley, Brian Cole, and the Methodist minister, Ian Lewis, in Copley itself and at the General Hospital. Her position was funded in part by the diocese. The collaboration seems to have lasted for five or six years.

The most radical steps came with the sharing of churches. Here a degree of pragmatism was coupled with an acceptance of the ecumenical philosophy. The use of St Peter's, Gildersome, for a Roman Catholic Mass from Easter Sunday 1968 was possibly the first in the country. Shortly afterwards the Catholics began to hold services at St Paul's, Hanging Heaton. In 1971 negotations with Peter Spivey, Vicar of St Bartholomew's, Meltham, and the parochial church council led to the Roman Catholics celebrating mass there on Sundays. Somewhat later, following revisions to the boundaries of Roman Catholic parishes, St Paul's, Shepley, too began to accommodate services for the parish of the Immaculate Heart. The arrangement at St Peter's came to an end when the old church was demolished in 1984. For a time while the new church was being built, the congregation of St Peter's held services in the nearby Methodist church.

An early scheme for shared worship with Methodists began in 1967 at All Saints, Whitley, the daughter church of St Edmund's, Kellington, when joint evening services were held once a quarter, alternating between the church and the Methodist chapel. During Barbara Lydon's ministry there were again some joint evening services in the early 1990s. Another scheme was initiated by Colin White in 2007 following a service in St Edmund's in January for Churches Together. Services took place either at Kellington or Eggborough Methodist Church when there was a fifth Sunday in the month; the arrangement was discontinued when the Anglican services were poorly attended by the Methodists.

In 1969-71 a scheme was pursued to make St Thomas's, Claremount, redundant and, despite the parish being 'moderately high church', to continue worship in the nearby St Thomas Street Methodist Chapel. St Thomas's, perched on a hillside above Halifax, required substantial repairs and the long-term stability of the building was in doubt. Bishop Treacy was insistent that the repair work be undertaken and in 1971 the parochial church council decided to take down the unsafe spire and reduce the level of the tower. Albeit now united with St Anne in the Grove, Southowram, the church remained in use in 2012. The Methodist chapel closed in 1990 and later became a motor repair workshop.

Shared services with the local Methodist church began in Alverthorpe in February 1970 with the Methodists invited to share the parish communion at St Paul's on Sunday mornings and the Anglicans invited to the Methodist chapel for the evening service. There was to be a shared communion at the Methodist chapel once a quarter although Treacy made it clear that no one from the Church of England need feel in any way obliged to take the sacrament there. There was a more radical step at Alverthorpe in 1983 when the United Reformed Church Chaplain from Silcoates School began to assist with worship at St Paul's.

At the same time as the congregation at St Matthew's, Rastrick, studied the course The People Next Door, the nearby Crowtrees Methodist

Church was facing closure. In 1969, St Matthew's parochial church council articulated its commitment to ecumenical co-operation 'wherever this is possible', and resolved, under the guidance of the bishop, to offer the hospitality of their church 'either ecumenically or on a shared basis'. The sharing agreement that followed in 1970 was the first to be made by the Methodists in the country. In 1971, the two congregations began to hold a joint service of evensong tailored to suit both denominations rather than continuing to hold their own on alternate weeks. The two denominations signed a covenanted partnership and declaration of intent in 1990 to 'share the riches of each tradition', coming together as a single congregation with one church council in 2004.

In 1971, the Methodist Church at Hinchliffe Mill was declared unsafe but its congregation was reluctant to amalgamate with their churches at either Holmfirth or Underbank. At the time, the congregation at St David's, Holmbridge, was quite modest. The sharing of its church with the Methodists was seen as something of a lifeline. A shared building agreement was signed in November 1971. The Anglicans had no Sunday School but the Methodists brought theirs, which Anglican children joined. The two bodies provided a joint over-60s group and held a joint Autumn Fair. Over the years various patterns of individual and shared services were tried. A review of the Local Ecumenical Partnership in 1996, by which time Holmbridge was a part of the Upper Holme Valley Team Ministry, took encouragement from its reaching its twenty-fifth anniversary but noted that the apportioning of expenses between the two denominations had never been fully addressed. The Methodists were invited to the Christ Our Light commissioning service at the millennium and the two bodies held joint baptism services and jointly pursued an Emmaus course. As their numbers declined, the Methodists ceased to provide services in 2003 and most of the remaining members became regular attenders at the morning Anglican services.

When their own church was vandalized in late 1974, the Methodist community at Lundwood, Barnsley, held their services in St Mary Magdalene's. Although the arrangement came to an end in due course, the local Methodists continued to come together with the Anglicans for their annual Christmas carol services at St Mary Magdalene's and at Monk Bretton Priory. When All Saints, Paddock, closed in 1982, services continued, until it, too, closed, in Paddock Shared Church where services were already held by both Methodists and the United Reformed Church. In 1987 following the fire on 27 February at the newly renovated St Paul's, Armitage Bridge, the congregation held its services for a time at Newsome South Methodist Church.

Ecumenical sharing at West Bretton was a case originally of the Anglicans moving in with the Methodists rather than the other way round. The Anglican church at West Bretton was in the grounds of the Bretton Hall estate. In winter in particular it was difficult to access. The Methodists had a chapel in the village itself, converted from three cottages. The Anglicans asked to hold their communion services there in 1978. The sharing developed in 1982 into a Local Ecumenical Partnership with the signing of a declaration of intent 'to do together all that we can and not to do apart what we should do together'. Following a decision in 1987 that the existing Methodist church was inadequate, a new church and meeting room for the partnership were dedicated in 1994.

The church in West Bretton

The Anglican church was sold to Bretton Hall College in 1996. Following the closure of the college it became an exhibition space for Yorkshire Sculpture Park. The parish boundary was changed to bring Bretton into the parish of Woolley.

Not all Local Ecumenical Partnerships have involved the sharing of a church building. The partnership formed between St John's, Newsome, St Paul's, Armitage Bridge, and Newsome South Methodist Church in 1989, covered shared projects rather than shared worship space. At the core of these was a community shop, providing second-hand goods for people with limited means. Proceeds from this have funded a community worker for the local housing estates and a community gardener for those who cannot tend their own.

The Community of the Resurrection at Mirfield marked the Octave of Unity in 1973 in what they regarded as 'a bit of a triumph' by bringing together for the first time Anglicans, Baptists, Methodists, Moravians, Roman Catholics, the Salvation Army and the United Reformed Church. The arrangements, initiated by Father Godfrey Pawson, were made in association with the Mirfield Council of Churches. Addresses on successive evenings were given in the Community's chapel by a bishop from the Moravians, men from the United Reformed Church and the Baptist Church, one of the Brethren from the Community itself, a Roman Catholic French Canadian nun, and the priest from St Aidan's Roman Catholic Church in Mirfield. In the middle of the week the service was held in St Aidan's when the address was given by a Methodist.

The mid 1970s saw dialogue between representatives of the Ecumenical Commission of the Roman Catholic Diocese of Leeds and the Diocese of Wakefield, the latter including Bishop Richard Hare, when they considered Agreed Statements of 1971 and 1973 on Eucharistic Doctrine and on Ministry and Ordination issued by the Anglican–Roman Catholic International Commission. A report of one meeting notes, 'The present-day movements of the Holy Spirit and the renewal of Christians led us to agree that the unity in Eucharistic belief and practice should be based on common discipleship and not on formal statements and definitions. When Jesus comes alive to his people, and they open their lives to His Spirit of holiness, God is glorified and fellowship can be expressed more deeply.'

When he came to the diocese in 1977, Bishop Colin James was concerned that very little was happening on the ecumenical front. On the other hand, he was conscious of the dangers of attempting too much too soon. He wrote to the Ecumenical Officer, Ian Harrison, 'I do not think it matters particularly, indeed it may be a positive advantage, if you do not see yourself as a dedicated ecumaniac. The real work I am sure is to give confidence in the parishes to keep abreast of what is happening on the unity front and to encourage projects for co-operation and sharing wherever they are practical.'

By no means all clergy supported ecumenical moves. In 1977, the Vicar of Coley expressed doubts about the wisdom of the pulpit exchanges being proposed by his local ecumenical council, 'The URC pastor is very firm in his Calvinism and I am not at all keen on this being preached from the Coley pulpit. It seems to me we are trying to do this the wrong way.

At a local level we should get to know each other as friends and share in Bible studies and discussions. Then at top level dialogue would be easier and, if physical reunion became possible, we should enter it with all the spiritual richness and insight that God has given us. Actually I am not yet convinced that large-scale organic union is a perfect solution or God's answer.' Two years later he remarked, 'People are beginning to say that it doesn't matter what you believe and one belief is as good as another.'

Bishop James and the Roman Catholic Bishop of Leeds, Gordon Wheeler, agreed together in 1977 that, in accordance with his wish for his funeral to take place in a pre-reformation church, a Requiem Mass for a prominent Elland Roman Catholic should take place in Halifax Parish Church. In thanking James for his guidance on how the Mass could be conducted in a true ecumenical spirit, the Vicar of Halifax said, 'I can imagine that it might cause a bit of a stir in the churches in this town – but with the authority of our bishops behind us we ought not to be afraid of outmoded prejudice and bigotry.'

The first Roman Catholic Mass to be held in Wakefield Cathedral since the Reformation took place on 9 May 1979 when, required because of its size, it was made available to mark the centenary of the Diocese of Leeds. Mass was celebrated by Gordon Wheeler, assisted by Gerald Moverley as auxiliary bishop, and Monsignor Henry Thompson, parish priest at St Austin's, Wakefield.

An ecumenical chaplaincy centre at Huddersfield Polytechnic was opened in September 1980 served by Anglican, Methodist and Catholic priests. The chaplaincy at Wakefield Prison became a local ecumenical partnership in 1990.

Colin James was happy to recommend in 1985 that a priest coming new to the diocese should send his son to Silcoates School which had been founded in the nineteenth century for the sons of Congregational ministers and where the Trust was still in the care of the United Reformed Church. In the event both the priest's children went to St Wilfred's Catholic High School in Featherstone.

In the 1980s, the Methodist minister in Crosland Moor, as his own ecumenical gesture, administered the chalice at the Tuesday morning Eucharists at St Barnabas.

For a time, starting in May 1993, there were monthly multi-media presentations aimed at young people held in Wakefield Town Hall, run in turn by different denominations, under the title, 'The Big If'.

An ecumenical Vigil for Peace was established at the cathedral in October 1983. Originally this lasted for twenty-four hours but was later reduced to twelve. It involved a succession of leaders from different denominations taking part at half-hour intervals. The Society of Friends brought a period of silence. St Andrew's, Wakefield, brought a period of charismatic song and dance.

In 1985 a joint development education project was set up between the Roman Catholic Diocese of Leeds, Christian Aid, and the Diocese of Wakefield, following the Brandt Report. It was launched jointly by Bishop David Konstant and Bishop Hope. Elizabeth (Lissa) Smith was appointed as the Development Education Officer devising, with help from Oxfam, educational materials on development issues in countries such as Nicaragua, South Africa and the Philippines. These were tried out in schools, primarily in Leeds and Bradford, and training was provided for teachers. Smith's managers were the Roman Catholic Justice and Peace Commission and Christian Aid.

The British Council of Churches' initiative of 1984 led to an informal consultation of church leaders from Yorkshire dioceses beginning with a meeting at Bishopthorpe in December 1985. This was attended by the new Bishop of Wakefield, David Hope, the Wakefield Ecumenical Officer, Ian Harrison, and representatives of Methodism, the Roman Catholic Church, the Salvation Army, the Society of Friends, and the United Reformed Church. The meeting urged that leaders of all the churches should commend the 1986 Lent study course, 'What on earth is the church for?', to their flocks. Urging it on the parishes in the Wakefield Diocese, Hope wrote of its aim to stimulate thought and prayer and living in a wider context than the 'often suffocating parochialism in which we as church folk are too content to be'.

After a further meeting at Bradford, the West Yorkshire Ecumenical Council was established in 1986 as a more formal successor, although without any representative from the Society of Friends. Its first officer, the Reverend Dr Lewis Burton, then the Ecumenical Secretary of the West Yorkshire Methodist District, was appointed the following March. He was the first full-time county ecumenical officer. Notwithstanding the differing administrative boundaries of the constituent bodies, the Council was based simply on the geographical county. Churches in the diocese that were in South Yorkshire were not covered by its remit. The principal roles of the Council lay in 'establishing an underlying philosophy and setting the overall direction for ecumenical work in the region', in supporting existing Local Ecumenical Partnerships , and in promoting new ones. These might take one of four forms: local churches pledging to work together, churches sharing a building, a shared congregational life involving shared worship witness and pastoral care, or a shared ministry with agreement reached over all sacramental services except marriage. It was expected that the Council would be able to speak with a united voice on issues raised by the media. The officer was financed by contributions from the constituent Churches but with the three Anglican dioceses contributing half of the cost between them. District, rather than Diocesan, Ecumenical Councils were to be formed as a second tier. On 14 October 1987, the church leaders came together at St Anne's Cathedral in Leeds to sign a convenant to work together and for the induction of Dr Burton. The Lutherans were represented on the Council from the early 1990s.

David Hope's 'Bread not Stones' project had a significant ecumenical dimension. He wrote in the *Wakefield Diocesan News* in May 1987 of the ecumenical significance of the Who are our Allies section in the audit booklet: 'Some parishes are engaging in this in fellowship and co-operation with other Churches in the parish area ... Christian unity must be for the sake of and in service to others that God's kingdom on earth may be proclaimed and celebrated with one voice, and the church spend itself and be spent in healing the divisions between peoples and nations.'

Since 1988, Holy Trinity Senior School Halifax and the Halifax Catholic High School have had a shared sixth form. In 2010, Holy Trinity became an academy.

There were very many and very varied ecumenical ventures at a parochial level. For example in 1980 Huddersfield Parish Church and the town centre Methodist church embarked on a shared magazine, *Network*. Shortly afterwards St Mary's, Illingworth, produced a magazine jointly with both Methodists and Roman Catholics. Many schemes involved community outreach. In 1994 St Helen's Church, Sandal, established a community centre on the Portobello estate in collaboration with the local Baptist and Methodist Churches.

Churches Together in Wakefield organized a Christian Festival, Wakefield Awake, on an ecumenical basis in April–May 1994.

In September 2009, because of the dangerous state of the parish church, a temporary licence was granted for services for St Mary's, Illingworth, to be held in Illingworth Moor Methodist church. However, the services were at 12 noon and people felt that the time divided their day too much. The parish had been part of a team ministry that included Holy Nativity, Mixenden, since 1975 and, once it became clear that St Mary's was not going to be restored, the majority of services took place at Holy Nativity.

At the time of a fresh exploration of an Anglo-Methodist covenant in 2002, joint synods were held with the Methodists in 2002 together with the synod of Ripon and Leeds. Subsequently Methodists were invited to send an observer to the Wakefield synods.

Bishop Platten, who served from 1990 as a Governor of the Anglican

Centre in Rome, appointed the cathedral's first ecumenical canons in 2006. They were Malkhaz Songulashvili, Bishop of the Baptist Church of Georgia, Arthur Roche, Roman Catholic Bishop of Leeds, and Peter Whittaker, chair of the West Yorkshire district of Methodist Churches. Two further ecumenical canons, Anders Bertil Alberius, Dean of Skara, Sweden, and Elizabeth Ann Smith, Chair of the Leeds Methodist District, were installed in 2011.

There was a frisson of ecumenism in the choice of Ampleforth Abbey for the annual residential meeting of the Bishop's Council in 2006.

In 2009, Christ Church, Linthwaite, joined with Linthwaite Methodist Church in providing a Good Friday workshop for fifty children from junior schools.

Roman Catholics from the Dioceses of Hallam and Leeds shared a Lent course, 'Praying the Scriptures', in 2011 devised by a group drawn from the three bodies. This included June Lawson (Chair), Matthew Bullimore, Glenn Coggins and Simon Moore, together with John Wilson (from the Roman Catholic Diocese of Leeds) and Mary Dolan (from the Diocese of Hallam). The initiative followed a historic joint assembly between the two Churches following the meeting of the diocesan synod in March 2009. The course was designed to be studied in ecumenical groups drawing people in from other denominations. Alongside it, four central evenings were held during Lent in Wakefield, Barnsley, Huddersfield and Halifax. Each service was led jointly by an Anglican and a Roman Catholic bishop.

One of the parishes drawing up its Transforming Lives' pledges in 2009 made a commitment to supporting the work of the Ecumenical Society of the Blessed Virgin Mary (founded in 1967).

Much ecumenical work has been led by the local groups of Churches Together.

Possibly the most popular and well supported of all ecumenical ventures have been the annual Good Friday processions of witness which take place not only across the Wakefield Diocese but throughout the country.

Social Responsibility and Community Service

Until the 1970s, social work in Wakefield Diocese followed the traditional pattern within the Church of England, concentrating on the support of unmarried mothers and their children via mother-and-baby homes and social-care work. Changes in attitudes, with more pregnant girls remaining with their parents, and the availability of both contraception and abortion, made the residential homes less necessary. In 1969, St Katharine's in Huddersfield, faced with both fewer clients and a diminishing income, amalgamated with the Methodist Home, Bryanwood. By 1972, when the Moral Welfare Council became the Diocesan Family Welfare Council, both the Halifax and Pontefract mother-and-baby homes had been closed and sold. By 1977, the role of Bryanwood had changed from accommodating unmarried mothers to providing emergency accommodation for women under stress and their children. However, in December 1977 responsibility for the homeless in Calderdale was transferred from the Social Services department to the Housing department, houses were made available immediately and Bryanwood no longer had any purpose. There remained two main institutions where social/welfare work was undertaken – St John's Training Home, which was an Approved School, and the House of Mercy at St Peter's Convent, which then cared for maladjusted girls. Under the Children's and Young Persons Act of 1969, St John's Home became a Community Home for thirty girls aged 15–19; it had 'controlled' status, with the new Wakefield Metropolitan District Council providing eight of its governors. Diminishing numbers of girls referred to the Home led to its closure in 1982. The work of the House of Mercy as a boarding school for maladjusted girls came to an end in 1980. The House of Mercy was sold in 1989 and the Sisters moved to the Retreat House.

The Chapel provided in the Retreat House when it became St Peter's Convent in 1989

As their number diminished, they moved again in 2011 to Spring End, a modern (1990) twenty-room bungalow a short distance away in Horbury.

There were ad hoc moves to widen social responsibility. At St Botolph's, Knottingley, for example, a community development scheme involved local councillors, social workers, teachers, trades unionists, clergy and ministers of the Free Churches. St Augustine's Church, Halifax, in an area suffering from planning blight, and where there were timid elderly householders, squatters, and immigrants, had been running a Community Centre since it began with a playgroup in 1964. In 1968, this became a family centre. Again in 1968, a Neighbourhood Project was established at Holy Trinity, Mixenden, with a counselling unit and caseworkers. But it could be said that the diocese as a whole awoke to the broader concepts of social responsibility and outreach in the early 1970s. The pace of developments quickened in the 1980s with Colin James's Church in the Eighties project and, following the publication of *Faith in the City*, the financial provisions of the 1988 Bishop's Centenary Fund and the Church Urban Fund.

One of the most pressing needs in the diocese in the 1970s lay in areas with growing numbers of Muslim and Sikh immigrants, and in 1972 the influx of Ugandan Asians, with the attendant problems of ignorance and suspicion of the new communities among the indigenous population. In 1971, Bishop Treacy appointed Bernard Chamberlain of the Community of the Resurrection as the Bishop's Adviser on Community Relations. Coming originally to the diocese as a curate in Brighouse, Chamberlain had subsequently served in South Africa. A well-built, tall, bald, charismatic Catholic figure, he worked tirelessly to achieve understanding of and support for ethnic minorities until leaving the Community (to be married) in 1985. He was a man who liked excitement, brought enthusiasm, and was full of bright ideas. He was seen usually in his Mirfield cassock and scapula. He organized conferences at the Roman Catholic Ecumenical Centre at Woodhall on aspects of Islam and Judaism, fostered numerous meetings between Christian groups, Muslims and Sikhs, and prompted schemes whereby British women visited Asian women in their homes to tutor them in the English language. He organized seaside holidays and social evenings for multi-racial groups. He built up relationships with Christian West Indian immigrants who had been living within the diocese for some fifteen or twenty years – there were 6,000 in Huddersfield – but who still felt alienated and experienced discrimination. His main purpose was to draw them in to the existing church communities. He encouraged churches to take part in an annual vigil for racial harmony. He went to Pakistan for eight weeks, visiting both Christian and Muslim homes and institutions in the hope that the experience and understanding gained of the backgrounds of the immigrants would be of help in building bridges in the diocese. He also visited the West Indies to gain first-hand experience of the Christian churches there. He worked with the Council of Churches to secure the redundant St Michael's School in Wakefield as a mosque. He gave numerous talks at meetings of deanery synods, to schools and to other organizations. Soon after coming to Wakefield, Colin James spent a day in April 1977 with Chamberlain, meeting some of the individuals and groups with which he was in contact. He met the Community Relations Officer in Dewsbury, visited the Community Relations Offices in Huddersfield and Halifax, met a Muslim Imam, and went to St Augustine's parish, Halifax, where the church school had some Muslim pupils.

In the late 1970s, members of local churches helped to teach English to some thirty Vietnamese refugees living at Ockenden House, Thornhill Lees, where the wardens were a Christian couple.

Chamberlain was followed as the Adviser for Community Relations by Bill Jones, a teacher and missionary who aimed at supporting and developing the church's ministry in the multi-cultural communities, and to show the Church's sympathetic attitude to problems faced by ethnic minorities.

In 1973, the diocesan synod appointed a Commission on Christian Social Responsibility to consider what further work the Church should undertake. Father Bernard and Miss M. G. Westwood, organizing secretary of the Diocesan Family Welfare Council, were among its members, as was Stuart Pearson, then Vicar of Knottingley. In its report it recognized the need to move from one-to-one social work to a broader community activity. The report noted, 'For the neighbourhood, the church can provide a solidity and resources which are hard to obtain otherwise, especially in deprived areas. In the wider context of local authorities and officials, there is an unrivalled opportunity to bring a broader, more humane and more Christian approach to their work.' It warned that there might not be a flood of volunteers, noting that vicars' wives now went out to work as did other married women. Importantly, it recommended the appointment of a Diocesan Social Responsibility Officer whose tasks would include initiating and encouraging ways of educating church people in Christian social responsibility and service, creating working relationships with statutory and voluntary social work agencies, and being aware of the possibility of inter-diocesan and ecumenical co-operation. The post could be financed, it suggested, from the money invested following the sale of the mother-and-baby homes.

Although Synod approved the report, little happened immediately except that a working party was set up to consider its feasibility. The sixteenth synod, in May 1976, was told that it recommended the establishment of an ad hoc body, with a life of no more than five years, to be set up by the bishop and responsible to him. Its remit would be to mount an educational operation in the deaneries and parishes to arouse awareness of opportunities for social responsibility among church people, to discover what pieces of social work were being undertaken already in the diocese (and, by implication, show what was not being done), to encourage and stimulate practical work by a personal approach to active and informed individuals, both clerical and lay, and to explore the possibilities of inter-diocesan and ecumenical co-operation. It recommended that a part-time executive officer should spearhead this. The Family Welfare Council should be asked to use the income from its capital to underwrite the expenses.

Meanwhile ad hoc community work continued. Efforts to assist the Muslim communities included a visit to churches in both Halifax and Wakefield by a Christian Pakistani woman, Prio Manget Rei, who called on the families of Muslim children attending church schools. In Huddersfield, the Council of Churches provided a field worker, Eileen Slater, who ran two community centres in multi-racial areas, providing classes and dealing, it seems, with rather a number of marital problems among Asians which the local Social Services had been unable to cope with adequately. She was assisted by a missionary who had worked in Pakistan and who could speak both Punjabi and Urdu.

The Kirklees and Calderdale Faith Fellowship, was established with the aims of promoting racial understanding and working for a multi-racial society based on justice and equal opportunities.

Immigration became a 'hot potato' in 1978. Father Bernard spoke to Synod about 'the irresponsibility of certain politicians and their "emotive language from tongues and pens" causing embarrassment, hurt and fear to fellow citizens from Asia and the West Indies who have come to regard this country as their home'. He added that they rendered Britain, 'in danger as a nation of elevating groundless fears about colour and numbers above the real crucial problems of our Society – housing, unemployment, education, industrial relations, marital breakdown, and crime'.

Bishop James and the Bishop of Ripon, David Young, both took part in the March for Racial Harmony in Leeds on 15 April 1978 as did leaders of Methodist, Roman Catholic and United Reformed Churches. James responded to critics by reminding them that the British Council of Churches wanted all Christians to sign a statement affirming the need to live together with all the peoples of England.

It was in 1978, too, that, after the Diocesan Social Responsibility Group had been formed under the Board of Mission, Stuart Pearson moved from Knottingley to the rural parish of St Peter's, Woolley, and was appointed as the Diocesan Adviser for Social Responsibility. The Group hoped to be concerned with industrial mission, community relations, community care and structural planning.

Unemployment in the late 1970s and early 1980s saw the setting up of national schemes under both Labour and Conservative governments to provide short-term work and training. St Mary's, Horbury Junction, was redecorated under a Community Industry scheme in 1978. With help from a job creation scheme in Halifax, substantial cleaning and repairs were effected at St Hilda's in 1978, including cleaning oak panelling and the 1952 tryptich. By January 1981, twenty parishes in the Pontefract and Wakefield Rural Deaneries were offering work for six months at a time for unemployed school leavers under the Youth Opportunities Programme. This was primarily outdoor work and involved pointing, dry stone walling, laying drives and clearing graveyards. Parishes were invited to contact Pearson about setting up further schemes. At St Catherine's, Wakefield, where the vicar, Ray Adair, led the Belle Vue and Agbrigg Community Association, there was a scheme to convert two houses into a Community Centre. (Adair had formerly been a Church Army Captain working at Wakefield prison.) A Community Action team worked at Badsworth in 1981 converting the former school to a parish centre.

On the initiative of the vicar, Robert Ferguson, the parochial church council at St George's, Lupset, set up Lupset Community Projects in June 1981 in association with the Manpower Services Commission (MSC) as a response to the growing problem of youth unemployment on the Lupset Estate. It took in youngsters of every ability, including those classed as educationally sub-normal, and gained an excellent reputation despite, apparently, considerable administrative difficulties in working with the MSC. Youths came from the Portobello and Kettlethorpe estates as well as from the immediate area. They learned skills in painting and decorating and in horticulture. Many went on to apprenticeships or employment. By 1983, fifty-six trainees had passed through the scheme.

At Upper Hopton a team under the Manpower Services Commission worked to rebuild and extend the church hall in 1982. The redeveloped premises opened on 9 July 1983. At the same time an MSC team worked on the church hall at Altofts.

Social responsibility extended to the colliery communities in the diocese when there was a prolonged strike in 1984–85 against threatened pit closures, to be followed by further devastation by the closures themselves. During the strike period, local churches provided facilities for meals for miners and their families. At St Michael's, Castleford, the Kitchen Miners' Support Group served 350 meals a day. Castleford Women's Centre was set up in 1984 with the help of the Social Responsibility Department with the aims of promoting the self-esteem of both women and men. It was linked, for the provision of courses, with Leeds Metropolitan University and Wakefield College. A grant from the Church of England Children's Society enabled Bishop James to provide a little help to miners' children. At Dodworth, where there were 'violent scenes' in November 1984 when a contingency of police came from Birmingham, the incumbent, Peter Ford, made pastoral visits to the picket lines and lit candles daily in the church for peace in the industry.

As pit closures loomed, Bishop Nigel McCulloch appointed Ian Gaskell as his Chaplain to the Coalfields. In 1992 and 1993 McCulloch himself played a prominent part in opposing the programme of closures. Having visited the parishes which would be affected, he went with Ian Gaskell and Elizabeth Peacock MP to confront Michael Heseltine, the President of the Board of Trade, who was, it was reported, shaken by the statistics McCulloch and Gaskell produced. McCulloch attended the Fight For Coal march and rally in Barnsley on 7 November 1992, organized by Barnsley Labour Party. At the rally he said that the plans to close thirty-one collieries were 'disgusting, disgraceful and unjust'. He spoke of the Government's betraying its moral duty in that it did not care about the ensuing financial hardship, depression and stress. At Christmas 1992, working with the Barnsley-based Coalfield Community Campaign, McCulloch accompanied schoolchildren and students from all the thirty-one communities facing the closure of their colliery to a Carol Service in Westminster Abbey. Grimethorpe Colliery Band played for the service, which was attended by both David Hope, then Bishop of London, and Cardinal Basil Hume. McCulloch also joined a protest march at Sharlston Colliery in July 1993. Again in 1993, Tony Macpherson, then Vicar of St Luke's, Grimethorpe, addressed a rally in Hyde Park organized by the Trades Union Congress.

The impact of pit closures extended over the next decades. A comment in 2009 from St Mary's South Elmsall for Bishop Platten's' Transforming Lives project is telling. 'With the development of this mining community came a distinct form of working-class culture which was based on hard dangerous work in the mines, hard drinking on the surface and a closely-knit extended family-based pattern of social relations. The pattern of family life made South Elmsall strong in many ways: the tradition of extended families living in close proximity to one another complemented the powerful influence of the miners' union which not only protected the interests of the miners themselves but also their families and the life of the town in general. With the miners' strike in the 1980s and the closure of the pit in 1993, this unique form of working-class culture received a severe blow. Unemployment soared and a range of problems began to develop within the social life of the town. Increased strain was placed on families resulting in relationship breakdown and a general deterioration in social life generally resulting in some of the highest social deprivation scores in the European Union.' What was lost included the cinema, the bingo hall, and the public houses, and membership of the Working Men's Club was declining.

The momentous report of the Archbishop of Canterbury's Commission on Urban Priority Areas, *Faith in the City*, was published in 1985. It highlighted the environmental, social and economic problems of inner-city areas and some of the suburban housing estates. It was forthright in laying some of the blame on contemporary government policies. It noticed the preponderance of the 'unemployed, the unskilled, the uneducated, the sick, the old, and the disadvantaged minority ethnic groups'. Marriage breakdown was common. 'To describe UPAs', it said, 'is to write of squalor and dilapidation. Grey walls, littered streets, boarded-up windows, graffiti, demolition and debris are the drearily standard features of the districts and parishes with which we are concerned.' Vandalism was rife and crime rates higher than elsewhere. In regard to the Established Church, it noted the problem of barn-like Victorian churches which were difficult to heat and maintain. Church attendance was proportionally lower than elsewhere. The report argued that the majority of Church members living outside such areas appeared to be unaware of the 'concentration of human suffering'. It suggested that in the Urban Priority Areas, the Church must become far more engaged in community action. It (successfully) recommended the setting-up of a Church Urban Fund to support a variety of initiatives.

A series of lectures on the implications of *Faith in the City*, arranged by Colin James at the time of his translation to Winchester, took place in the cathedral in April and May 1985. They included ones on Christ, the Church and the World, given by James himself, Education in multi-faith communities (Jennie Chesters) and the Church in outer estates (Anthony Hawley).

In 1986, Bishop Hope set up a working group to consider the diocesan response to the Report, with John Allen, Provost of the Cathedral, as its chairman. Its members visited thirty parishes, identified six types of Urban Priority Area parishes, and fundamentally recommended that the Church must move from the prevalent, inward-looking 'congregationalism' back to its original role of caring for the whole community. It envisaged an enhanced role for deanery synods in requiring annual reports from their parishes as a means of monitoring their progress in following their 'Bread not Stones' objectives, and in drawing up a strategic plan for staffing across the deanery as a whole. It suggested some revision of parish boundaries to facilitate closer working between the Church and local authorities. It recognized that congregations felt inadequate in knowing how to respond to the needs of their Urban Priority Area and proposed the setting up of a Task Force, drawing on the sector ministers, which might work for six months in a specific area 'to show them what to do and how to do it'. While recognizing the value of the Shared Ministry training, it recommended more targeted courses, for clergy as well as laity working in an Urban Priority environment. The working group understood the problems of the small congregations in UPA parishes in funding the expenses of their clergy and suggested that the diocese as a whole should take responsibility for these. Radically, in its report, *Looking Forward*, it suggested replacing the parish and its church with a family centre with a community worker or Church Army captain at its head, or with the incumbent priest as its first warden. It offered no suggestions otherwise as to particular projects to adopt, tending to assume that these would spring from 'Bread not Stones', and observing that what *Faith in the City* demanded was a change in attitudes.

Some concern was expressed in response to *Looking Forward* that the emphasis on family centres might impact on the provision of worship and give the impression that the church was no more than a branch of social services.

By 1987, the volume of work in Wakefield Diocese – and the potential for much more – was such that the diocese needed a full-time Social Responsibility officer. An advertisement in the *Church Times* brought George Nairn-Briggs who was at that time working in a south London parish with a 'tough' housing estate. His overall purpose was to make the Church relevant whether among the homeless, the unemployed, those in debt, those facing marriage breakdown, families where the father was in prison, or those affected by long-term health issues such as AIDS. In his first year Nairn-Briggs set out to visit every parish in the diocese and to identify its needs and opportunities He spent time in the coalfields areas, where there was a lack of enterprise and an absence of any substantial middle-class, setting up community projects. There were problems in Halifax with the collapse of Nissan and in Dewsbury and Huddersfield with the decline in the textile industry in addition to the ethnic mix. He was joined for a time by a Homelessness Officer, Liam Gallagher, who was funded by the Rowntree Trust. Two women (job sharing) worked with him in the field of Family Life, funded by the Family Life Trust. (FLAME, Family Life and Marriage Education, was born in 1989 after a major national conference drawing people from almost every diocese and focusing in particular on sexual abuse.) Others worked with him in a voluntary capacity in the fields of health, homelessness, unemployment and poverty. Before he moved on, he helped parishes to access over £1 million from the Church Urban Fund which, in turn, because of the respect for the Fund from other grant-making bodies, facilitated access to a further £8 million from other sources. The fund supported projects ranging from the reordering of churches and renovation of church halls to provide community facilities, to employing community workers, a debt adviser and a domestic-violence worker. St Andrew's, Holmfield, was the first church to host a conference for full-time HIV and AIDS workers in Yorkshire. Its focus was on the spiritual well-being of victims.

Addressing the diocesan synod in 1988, David Hope spoke of using church buildings and facilities 'to meet the particularly pressing needs of the locality'. He suggested providing starter units for small enterprises, or facilities for the unemployed or the disabled.

The Diocesan Board for Social Responsibility was formed in 1989 separating this area of work from that of the Board for Mission and Unity. The Department published information packs on many social problems including homelessness and debt.

Among significant ecumenical projects was the founding of the Calderdale Ecumenical Housing Association by clergy in Calderdale bringing together Anglicans, Baptists, Methodists, Quakers, Roman Catholics, the United Reformed Church and professionals from the local authority with the aim of providing affordable housing.

The two new parish churches of the 1990s were designed with opportunities for outreach in mind and as much as community centres as places of worship.

St Peter's, Gildersome, was consecrated in June 1992. The former church had been demolished in 1984 when its foundations, deteriorating because of water from small streams beneath them, were found to be too weak to warrant repair. The small and struggling congregation was galvanized in 1985 by the impact of the nurture course, 'Saints Alive'. Groups were formed for Bible study, prayer and healing. Additionally the congregation founded a lunch club for the elderly and a fellowship group for the lonely. Numbers of worshippers trebled and a new church was planned with a coffee bar and meeting rooms as well as a very flexible worship space. When St Catherine's, Sandal, was destroyed by fire, its congregation

St Peter's, Gildersome

turned to the Gildersome model and a church complex with very similar facilities was planned. Its chapel was consecrated in March 1995. The incumbent set up a co-operative, Campitor, to run its community and business projects. By 1997, it had issued a leaflet offering its facilities on a commercial basis as a conference centre, with the aim of using the profits for other community enterprises. (It was the only scheme in the Wakefield Diocese cited in the 2006 ecumenical report, *Faithful Cities 2006*.) Campitor was wound up in 2010 with a new management group established under the control of the parochial church council.

In 1992, both Barnsley and Kirklees local authorities won recognition from the Government under the City Challenge scheme. Barnsley thanked George Nairn-Briggs for his part in this.

In 1993, the diocese achieved a historic agreement with one of its local authorities, Kirklees, to work in partnership towards the regeneration of inner city and outer estate areas in the fields of childcare, community care, and social housing. The agreement involved raising funds for joint schemes for the community use of churches and for new children's centres. A Community Development Worker was appointed at Purlwell with the aim of bringing together the various communities living in the area. A scheme financed in part by the Church Urban Fund, provided Community Link Workers based at Woodhouse Church of England Schools. The agreement was signed by the Bishop and the leader of Kirklees Council in July 1993.

The problems of the young homeless were addressed in 1995 by the founding at the cathedral of the Wakefield Rent Deposit Scheme which involved helping them to find somewhere to live – usually in private rented property – and providing a guarantee that the rent would be paid.

On a lighter note, to mark the tenth anniversary of the publication of *Faith in the City*, in 1995 George Nairn-Briggs persuaded the Wakefield-based Clark's Brewery to create a special beer. He named it City Pride and added the strap-line, 'The Church grows in little hops!'

Many parishes have found difficulty in maintaining and repairing their church halls and often these have been closed and sold. However, at St George's, Lupset, a company, St George's Lupset Ltd, was formed in 1997 to take over the hall and manage it as a community resource. The hall was extended and upgraded and the company acquired a range of partners, including the local authority, the NHS Wakefield District Primary Care Trust, Wakefield College, the Workers' Educational Association, the Royal British Legion, and Yew Tree Theatre. A further partner, the British Trust for Conservation Volunteers, manages a community allotment which developed as a green gym for those with learning difficulties. In 2012 the company was able to employ thirty-five people. It has offered a range of child-care services, a full adult-education programme with both accredited and non-accredited courses, a response to many health-related problems, social provision for the elderly, and a food-preparation service which includes a community café but also serves the wider community.

Bishop McCulloch's determination to work in an even-handed manner with the 'two integrities', led him to appoint George Nairn-Briggs, a leading light among the traditionalists, as Provost of the Cathedral in 1997.

In 1999, the Bishop's Lectures, held in the Treacy Hall, Wakefield Cathedral, concentrated for the first time (it was said) on social rather than theological issues when Sir David Ramsbotham (son of Wakefield's bishop) spoke about his role as Chief Inspector of Prisons, and Keith Hellawell, the so-called Drugs Czar, spoke on the Government's anti-drugs strategy.

Ian Gaskell followed George Nairn-Briggs as the Social Responsibility adviser. The Department continued to promote good interfaith relations and pursue wider issues of social justice in the first years of the twenty-first century. In 2004, it reported that more than two-thirds of the parishes had projects reaching out into the community.

At St Helen's, Athersley, which is among the most deprived areas of the diocese, the Romero project was founded in 2004 to provide support of many kinds and in particular for alcohol problems and debt. Two staff counsellors, plus volunteers, work in partnership with other agencies from Age Concern to a Credit Union. The project was named after Archbishop Oscar Romero who campaigned in El Salvador for the poor and who was shot dead in 1980.

The diocese worked with the Muslim community to host a seminar at the National Coal Mining Museum in July 2005 on 'The Tolerance of Difference', which was attended by the Archbishop of Canterbury, Rowan Williams, who had come to the area to learn more about its Muslim population.

Ian Gaskell's role as the Social Responsibility Officer for the diocese in 1997–2006 focused primarily on issues relating to the coalfields communities in the wake of the closure of most working pits in its area.

In the summer of 2008, Bishop Platten invited Maureen Browell to take on the role of Social Responsibility Co-ordinator working with a group of officers who advised the bishop and senior staff on relevant issues. Browell had been appointed in 1999 as the Social Responsibility Officer for the Diocese of Ripon and Leeds. While there she trained on the North East Ordination Course as a self-supporting minister, and served as a curate in 2005–08 at the united benefice of Hoylandswaine and Silkstone. She relinquished her post with Ripon and Leeds in 2008 and moved into full-time ministry in the Team Parish of Almondbury with Farnley Tyas. The officers in the new Social Responsbility (SR) team – all clergy – were Keith Griffin and Maggie McLean (Advisers in Theology and Society), Hugh Baker and Dennis Handley (Advisers on Farming and Rural Affairs), David Fletcher and David Nicholson (Advisers on Urban Issues), Carol Wardman (Adviser on Older People's Issues) and Bill Halling (Adviser on the Environment).

The SR Group produced and published four copies of 'Theology and Society' between Spring 2009 and Summer 2010. These focused on poverty, family, the right to die and the environment.

The issue of the right to die was timed to coincide with an evening of Open Conversations which the group arranged and which took place in February 2010 at Dewsbury Minster. Despite heavy snow, the evening attracted over 100 participants who were keen to listen to the four speakers who were each presenting a different perspective on assisted dying. The speakers were Debbie Purdy (Dignity in Dying), Dr Charlotte Clare (Clinical Director at Kirkwood Hospice), Carol Wardman (Age Concern), and Mark Cobb (Sheffield Teaching Hospitals). The event was covered by local media, featuring in the press and also local television.

In the spring of 2011, increasing parish responsibilities led Browell to stand down. As well as chairing an annual meeting of all the advisers himself, in late 2011 Platten invited Roy Clements to chair a newly formed group entitled the Bishop's Advisory Group on Theology and Society, to advise parishes and the bishop's staff as appropriate. It aimed to be open to questions from any quarter and from time to time it may publish what resources it can find on issues that arise of public interest. Roy Clements chairs the group and its members, again all clergy, are James Allison, Stephanie Buchanan, Matthew Bullimore, Keith Griffin and Stephen Spencer.

Work in the field of social responsibility has played a major part in keeping the Church presence to the fore in the diocese.

The Link Dioceses – Mara, Faisalabad, and Skara

The link between Wakefield Diocese and that of Mara, Tanzania, made in the centenary year of 1988, was in 2012 one of the strongest and most effective between any two dioceses in the Anglican Communion. In 1990, Bill Jones became the head of Mara's first secondary school, Issenye. The link is overseen on behalf of the diocese by the Mara Link Committee which is appointed by the Bishop's Council and an officer in the Diocese of Mara with a counterpart in the Diocese of Wakefield. By 2010, over £1.25m had been contributed from Wakefield. Individual parishes in the diocese have forged links with parishes in Mara. There are also links between schools: Lightcliffe Primary School became linked to Mara Primary School in 2003 when its headteacher came to Lightcliffe. There was a reciprocal visit by Catherine MacDonald, Deputy Head at Lightcliffe in 2005. The theological college in the village of Kowak is also given practical support from Wakefield. Donations from Wakefield assist the church in Mara to provide health care, housing, safe water, and aids for people with disabilities. When the drought of 2006 brought widespread famine to Mara, the diocese was able to send over 200 tons of maize directly to villages throughout the link area. Stephen Platten's Lent appeal in 2007 raised £6,500 towards providing a mobile health clinic and 1,600 mosquito nets. Quality second-hand goods are shipped to Mara each year in containers packed at Lindley and St Thomas's, Batley. A Key to Life fund was initiated at the Church of Christ the King, Battyeford, to provide money for poor parents to fund their children's education and was taken up by parishes across the diocese.

The Anglican Church in Tanzania grew so much that the Diocese of Mara was split in 2010 to create the Dioceses of Rorya and Tarime, with thirty-six and thirty-eight parishes respectively. Of the sixty-eight parishes of the 'new' Mara, forty-two have links with Wakefield parishes. The link with Wakefield, now embracing all three dioceses, has been maintained.

A link with the Pakistan Diocese of Faisalabad was forged in 2002. There had long been Asian Christian immigrants from the area living in

Huddersfield, among them Yacub Masih who had moved there as a teenager and who by then was the General Secretary of the Asian Christian Fellowship. The closer relationship began with conversations between McCulloch and Bishop John Samuel of Faisalabad at the 1998 Lambeth Conference. A visit proposed to Pakistan for 1999 was postponed after the military coup but at the beginning of 2002 Bishop James, accompanied by Masih and Bill Jones spent a fortnight in Faisalabad visiting some of its villages (where the sick and disabled were brought to James for blessing) its churches, its schools, and its Christian Study Centre in Rawalpindi.

Bishop Platten was instrumental in the Church of England's signing up to the Porvoo Agreement of 1996. This created a Communion of churches, most of which were in Northern Europe, committed to 'share a common life in mission and service'. The churches which signed the Agreement were the Evangelical-Lutheran Churches of Estonia, Finland, Iceland, Lithuania, Norway, and Sweden, and the Anglican Churches: the Church of England and of Ireland, the Church in Wales, and the Scottish Episcopal Church. When he came to Wakefield, Platten was keen for the diocese to be twinned with one in the Porvoo Communion. Since 2003 links have been fostered between Wakefield and Skara in Sweden through exchanges, sharing in training, and a flourishing link between the two cathedrals. It happens that the choir of Wakefield Cathedral went on tour to Skara in 2001, sometime before the link was envisaged.

The Diocesan Mothers' Union has for many years (since *c.*1966) had its own link with the Australian Diocese of Adelaide. Bishop Platten has sought to widen this at the same time as making contacts between the diocese and churches in Georgia, Germany.

Catholic and Charismatic Renewal and New Forms of Worship

Since the 1960s many of the churches in the diocese have seen changes in styles of worship, influenced in some cases by the Pentecostal movement of America. Although Richard Giles lamented in 1993 that Anglo-Catholics had ignored the 'dynamic of the Holy Spirit' and 'fled panic-stricken from Charismatic renewal', both Anglo-Catholic and (rather more) evangelical churches in the diocese have responded to the greater emphasis on the power of the Holy Spirit working within the individual, on personal experience of spiritual renewal, on spontaneity and emotion, and on the need to express joy freely. New worship songs have been introduced with guitars and percussion instruments in place of organs. In some churches 'speaking in tongues' has been encouraged. Giving the lead in charismatic worship were the churches at Kirkheaton and Normanton, but a Renewal Fellowship was also formed by Harold Ingamells at the Anglo-Catholic church at Monk Bretton in 1978. Finding a successor for Ingamells in 1983 proved difficult as, it was said at the time, 'Catholics involved in the renewal movement seem thin on the ground.'

Tensions between members of a congregation who wanted a modern, charismatic style of worship and those who wished to keep to traditional forms surfaced in a number of churches. At All Hallows, Almondbury, for example, the incumbent commented in 1978, 'A charismatic group within the parish is beginning to get a bit frustrated. They expect almost instant changes – their way – and we are trying to show them that people do like to worship in traditional ways still and should have the opportunity of doing so.'

In November 1981, the General Synod debated a report from a working party looking at the Charismatic Movement. Canon Colin Craston, who introduced it, acknowledged that there were criticisms but said that many church members had been led by it 'to know experientially much more of the riches of Christ pledged by God in baptism' (but the tone of the debate was so hostile that it was curtailed).

Bishop Richard Hare emphasized the need for joy at his confirmation services. Giving the eulogy at Hare's memorial service in the cathedral in 2010, John Flack recalled the confirmations at Rishworth School where Hare would begin the service with a loud, 'We're going to make whoopee this evening!', and would process up the aisle decked in a highly colourful vestment which he called his 'butterfly' suit. Hare, it was said, always carried his oils in his pocket, ready to anoint anyone at the slightest opportunity.

From 1993, charismatics were invited to 'mega' services of prayer and praise in the cathedral at Pentecost and Advent. Hare was a pivotal figure here and, as John Flack recalled, his dynamic presence meant that there was often standing room only. He took part in the preparation of the events, bringing in the music groups from Kirkheaton and Normanton and drawing in all other parishes in the charismatic tradition.

New forms of worship have not always been acceptable to long-standing members of congregations. There were complaints to Bishop James from one church in the late 1970s of Readers being compelled by their incumbent to take part in the laying-on of hands and of worshippers coming forward and then falling on the floor in ecstasy 'not with any reverence but just like a spectacular show'. The incumbent of St Cuthbert's, Ackworth, reported to James in 1979 that 'the Pentecostalist wind has blown into Ackworth' and brought an adult study group, some members of which proudly proclaimed that they had spoken in tongues and even sung in tongues, although not in his presence for which he was grateful. He added that they would like to be able to cry in church (a feeling with which he was himself not unfamiliar!). At St Andrew's, Wakefield, in the 1980s, Bryan Ellis offered lively worship and lively music while understanding the problem of a rather hysterical reaction to charismatic worship. He preferred not to encourage dramatic exhibition, instead suggesting to the congregation that they should react quite simply to what they felt, perhaps just waving their arms if they wished. The services were popular not just with local Anglicans but with members of the Baptist Church and students from Bretton Hall College. One church seeking a new incumbent in 1994, specified that it wanted 'a man (*sic*) of sound Bible-based evangelical views in sympathy with the recent renewal movement but not a man of extreme charismatic outlook as we do not feel this would help us to welcome people of all shades of churchmanship into our parish'.

The healing ministry

Bishop John Ramsbotham had been anxious to promote the ministry of healing within the diocese. In 1966, he referred to the work of the Guild of St Raphael which, since its foundation by Anglo-Catholics in 1915, had contended that healing was a part of every priest's role. He tried to encourage those who 'are doing their best to make sure that the Ministry of Healing is fully accepted as normally belonging to the priest's office and not thought of as something exceptional for people with exceptional gifts'. However, he noted, 'Many of the clergy and parishioners in our own diocese are still unaware of the good things provided for us through the ordinary channels of grace. It would be a good help if every parish priest were to demonstrate to such parishioners as would come, each year, just what should happen in the case of any kind of illness, whether in hospital or at home.'

In 1969, the Rector of Emley, Donald Baker, established monthly healing services on Saturdays, with a team of clergy including Bernard Chamberlain and other members of the Community of the Resurrection, Cyril Hartley of Woolley, Godfrey Higgins of High Hoyland and Clayton West, John Howard of Skelmanthorpe, and Bill Verity of Thorner, Leeds. Kenneth Bevan, who had been a bishop in China and come to the diocese as Master of Holgate Hospital, also took part in some of the services. Baker, who later wrote that he had been praying for five years for open healing services, was directly influenced by Sister Ursula of the Whitby

Order of the Holy Paraclete. By 1972, when it met at the Community of the Resurrection for a talk by Donald Baker on 'The Healing Ministry in the Parish', the diocese had a Council for Health and Healing. In June 1974, there was a service of thanksgiving in the cathedral for the return of the healing ministry to Christ's Church. In 1978, there was a four-session course at the Community of the Resurrection for lay people on Christian healing. Writing in the *Wakefield Diocesan News* in February 1979 in his capacity as Bishop's Adviser for Social Responsibility, Stuart Pearson noted the return to the ancient practice of the church in sacramental healing. He held healing services at Woolley on the third Sunday of each month which conformed to the standards of the Guild of St Raphael and the Churches Council of Healing, and were sponsored by the Diocesan Council of Mission and Unity.

In time many more places of worship, whatever their churchmanship, have provided similar services. Some churches have developed healing-ministry teams of lay people. In 2000, a parochial church council indicating what it looked for in a new incumbent asked to have someone 'deeply committed to the ministry of Bible teaching, prayer and the healing ministry'. A number of parishes included the fostering of the ministry of healing in their 2009 Transforming Lives pledges: St Giles's, Pontefract, proposed holding a healing service quarterly, preceded by teaching about the healing ministry; St George's, Barnsley, planned to explore resources which would help people in evangelism and healing ministry; St John's, Warley, would continue to plan special services including healing.

Healing, for some, embraced the concept of deliverance from evil spirits. It was taken up in the 1970s not only by the Established Church but by ad hoc Christian groups with their own self-styled missionaries who took little account of the possibility that what they interpreted as devil-possession might be a psychiatric illness better treated by therapy. In 1974 there were tragic consequences in the diocese when a disturbed member of such a group, Michael Taylor, was taken 'for exorcism and healing' to Gawber where the vicar, Peter Vincent, his wife Sally, a Methodist minister, Raymond Smith, together with a Methodist lay preacher and his wife, 'strove' with him through much of the night 'casting out his demons'. They then, with some anxiety at his continuing irrational state, took Taylor and his wife home. Their immediate attempts to secure either medical help or police intervention failed. Shortly afterwards Taylor killed his wife by gouging out her eyes and pulling out her tongue. He was tried at Leeds Crown Court and found not guilty by reason of insanity and was remitted to Broadmoor. The case caused a national stir with sensational and hostile newspaper reports claiming that the defendant was changed from a normal person into a homicidal killer through the influence of a religious group. Although it was not customary to hold an inquest after there had been a criminal trial, the Wakefield coroner, Philip Gill, decided that the public concern was such that an inquest would be expedient. This was held over a three-day period in April 1975. Recording a verdict of death by misadventure, Gill observed that 'the spiritual problems of others were not for well-intentioned amateurs without specific training and careful preparation to meddle with'. Peter Vincent remained at Gawber for a further two years, with the support of Bishop Treacy, who spoke of the episode as 'unwise' but said that the clergy involved in it were 'activated by good intent', but he never overcame the hostility of some of his parochial church council.

Bishop Treacy regarded the renewal of the practice of exorcism as a consequence of the Charismatic Movement which he saw as 'a judgment on the spiritual barrenness of the Church'. He was critical of those who undertook exorcisms without consulting him or the medical profession. In fact the Church had issued a rule in 1604 making clear that no priest could engage in exorcism without the permission of his diocesan bishop. A new Code had been drawn up in 1963 to provide guidance on exorcism which stated that no exorcism of an individual should take place without medical opinion. However, it had not been published until 1971 and had never been formally adopted. Treacy wrote in the *Wakefield Diocesan News* shortly after the Taylor inquest that those interested in charismatic religion must be aware of its danger.

Following the Gawber case, the Archbishop of Canterbury set out fresh guidelines for the conduct of exorcisms.

Bishop Hare became very concerned when a little later in 1975 a visit was proposed by a prominent national 'exorcist', Trevor Dearing, to conduct a healing service at All Saints, Darton. Dearing asked for 'maximum publicity' for his role as an exorcist. Fearing that the event would attract a great deal of sensational reporting, Hare advised the incumbent that he ran 'the gravest risk of bringing the whole charismatic renewal in the diocese further into disrepute'.

The demand for deliverance, whether in terms of responding to the needs of an individual who was experiencing fear or guilt, or to a problem with a building where strange manifestations had been reported, led in the early 1980s to the appointment of a Bishop's Adviser for Deliverance and Healing and the establishment of a team of men and women, both Anglo-Catholics and Evangelicals, authorized by the bishop to provide help. They were trained by the National Delivery Advisory Team. 'Delivering to Jesus' replaced the notion of delivering from demons. Following the publication of the House of Bishops' report, *A Time to Heal*, in 2000, the synod voted unanimously to promote the ministry of healing throughout the diocese.

Further revival and innovation

For Anglo-Catholic priests, the revival of the annual blessing of oils on Maundy Thursday, the Chrism Eucharist, became important certainly by the 1960s. Some clergy took their oils to the Community of the Resurrection to be blessed by one of the bishops who had retired there. Bishop Ramsbotham was happy to bless the oils in the chapel at Bishop's Lodge. In 1967, there was an evening 'solemn eucharist and blessing of oils' in the cathedral with Provost Philip Pare as the celebrant, but it was in 1971 in the time of Eric Treacy that the Maundy Eucharist and blessing of oils by the bishop first took place openly in the cathedral. In the first years the numbers attending, primarily Anglo-Catholic priests, were modest. The service was later coupled with the clergy's renewal of vows and grew to become popular with men and women of every strand of churchmanship. However, 1994 brought the problem, for some, of the bishop's having ordained women. Some Anglo-Catholic clergy chose subsequently to attend a separate service where the celebrant was the Provincial Episcopal Visitor. When Bishop Nigel McCulloch became the Royal Almoner with attendant duties elsewhere on Maundy Thursday, the blessing of oils took place on the Tuesday of Holy Week. For some churches, for example St Thomas's, Claremount, where it was introduced in 1983, the Sacrament of Unction, using the oils that had been blessed, became part of healing services.

Parish pilgrimages to Walsingham remained important to Anglo-Catholic parishes, or perhaps at least to their priests. In 1974, All Saints, Paddock, obtained a faculty for the installation of a statue of Our Lady of Walsingham. For a few years in the 1970s and early 1980s, a notional pilgrimage to Walsingham was held at Paddock itself in the garden; it included the setting up of Stations of the Cross, and Adoration. In 1982, the incumbent, Cyril Thomson, retired to Walsingham to serve as Chantry Priest at the Guild of All Souls Chapel.

Bishop Colin James preached at the Walsingham Whitsuntide service in May 1981. His theme was the reconciliation of the churches. Bishop Robinson was the celebrant at the Whitsuntide Eucharist in May 2011. Continuing the long association between the Community of the Resurrection and Walsingham, Anselm Genders blessed the site of the new St Joseph's wing in 1984, and John Gribben CR was elected a Guardian in

1993. Brian Bell, the incumbent at Horbury, was elected as a Guardian in 2011.

The practice of reserving the sacrament after the Eucharist, noted in earlier pages as being revived, continued to become acceptable to an increasing number of churches. In 1975, the parochial church council at Christ Church, Liversedge, voted unanimously to seek a faculty to place an aumbry on the north wall of the sanctuary. The cost would be borne by the children of a parishioner to whom the incumbent had taken the sacrament until her death. St Cuthbert's, Ackworth, sought permission for 'perpetual reservation' in 1977, accepting that they would need a faculty for an aumbry. At St John's, Bradshaw, an aumbry was placed in the newly enlarged sanctuary in 1981. All Hallows', Almondbury, sought to have an aumbry in 1985 but suggested that it should be fixed to a gradine shelf at the back of the altar, thus giving Bishop James some concern that it might prove to be a (proscribed) tabernacle. All Saints', Crofton, was granted such a tabernacle in 1990 by the Confraternity of the Blessed Sacrament and it was installed on the remains of a medieval altar stone standing beside the altar itself. In the early 1980s, both St Helen's, Hemsworth, and All Saints, Kirk Smeaton, obtained faculties for the much more elaborate sacrament houses but in neither case were these installed.

In 1991, in a further renewal of past practices, the Diocesan Spirituality Group noted that 'many were coming to value confession to a priest'.

Among Transforming Lives pledges given in 2009 was one to renew the festival of Corpus Christi.

The twenty-first century has seen further innovation in forms of worship in the sacramental tradition both in the United Kingdom and in the Anglican Church more widely, some of these prompted by the Church of England report, *Mission-shaped Church* (2004), and its subsequent movement Fresh Expressions. A different and so far unique Eucharist, Missa, was held for the first time in the cathedral on 1 November 2008, devised by Bishop Tony Robinson and the Canon Missioner, Tony Macpherson. Described as 'radical, contemplative, and very different', it relies on candlelight, darkness and colour and goes back to an ancient tradition. In 2010, Canon Macpherson began leading Missa from time to time in the Chantry Chapel.

There has been a growing interest in the contemplative chanting associated with the Taizé community. During his time at St Hilda's, Halifax, Kit Widdows organized camping holidays at Cluny when they 'had a profound time' at Taizé itself.

Cursillo, a three-day course for spiritual renewal and development, was introduced into the diocese with the approval of Bishop David Hope in the 1990s by Jenny Lowery who had been introduced to it in the Diocese of Southwell. Originating within the Roman Catholic Church in Spain, and taken thence to the United States, it was adapted for the Anglican Church in 1972 and brought to England and Wales by leaders from Dallas in 1981. The first Wakefield Cursillo weekend was in February 1992 at Whirlow Grange, Sheffield. Bishop Nigel McCulloch and his wife made their Cursillo in 1995 and were hugely supportive of the movement. In 2002 the diocese celebrated the tenth anniversary of Cursillo in Wakefield by hosting the 21st birthday celebrations of British Anglican Cursillo, the National *Ultreya* – a Spanish word meaning 'encouragement' – when Cursillistas from some thirty dioceses in England, Scotland and Wales took part in a Walk of Witness through the city centre to the cathedral, and celebrated the Eucharist, led by Bishop Nigel. Wakefield offers one or two weekend courses each year. Cursillo is aimed at 'mature' Christians, to help them be more effective in their Christian witness, and more honed in their discipleship. The unique thing that Cursillo offers the Church is the ongoing support structure, by way of regular small group meetings, and larger diocesan meetings. Cursillo also encourages people to seek spiritual direction, and to develop a Rule of Life. Though its roots are from the Roman Catholic tradition, by 2012 Christians from the whole spectrum of Anglicanism have taken part in weekends, finding personal renewal and being more fruitful and active in their parishes.

Julian Meetings began in some other parts of the country in the 1970s following a letter in church newspapers in 1973. Ecumenical in intention, they are Christ centred. They take their name from the medieval anchoress Julian of Norwich simply because a number of the originators were in the Norwich Diocese and because she advocated the 'waiting on God' which is the essence of contemplative prayer. Participants, perhaps a dozen or so people, sit in a circle or facing each other in another simple formation. After a few spoken words by a member, providing a lead, there is a period of about thirty minutes of silent contemplative prayer. The meeting concludes with a few more words leading out of the silence. There may then be refreshments and an opportunity for conversation. The first meetings in the diocese were held in the chapel at Pinderfields Hospital in the early years of the twenty-first century. These moved to the Chantry Chapel on Wakefield Bridge in 2011. Further meetings were founded in the diocese at St John's Church, Wakefield, and at Halifax and Holmfirth.

In the early years of the twenty-first century, the spectrum of churchmanship across the diocese remained wide. At the Anglo-Catholic end it was thought that in 2012 some twenty priests were member of the Societas Sanctae Crucis. However, the lack of any rigidity can perhaps be seen in the words of one parochial church council secretary in setting out the requirement of a new incumbent: 'Traditionally we are regarded as a "low" church in that we do not offer incense or make intercessions to the blessed virgin (*sic*) and our Eucharist is not referred to as the mass. We are accustomed to the practice of confessions by appointment and the reservation of the sacrament. Vestments are always worn.'

The Reordering of Churches

While some changes took place earlier, the reordering of churches became especially popular in the 1980s and 1990s. Alterations might simply be pragmatic, to secularize (the term used by Eric Treacy) a part of the worship space – especially its western end – to provide a meeting room, lavatories and kitchen facilities. However, increasingly two influences came to bear: on the one hand, as outreach projects developed, churches were seen as amenities for community use (a possibility strongly advocated in *Faith in the City*), on the other, as new styles of worship evolved, particularly under the influence of charismatic renewal, there was a need for greater flexibility in the worship space itself and for alterations which removed the traditional separation of priest and people. Reordering might involve the removal of fixed pews and the rood screen, the choice to keep the lectern rather than retain a pulpit, and the provision of a nave altar. Such changes facilitated a much greater participation by lay people in the rituals of worship and, at a very basic level, have meant that people can move freely to one another during the sharing of the peace.

There had been a call for the reordering of the cathedral as early as 1963 when a letter to the *Wakefield Express* complained of the 'sense of detachment' the congregation must feel in view of the large chancel screen cutting them off from the priests seated behind it and because of the distance of the altar from the public.

Eric Treacy was ambivalent about reordering. In 1969, he wrote of the expense involved in maintaining a parish hall and suggested that there was much to be said for secularizing the west end of the church so that it could be used for social purposes. He noted that this was happening in some of the Huddersfield parishes. However, when the parochial church council at St James's, Thornes, was, in the same year, considering selling the church hall and screening off the west end of the church, he expressed concern about the same building serving both spiritual and secular uses.

Among the most ambitious and transformative schemes of the 1970s was that at the 1868 St John's, Lepton, where a 'traditional dark and rigid vault' was changed into a light, flexible, and welcoming family church with meeting and counselling rooms. The changes were paralleled by innovations in terms of shared ministry, with a six-member team acting as a 'think and pray tank' and leading worship, with dance and drama, as well as exercising pastoral care.

A residential weekend in 1970 which drew thirty-seven members of the congregation of Halifax Parish Church and its Youth Fellowship, produced wide-ranging suggestions and reflected the widespread thinking of the time. Some of the concerns lay with the lack of community feeling and fellowship because of the geographical position of the church in the town, the way in which members lived not so much in the parish itself but scattered all over the town, and the small size of the congregation compared to the size of building. But there was a clear focus on reordering at the heart of a desire to become an ecumenical centre for worship and to foster community service. Traditional church music might increase a feeling of 'aloofness'; change here too was to be recommended. The report on the weekend's discussions advocated a study of the church building in regard to its suitability for worship, its use for worship by people of other races and religions, and its use for entertainments such as concerts and drama, and for art exhibitions. It proposed the removal of the screen to give a clear view of the east end of the church and to make the choir more audible, the removal of some pews from the front of the centre aisle to create space which could be used for a nave altar, orchestras, plays, or the needs of special services, and the removal of some other pews to make room for exhibitions. Stacking chairs could be acquired to provide extra seating.

In 1972 Christ Church, New Mill, was reordered, to the design of local architect Arthur Quarmby, to provide rooms in the gallery.

At St Mary the Virgin, Illingworth, people on the Government's Job Creation scheme gave help in 1978 in secularizing the west end of the eighteenth-century church. (The church closed in 2011.)

Reordering could not take place without the support of the Diocesan Advisory Committee and a faculty granted by the diocesan Chancellor. Some schemes created controversy. There might be objections to the loss of 'heritage' features, or fittings which had been given as memorials. At St John the Baptist's, Penistone, opposition to reordering led to a hearing of the Consistory Court in 1979. The tensions lay between those members of the congregation who wished to retain the 'traditional' church and those who wanted to adapt it to contemporary needs. At St Helen's, Sandal, there was controversy in 1981 when proposals, unusually to adapt the east end of the church, included the removal of the nineteenth-century reredos which had been given by the local landowner, Sir Lionel Pilkington of Chevet Hall.

The most ambitious, radical, and inevitably controversial reordering took place at Dewsbury Parish Church in stages between 1978 and 2003. In the 1970s the church, founded in the seventh century, was experiencing similar problems to urban churches elsewhere, increasingly isolated from any residential area and with a building that had become far too large for a declining congregation yet might well have a substantial weekday role for the wider community. Social facilities were lost in 1973 with the compulsory purchase of the parish hall for a road-widening scheme. In the first stage, the oldest part of the church, lying at its west end, became the worship area, leaving the eastern part for use as a hall and for storage. In 1994–95, inspired by the vision of the team rector of 1991–2002, John Hawley, this remaining, vast, part of the building was divided up to provide a heritage centre, meeting rooms, and a spacious café. It was thought that Paulinus, first Bishop of York, had preached close to the River Calder in Dewsbury in 627 and a small shrine to the saint was created on a

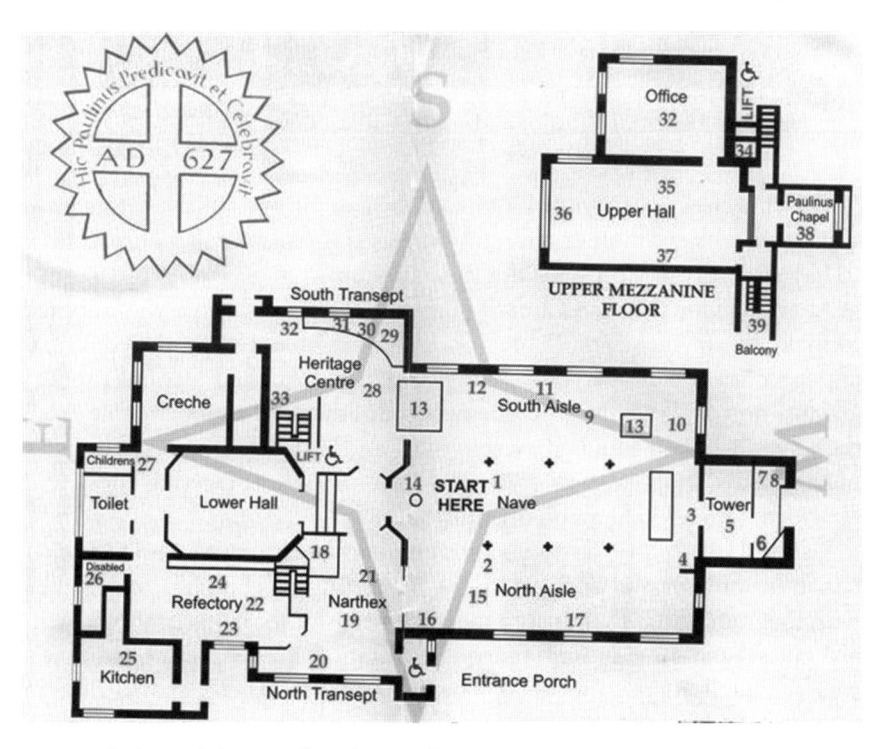

Ground plan of the reordered Dewsbury Minster

mezzanine floor. The worship area was much enhanced in 2004–07 and the refurbished organ was installed. It was rededicated by Bishop Platten in 2007.

The Heritage Centre, Dewsbury Minster, Gillian Gaskin

The church was designated a minster in 1993 in recognition of its position as the ancient mother church of the area. It was the first such church to have that distinction since the Reformation.

At Huddersfield Parish Church in the late 1980s a scheme was adopted to make use of the crypt. Some 300 tons of rubble were removed, creating space for a café, playgroup, advice centre, drug and alcohol support groups, and facilities for the unemployed. Financial support came from the Church Urban Fund. Between 1986 and 1989, the rear of the nave of St Hilda's, Halifax, was converted into a spacious meeting room and provided with a kitchen and lavatories.

Bishop Hope particularly encouraged parishes to move from maintenance to mission and supported the reordering of churches undertaken with that aim rather than just to meet the needs of the congregation. Richard Giles, who already had a strong reputation for reordering churches, was recruited to the diocese in 1987 as Canon Theologian, Priest in Charge of St Thomas's, Huddersfield, and in an entirely new post as Parish Development Officer, in which position it was anticipated that he would help parishes to make more imaginative use of their buildings. Giles had trained as a planner and had considerable interest in art and design. In his later book, *Re-pitching the Tent* (1996), he presents a clear argument for altering church interiors to meet the spiritual and theological needs of the contemporary church and the community and culture it serves. In essence he advocated doing away with 'gothic clutter', to provide space, or spaces and flexibility. He saw reordering as fundamental to revitalizing the body of worshippers. Duplication, whether of fonts, lecterns/pulpits, or altars was in his view simply a distraction. He advocated a liturgical movement from separate spaces for gathering and for words, to a space where all can stand around an altar for the Eucharist.

In 1989 Hope chaired a conference at Heptonstall on reordering.

A hearing in the Consistory Court was necessary in the early 1990s when reordering was proposed at Golcar. Controversy focused on the plan to remove the chancel screen and pulpit, although the Rood beam would be left in place. Petitioners for the faculty saw the screen as a serious hindrance to visibility; they were concerned with mission and they argued that the building conveyed a negative image. Seventeen members of the parochial church council supported the application but two opposed it. The concerns of the objectors lay with the fact that the screen was a memorial and was a fine architectural feature; they saw no point in the changes which were ' just being trendy'. The Chancellor pointed out that there had always been changes to the building in line with contemporary beliefs and practices. The west end had been reordered three years earlier without much controversy and had brought benefits. After taking advice from architects, the Chancellor granted the faculty. The reordered church was opened by McCulloch in January 1993.

The seating capacity of churches was radically reduced by reordering schemes, rendering them more appropriate for the diminished congregations of the late twentieth century (although it should be noted that very many churches were built originally in the nineteenth century on an overambitious scale!). When Holy Trinity, Huddersfield was extensively reordered in 1994-95 seating accommodation was reduced from 1,500 to 350. The changes created a more flexible worship space, meeting and fellowship space, lavatories and a kitchen. Additional rooms were created above the meeting and fellowship space which proved excellent for work with children and young people.

Church towers could present an opportunity to create an upper room as happened at St Michael's Cornholme in 1982

Shrewd reordering might allow a parish to save money by closing and selling its church hall. *Helping the Stones to Speak* (1991, the Diocesan

Board for Mission and Unity), noted the scheme at Christ Church, Moldgreen, where in 1990 new rooms were opened in the church itself: the altar and reredos were brought forward into the nave, the former chancel area was walled off and a second storey created, and a kitchen and lavatories were provided in the former organ space. Among the other seven schemes noted in the book was that at Choppards Mission Church, Holmfirth, where in 1979 the decreasing congregation determined to convert it into a retreat centre at the heart of the 'summer wine' country: some work was undertaken by members themselves, some by a team provided under a Manpower Services Commission scheme, and some was financed by the Bishop's Centenary Fund. Work was completed in 1990.

Following the fire in 1987 which destroyed much of the church at St Paul's Armitage Bridge, the building was redesigned to provide meeting rooms on two floors in the two bays at the rear of the nave. A symposium on church buildings was held there on 20 October 1990.

One of the most successful examples in the diocese of reordering remains the 1990 changes to Giles's own church, St Thomas's, Huddersfield. Here a spacious open area was created at what had been the west end of the nave, allowing for the welcoming of those coming to worship and the freedom to socialize afterwards. Such spaces were greatly favoured by Giles, who applied the Greek term, Narthex, to them. (The term had been used in the early 1960s at St George's, Leeds, when after the collapse of the steeple in 1962, the west end was redeveloped with a space distinct from the nave.) The former nave and chancel, and the side chapels, were converted into one open space. The Lady Chapel retained its figure of the Virgin and Child but the altar was removed.

One of the schemes that excited the most controversy – and certainly the most adverse public comment – was not the reordering of a church but the addition of an extension to provide a meeting room, kitchen and lavatories. This was in 1990 at Almondbury, where the removal of pews and the creation of a nave dais for an altar had already caused friction in 1983. Prior to the mid 1980s, the church and the community had been able to use the facilities of the National School, but this had closed and there were complexities surrounding its sale, hindering a scheme to buy it for church use. Hence the church council determined to build an extension on the north side of the church itself. They fulfilled all the legal requirements to obtain a faculty for the work as well as planning permission from Huddersfield Council. The non-church-going inhabitants of Almondbury seem to have realized what was happening only at the time the work was due to begin. There was a public outcry with a petition signed by some 1,637 people, a spate of letters to the newspaper and appeals to both the Prince

The controversial extension at All Hallows, Almondbury, Brian Holding

of Wales and the Archbishop of Canterbury to intervene. The protesters enlisted a solicitor to try to demonstrate that the law had been broken. An inspector from English Heritage provided adverse comments on Peter Marshall's design for the extension. An article appeared in *Private Eye* in April 1990:

> This column, I fear, could devote itself entirely to the Church of England's bold policy of coming to terms with the challenge of the twenty-first century by providing the faithful with essential facilities for the Rite of Coffee and for going to the toilet afterwards. I am regularly sent examples of monstrous church extension schemes, almost always as gratuitous as they are twee. But here is one that deserves comment. This is for All Hallows, Almondbury, near Huddersfield. In April 1988, the district church council decided to build a church hall attached to the north side of this medieval church. This involves breaking through a wall, chopping down trees and removing graves from the ancient churchyard. In October Mr Peter Marshall was appointed architect; he came up with the charming essay in the neo-vernacular scout-hut style ... A faculty was requested from the Diocese of Wakefield and granted in March 1989. The scheme put in for planning permission in February (fortunately, the scandal of ecclesiastical exemption does not apply to lavatory extensions) and permission was obtained in May. Only then

did the village seem to become aware of what was proposed and an appeal was launched. A petition attracted 1,637 signatures but too late, the bulldozers have already moved in.

David Hope invited representatives of the protest group to a meeting at Church House and, seeking to mollify them, promised to do what he could to progress the possibility of the redundant National School building becoming available for community use.

A radical scheme at Normanton of the early 1990s (and one much criticized subsequently) changed the orientation of the worship area from the traditional east-facing layout to one facing north.

By the time Giles gave a presentation to the diocesan synod in March 1993, 121 of the 191 parishes had sought advice on reordering.

All Saints, Salterhebble (later designated All Saints, Halifax), was re-dedicated after reordering when Bishop McCulloch went there for the Christ Our Light commissioning in January 2000. The scheme, initiated nine years earlier, was celebrated as providing a building 'more suitable for the church's task of worship, outreach, and service for the next century'. It won a Civic Award. The Church was equipped with kitchen, office and lavatories, a crèche, a lounge (used several times a year by a men's breakfast group) and other meeting rooms, a refurbished worship area and new furniture. An upstairs room had a pool table. The heating, lighting and sound systems were renewed. Except for a grant of £7,000, the whole £245,000 cost of the scheme was met by the congregation. The architects were Nick Rank (initially, and the basic plan) and Stuart Beaumont (the detailed design). From the start the congregation agreed to tithe the income, thus giving ten per cent of whatever was received for the building fund to charities at home and abroad. Among achievements from this was the building and equipping of a church in India.

The reordering of All Saints, North Featherstone, was also completed in 2000, providing meeting rooms within the church itself. Plans for development had already been made when a fire on 12 August 1998, which destroyed the south aisle, the vestries and the organ, brought the renewal rather sooner than had been anticipated.

When St Thomas's, Batley, was reordered in 2004–05, the original entrance on the south side was closed and a small prayer-room was created there. The north-western end of the church was converted into a kitchen and coffee room, with the west door becoming the principal entrance.

Some churches have been altered more modestly. At St Paul's, Monk Bretton, for example, the choir pews were removed and nave altar introduced but no other change was effected.

Reordering continued after the millennium, for example at St James's, Heckmondwike (2001), St Paul's, Birkenshaw (2001), St Mary's, Gomersal (2004), St Michael's, Emley (2005), St Peter's, Morley (2005), All Saints, Batley (2006), St Luke's, Sharlston (2009), and St Paul's, Drighlington (2009). The work at Emley was funded in part by selling its decaying church hall. The reordering of St Michael's, East Ardsley, was completed in 2011 after a major donation from local businessman Cyril Gay. The sale of St Mary's, Gawthorpe, enabled reordering at Holy Trinity, Ossett.

The Cathedral

There was some modest reordering of the cathedral in 1974 when the first four rows of pews on either side of the nave's centre aisle were removed and a low nave platform was installed for a nave altar. The spiral staircase by the south porch was fitted to create office space for the Cathedral Secretary in the room above the porch (where anciently the records of the Trustees of the Wakefield Charities were kept).

The pedestrianization of Upper Kirkgate in 1974–75 took heavy traffic away from the vicinity of the cathedral but its grounds remained railed off.

Following the withdrawal in 1976 of the Sisters of St Peter's Convent, who had assisted at the cathedral since 1925, a small group of nuns from the Community of St Mary the Virgin, Wantage, Sisters Jean Mary, Millicent Olga, and Sara Maureen, came to the cathedral in their stead. For a time Sister Jean Mary assisted in the parish of St Helen's, Athersley.

As a memorial to Eric Treacy, the cathedral gained a major new building to the north of its churchyard in 1982. It was the second addition to the cathedral complex, its foundation stone laid eighty years after that of the great extension on the east end which commemorated William Walsham How. It provided a large octagonal meeting room, with kitchen and first-floor offices. It was not without controversy: the actual site was changed from one closer to the cathedral after criticism from the Royal Fine Arts Commission which was concerned that some of the windows in the north aisle would be obscured.

An appeal for a massive £450,000 for the Treacy Hall, repairs to the cathedral itself and the renewal of the organ, was launched in February 1980. The Lord Lieutenant of the West Riding, Sir William Bulmer, was the president of the appeal fund, and the chairman of the Wakefield Cathedral Centenary Development Fund was Colonel Michael P. Robinson, chairman of the Yorkshire Weekly Newspaper Group. The architect for the Hall was Wakefield-born Peter Marshall and the principal contractor was J. Wimpenny of Linthwaite, Huddersfield. To facilitate fund raising, the diocese was divided into six areas, each with its own vice-chairman. The appeal was made not only to diocesan churches but also to industry, schools, other organizations and individuals. By the time the first sod was cut by Colin James on 18 May 1981, almost £200,000 had been raised. The foundation stone was hallowed by Bishop James and laid by Bishop Treacy's widow, May, on 26 June. At the same time a chest of memorabilia was buried in the foundations. Among other things it contained a commemorative plate given by Peter Jones and a mint set of 1981 coins presented by Barclay's Bank. Philip Gill, vice-chairman of the Appeal Committee, presented Mrs Treacy with the first of an edition of commemorative vases in cobalt blue. The Hall was opened by Roger Wilson and dedicated by Colin James on 25 April 1982.

The Treacy Hall from Cross Street, Brian Holding

The early 1980s saw a major project to provide embroidered kneelers. The designs were worked by people across the diocese.

In 1987, the three inner glass porches, each with its own 'heat curtain' designed by Peter Marshall, were installed, enabling the solid oak doors to be left open, and the cathedral to provide a more welcoming appearance.

YEARS OF CHALLENGE AND CHANGE, 1968–2012

The east and south sides of the cathedral grounds were brought into a new pedestrianization scheme by Tess Jaray in 1989 by means of a sequence of broad stone staircases.

In 1992, the cathedral became the second in the country to form a girls' choir.

The position of Provost became that of Dean in 2000 when the cathedral gained a new constitution and statutes following the Cathedrals Measure of 1999. At much the same time, parish boundaries were re-drawn under an Order in Council and the care of the Chantry Chapel of St Mary the Virgin, Wakefield Bridge, was taken from St Andrew's into the cathedral's parish and vested in the Dean and Chapter. The constitution allowed for further honorary canons and for the installation of lay canons although it was not until Stephen Platten became bishop that any of the latter were appointed. Platten chose lay canons for the depth of talent and expertise they brought to the diocese. He appointed ecumenical canons drawn from Methodism, Roman Catholicism, and the Lutheran church in Skara. George Nairn-Briggs, who became the first Dean of Wakefield, chose the first names for the new canonic stalls.

George Nairn-Briggs as Dean of Wakefield conducting the wedding in Wakefield Chantry Chapel of Pat Langham and Nev Hanley, John Briggs

Having been the Social Responsibility Officer, and recognizing that the names of more women were needed, he chose Josephine Butler for one. The presence of the Community of the Resurrection and its service to the diocese suggested Charles Gore as another. The link with Faisalabad, Pakistan provided Henry Martyn, the association with Skara in Sweden provided St Brigid, and the African Mara partnership Janani Luwum. Past priests at Huddersfield Parish Church, John and Henry Venn, gave their names to further stalls.

In 2003, a substantial house in Westmorland Street was acquired to provide office facilities and an education centre. It was opened in November by the Duke of Kent. Known at first as the Westmorland Centre, it was later named the Cathedral Centre.

It was the turn of Wakefield Cathedral to host the Queen's distribution of Maundy money in 2005, with 1,100 people attending the magnificent service and 158 of them receiving purses from the Queen's hand. Bishop Nigel McCulloch walked just behind Her Majesty as the Royal Almoner.

In 2009, the Dean and Chapter embarked on a massively ambitious campaign to raise £4.5m for the reordering of the cathedral in time for the 125th anniversary of the diocese in 2013. Numerous devices for raising the money included, in the autumn of 2010, a competition to complete the wording of a poster, 'I love Wakefield Cathedral because ...', to be displayed on the local Arriva buses. Funds were also raised by sponsored abseils from the cathedral tower, an exhibition of angels from around the world created by Celia Kilner, and events such as a barn dance, candlelit dinner, and 'pamper' evenings when varied therapies were made available in the cathedral and the Treacy Hall. Many local organizations were reflected in Wakefield in Flowers held over a weekend at the end of October 2010; they included the Paxton Society, formed eleven years before the diocese itself, and the even older Wakefield

HM Queen Elizabeth II at Wakefield Cathedral, The Wakefield Express

Trinity Football Club. Group Rhodes created a model of the cathedral tower which seduced donations by inviting people to throw coins at the bell hanging within it. In 2011, individuals and groups were invited to buy shares in the future of the cathedral for £250. Substantial sums came from the Heritage Lottery Fund, Wakefield Metropolitan District Council and the Garfield Weston Foundation, as well as many other grant-making bodies. Early in 2012, the nave pews, installed in 1874 under a renewal scheme designed by George Gilbert Scott, were advertised for sale individually as souvenirs. The project contributed to the impression the cathedral made on the Dioceses Commission which, while recommending the merger of three Yorkshire dioceses, originally recommended that Wakefield remained the diocesan see. The proposal in George Osborne's 2012 budget to levy VAT on alterations to listed buildings led to a flurry of activity. An e-petition to the Government was launched seeking continuing exemption. The Dean's wife, Pamela Greener, composed, sang and played a protest ditty, while she wore a safety helmet in the dismantled nave, which swiftly gained national publicity.

Jonathan Bielby, who had been the organist and Director of Music for forty years, retired in 2010.

The Mirfield Centre

The College of the Resurrection was threatened with closure in 1992 when the report, 'Theological Training: A Way Ahead', published for the House of Bishops, focused on its weaknesses. The Bishop's Council itemized its strengths: its training in the spiritual life, its ministerial priestly formation, and the relatively low cost of training there. It was held that its closure would be a significant loss to the north of England and that there was a danger of training being concentrated too much on Oxford and Cambridge. Bishop McCulloch joined a successful quest for its retention.

From 1996, the diocese has gained a base for the Northern Ordination Course (later the Yorkshire Ministry Course) in the College premises owned by the Community of the Resurrection. The building, originally housing just the College, also provided a training centre for the Wakefield Ministry Scheme in the 1990s. The Community, with the encouragement of the diocese, launched the Mirfield Centre in 1998, providing a programme of educational and spiritual events open to all, with its own director. Bishop Platten further strengthened the diocese's emphasis on education, forming the Wakefield School of Ministry, located at the Centre, in which diocesan staff train Pastoral Ministers, Readers, and some ordinands. Hence the diocese, in its partnership with the Mirfield Centre, has, since 2008, become a hub for the innovative Yorkshire Regional Training Partnership.

As Father Oswin Gartside has said, 'The whole venture, with the complications of meshing existing church bodies with differing callings and foci, embodies a pattern of developing mutual understanding and pooling of resources. The common factor is a shared desire for growth in discipleship of all Christian people as signs of Christ's presence within a culture that is forgetful of its religious roots.'

Changes to the Parish Structure

Already by the 1950s it had become apparent that the Church would need greater flexibility in the use of its resources of clergy as well as of buildings. There were decreasing numbers of the former and substantial problems in the maintenance of the latter. Finance was an ever increasing constraint. To seek solutions, a commission was set up in 1954 under the chairmanship of Lesley Paul. Its report, *On the Deployment and Payment of the Clergy* (1964), contributed to the provisions of the 1968 Pastoral Measure. This, taken with the Synodical Government Measure of 1969, was expected to 'be instrumental in shaping the Church's institutional life, so that it can minister most effectively in changing circumstances and with diminished manpower'. The measures allowed for a parish church to be declared redundant without necessarily providing another one and for parishes to be constituted without having a consecrated church.

A new Diocesan Pastoral Committee working to new national regulations succeeded the former Pastoral Committee in 1968. It was faced with the long (and often somewhat thankless) task of reviewing the parishes of the diocese, bringing some together as benefices held in plurality, uniting others, furthering group ministries, team ministries, and team parishes, and declaring some churches redundant. Before schemes could be effected by Orders in Council, there was a lengthy process of consultation with incumbents, parochial church councils and other church members, and where relevant with the patrons of one or each of the livings involved. There was also the often-difficult matter of addressing differences in churchmanship. The idea of a team ministry for the Barnsley town-centre parishes was mooted as early as 1977 but the evangelical bias of St George's was seen as a possible problem where St Mary's and St Peter's were Anglo-Catholic in tradition.

The pioneer of team ministries was the Venerable Arthur Smith who, as Archdeacon of Lincoln, established the first grouping of churches under a team in the Lincolnshire Wolds in 1949. He regarded the traditional pattern of one parish with one incumbent as outmoded and even undesirable as it left clergy isolated and lonely. His book, *Team and Group Ministry*, was published in 1965 and contributed to the 1968 Pastoral Measure.

Group ministries were to be established to bring independent parishes together as a collaborating body; conventional districts within such a grouping might be newly designated as parishes, thus changing the position of Priest in Charge to that of vicar. Team parishes created a single parish unit from the amalgamation of several former parishes (some of which might earlier have come together as united benefices) which would then be served by a team of ministers and lay people under a team rector. No member of the clergy of a team parish would hold a freehold, and appointments might be for a fixed term of, say, seven years. The new parish would have a single parochial church council although the churches of the former parishes might have their own district church councils. Team ministries similarly brought parishes together with a rector but with each parish retaining its own parochial church council. Each form of reorganization was expected to provide priests with something of a ministerial community which would counter their sense of isolation. Parishes would be better able to explore joint ventures. Problems where an incumbent was ill for any length of time, or where there was an interregnum, could be more easily addressed. There were attendant issues such as the status of the individual priest and the possibility, regarded as desirable in the Paul Report, of providing a modestly extended career structure for the clergy who might now progress not simply from assistant curate, to incumbent, and to rural dean (and perhaps onwards!) but also, now, from incumbent, or team vicar, to be the rector of a team. Some were critical of the added level of bureaucracy. One secretary of a parochial church council feared that clergy would become 'professional meeting attendees'. It was suggested that both groups and teams might have an ecumenical dimension. In one case a parochial church council feared that the good ecumenical relationships in their own parish might be lost in a grouping with other parishes with a less ecumenical orientation. Differences in churchmanship were, in theory at least, to be regarded as complementary rather than conflicting. It was held that benefits would come from both clergy and lay people pooling their resources and sharing their particular gifts across former parish boundaries. It was stressed, however, that the primary purpose of the new groupings was to advance the mission of the church. Some reorganization might involve making a former parish church redundant. Criticisms after team parishes had been formed, focused on the loss of leadership when churches saw a priest only once in three weeks, on failures of communication between the constituent congregations, and on the disappointing paucity of either joint services or other inter-congregation events.

In 1971, Kenneth Unwin, who later became Archdeacon of Pontefract, published a paper on 'The Parish in the Seventies' in which he argued that the old parish boundaries now meant very little in terms of people's actual lives. He wrote of the contemporary 'missionary situation', and referred to the advent of group and team ministries as 'not merely an expedient to relieve clergy shortage but a positive good to achieve specialization and to give the clergy companionship'.

Additional pressures to reduce the number of parishes came with the implementation in 1980 of the 'Sheffield formula' which imposed a restriction on the number of beneficed clergy for whom some funding would come from the Church Commissioners.

Looking Forward, the diocese's response to *Faith in the City*, which was presented to the Bishop's Council in December 1987, raised some concerns about the effectiveness of the team approach: 'There were teams where some members of the team looked forward to having specific geographical responsibility and looked simply to the team for support, while other members of the team appreciated that if it was to work creatively, different members of staff would have different responsibilities across the board ... (in) other teams ... worshipping members of the congregations saw little advantage in belonging to a team except that it meant they had a different priest each Sunday. They in fact found the pastoral continuity to which they had been used was disrupted rather than enhanced.'

Reorganization could be a painful business and one sometimes involving the lengthy suspension of benefices while Priests in Charge continued the care of parishes where no incumbent was appointed. The suspension of the benefice is a device for not appointing a priest with a freehold, with all the permanency that entails or entailed, on the basis that the parish was being considered as part of a contemplated reorganization. In theory, a Priest in Charge who had a licence, had less security than a priest with a freehold. Ministers in that position have certainly regarded it in that way. In fact it became almost commonplace when a living became vacant to appoint a Priest in Charge rather than a new vicar. In 1977, Colin James commented on the necessity of suspending presentations while the overall rationale for the next five years was determined. As the need to reorganize became more pressing and the scale of change much greater, the number of suspensions rose markedly. In January 2005, presentation was suspended in forty-eight benefices; in May 2011, the figure stood at sixty-nine; in almost all cases the reason given was 'reorganization' although there might be other grounds such as that a non-stipendiary minister currently had charge of the cure or that the Priest in Charge was there in a house-for-duty basis. The practice was criticized by clergy, one of whom argued that the parson's freehold was essential. 'Remove that', he wrote, 'and the parish priest becomes vulnerable to Episcopal displeasure, political expediency, and parochial pressure.'

Forming a happy and collaborative team ministry from disparate churches, each with its own traditions, alliances, loyalties, ad hoc committees, churchmanship, and forms of worship, must inevitably carry the possibility of failure. As with any other community, there is the risk of personality clashes. The role of team rector carries demands beyond that of simply a vicar of a single parish, and a man or woman who is excellent in one role may not necessarily prove able in another. While over the years the Diocesan Pastoral Committee sought long-term arrangements, some new groupings proved unsatisfactory, with resulting grief and anger, and some ceased to meet the needs of a changing situation. In time some further revisions became necessary.

The expansion of team and group ministries led to a question at the 96th synod about the position of woman priests. It was alleged that in the Wakefield Diocese, as elsewhere, a dominant parish within a group sought to impose a ban on women priests in other parishes in the group even where this was against the conscience of its parishioners.

The first really ambitious scheme in the Wakefield Diocese under the 1968 Measure was perhaps that made by Order in Council on 28 April 1972 when the three Sowerby parishes of St George, St Peter, and St Mary, together with St John the Divine, Thorpe, were formed into a United Benefice with the parish church of St John the Divine being declared redundant.

Also in 1972 came the Union of the Barnsley benefices and parishes of St Peter and St John, with St John's Church becoming redundant, and the Union of the benefices and parishes of Todmorden and Harley Wood with All Saints, Harley Wood, made redundant. The parishes of St Michael, Carleton, and St Stephen, East Hardwick, were to be held in plurality.

Looking to establish some group ministries, Bishop Treacy wrote in December 1974 that in the next few months he would ask groups of parishes in the large centres of the diocese to meet to discuss ways and means whereby four or five parishes serving such areas could develop new ways of working and to be ready for a sharing of their resources. At the same time he warned that they must ask themselves whether they would, in such a difficult time financially, otherwise survive beyond the decade.

The first legally constituted Group Ministry in the diocese came in June 1975 when the Illingworth Group was inaugurated. The initial idea had come from the clergy themselves who suggested it to Treacy in 1972. He referred it to the Pastoral Committee. The scheme embraced the two parishes of St Mary's, Illingworth, and St John's, Bradshaw, and the two conventional districts of St Andrew's, Holmfield, and Holy Trinity, Mixenden. Under the Order in Council the two conventional districts became benefices and parishes, Holmfield taking in a part of the parish of All Souls, Haley Hill. To mark the inauguration of the group, special services were held in each of the churches.

An informal group was formed in the mid 1970s by the 'Queen's Road' Halifax churches, St Augustine's, St Hilda's, and St Paul's, King Cross with St James's, Pye Nest. They agreed to co-operate in the fields of publicity, communication, worship, mission, fellowship, Christian education, and social responsibility. Their three vicars were to meet regularly together with any curates and licensed lay workers, forming the Group Chapter; a Group Council, to facilitate co-operation, embraced the clergy, the licensed lay workers, and three representatives of the parochial church councils of each of the three parishes. For a time they issued a shared magazine.

Meeting in April 1976, the parochial church council at Huddersfield Parish Church (St Peter's) suggested an ambitious scheme in which, in a union with Holy Trinity and possibly also St John's, St Peter's would become the centre of a team ministry, with an industrial chaplain, a hospital chaplain and a polytechnic chaplain in the team; the scheme would, they hoped, facilitate work with the Samaritans and in marriage guidance. Nothing came of it!

On coming to the diocese in 1977, Colin James asked the Pastoral Committee to advise on parishes of 'marginal viability'. He noted that four parishes in the diocese had populations of less than 1,000. Twenty-six further parishes were of less than 2,000. A few of these, he recognized, had geographical positions which made it hard to see how they could benefit from closer ministerial links with their neighbours and some should be regarded as providing a suitable parochial base for a priest engaged in some specialist or diocesan post. But he indicated clearly that he was looking for continuing reorganization. He asked for a five-year plan considering the establishment for the diocese as a whole which was to be presented to the Bishop's Council by September 1977.

One of the small parishes was St Lucius', Farnley Tyas, and when its incumbent retired in 1977 it seemed impossible to find a priest who would move there. A major factor was the work at Storthes Hall Hospital where the priest had been the chaplain. John Lodge, the Rector of Almondbury, suggested to Bishop James that the benefice and parish should be reunited with Almondbury itself, from which it had been carved in the mid nineteenth century. The presentation was suspended and Lodge was appointed as the Priest in Charge. The benefices were united in 1983.

While the union of benefices which had been taking place during Treacy's bishopric was to continue (St Peter's, Horbury, and St John's, Horbury Bridge, for example, were united in 1978), it was not until 1982 that the first team parish in the diocese was created. It had been ten years in the planning. It brought together three Halifax town-centre parishes, the 'parent' parish of St John the Baptist, Holy Trinity, and St James and St Mary. The new parish was named the Parish of Halifax and its Rector was to be known, retaining the traditional prestigious title, as the Vicar of Halifax. The parish was to have one other priest who would be called vicar and have the status of an incumbent albeit without a freehold. While there would be a single parochial church council (PCC), each of the former parishes could have its own district church council. The scheme was dissolved in 1994 when the parish of Halifax became again independent and a new Town Centre Group Ministry was formed with the Holy and Undivided Trinity becoming a new parish taking in the former parishes of St James and St Mary.

Just as new parishes had been created in 1975 to form the group ministry at Illingworth, so a new parish came into being when a smaller team parish was established in 1983 at Elland; here a parish was created for All Saints, the chapel of ease built in 1903, and this was at the same time united with its parent parish of Elland, with provision for the new team to have a rector and a vicar. In 2004, the daughter church of St Mary Magdalene, Outlane, was elevated to the status of parish church and the new benefice of Stainland with Outlane was created. St Mary Magdalene was consecrated on 31 January 2004.

Some proposals for change were contested. The scheme to create the Dewsbury Team Parish, the third to be implemented in the diocese, was delayed for a year because of an appeal against it which was referred to the Judicial Committee of the Privy Council. When the scheme was confirmed in 1983 it brought together All Saints (the 'parent' parish of Dewsbury), St Mark's, the previously United Benefice of St Matthew and St John the Baptist, St John's Dewsbury Moor, and Holy Trinity, Batley Carr.

Inevitably quite radical reorganization sometimes brought recriminations. The Team Parish of North Huddersfield was established on 1 December 1986, the first of a number of team parishes formed during David Hope's bishopric. It comprised the two Birkby parishes of St John the Evangelist and St Cuthbert, together with St Francis Fixby and St Hilda's Cowcliffe, and included a woman deacon, Jean Sykes, as one of the team vicars. Concerned congregations were told that the order setting up the team parish could be revoked (the word used at the time was 'unscrambled') if it proved unsatisfactory. Difficulties of many kinds arose, for example when unilateral decisions were taken in regard to the timing of services or changes to church furniture. An inquiry by Archdeacon David Hallett in 1993 found that the people felt the new structure had been imposed without adequate consultation but found, too, that the problems of relationships between different churches went back many decades and that St Cuthbert's, consecrated in 1926, had been 'born out of controversy'. Tensions were exacerbated when the Team's parochial church council decided that St John's, Birkby, should be declared redundant and a group of Friends of St John's was formed to ensure its survival. The proposed redundancy, which was never implemented, occupied the minds of the Diocesan Pastoral Committee over some years. The team parish was dissolved in October 2008 and new groupings were formed: St Francis, Fixby, and St Hilda's, Cowcliffe, became a new united benefice; St John the Evangelist, Birkby, was united with Christ Church, Woodhouse; and St Cuthbert's, Birkby, formed a new united benefice with St Philip the Apostle, Birchencliffe.

In 1984, the parish of Thurgoland was transferred to the Diocese of Sheffield to facilitate its becoming united with Wortley.

Penistone and Thurlstone were brought into a team ministry in 1986, with Thurlstone being added to the Penistone and Midhope Benefice which had also the mission churches of St Anne's, Carlecote, St Aidan's, Oxspring, and Snowden Hill Farm Chapel.

St James's, Midhope

In 1985, there was serious thought of combining the united parish of St Peter and St John, Barnsley, with St Mary's, and the presentation was suspended for three years but, following the work of a new Priest in Charge, the suspension was lifted in 1988.

When the Almondbury Team Parish was created in 1988 it was regarded explicitly as a means of securing a more stable ministry, with Team Vicars being more likely to stay than curates since they had a greater degree of independence, were better housed, and were better paid. It was an unusual creation in that there were no changes to the status of the constituent churches: Farnley Tyas had already been united with Almondbury in 1983 and the other two churches were the existing daughter churches of St Mary's, and St Michael's/St Helen's. All that changed was that the daughter churches were licensed for marriages. This led David Hope to remark to his Diocesan Registrar, 'The Church of St Michael and St Helen, Quarry Hill, is a dual purpose building and I really cannot imagine anybody wanting to be married there but nevertheless feel that if we have gone down this road of Team Ministries and Team Vicars then it could be conceivable that somebody may wish for this.' The Team Ministry was inaugurated on 7 February 1988. St Mary's was later closed.

In 1988, another quite complex scheme formed the Team Ministry at Brighouse. St Chad's, Hove Edge, became a parish church, the benefice of St John the Evangelist, Clifton, was dissolved, the new benefice of St Martin's, Brighouse, and St John's, Clifton, was created, and these were united with the new parish of Hove Edge, St Chad's, to become the Brighouse and Clifton Team Parish.

A new name was introduced when a complex and extensive scheme of 1989 created a team parish from parishes and daughter churches in the area of Holmfirth, New Mill and Thurstonland, designating it the Upper Holme Valley Team Parish; the scheme involved creating the new parish of Thongsbridge, dissolving the benefices of Holy Trinity, Hepworth, and St David's, Holmbridge, and transferring them to the team parish, and bringing together into the team All Saints, Netherthong, Christ Church New Mill, Holy Trinity, Holmfirth, St John the Evangelist, Upperthong, St Thomas's, Thurstonland, and St Andrew's, Thongsbridge.

There was the reintroduction of an old township name when in 1993 the benefices of Mytholmroyd and St John in the Wilderness, Cragg Vale, were united, the new benefice being termed Erringden. A new name was created in 2000 when the benefice of Went Valley was created by Order in Council, bringing together St Luke and All Saints, Darrington, St Martin's, Womersley, and St Peter's, Kirk Smeaton.

It was deemed in 1994 that by setting up the Diocesan Vision and

Strategy Group, a fresh programme of potential pastoral reorganization had commenced. As a consequence the Pastoral Committee was asked whenever a benefice became vacant to advise the bishop on whether the presentation should be suspended.

A working party was set up in 1996 to look at the needs of the Castleford area. A team ministry began to seem appropriate and to at least one commentator it would have the advantage of needing fewer clergy, of being able to sell one of the vicarages, and of being able to meet the 'parish share'. In 1998, All Saints, Castleford, and All Saints, Hightown, were brought together as a united benefice. A team ministry was established in January 2002, bringing this together with St Paul's, Glasshoughton. St Michael and All Angels remained, from its own choice, an independent parish. However, after having been served since 2010 by one of the vicars from the Castleford team, St Michael's joined the team itself in 2012.

Two further team ministries came into being at the end of Nigel McCulloch's bishopric. These were at Morley (formed from St Paul's, St Peter's and St Andrew's, Bruntcliffe), and on the outskirts of Huddersfield. The latter, named the Emmanuel Team Ministry, revived the name of a parish church which had been declared redundant sometime after the parish itself was united with Rashcliffe. The team comprised Lockwood and Rashcliffe and another earlier united benefice, Newsome and Armitage Bridge, and Holy Trinity, South Crosland. The proposal in 2004 to suspend the presentation met with considerable criticism: it was far too soon to consider 'tinkering with it' and would 'send all the wrong messages'.

In February 2006, a Group Ministry was created for Clayton West, Emley, Flockton, Scissett and Skelmanthorpe.

The Mirfield Team Parish was created in 2007 bringing together St Mary's, Mirfield, St Paul's, Eastthorpe, and St John's, Upper Hopton. A small group was set up to explore how best the church at Eastthorpe could be used. In 2012 it remained open within the Mirfield fold providing a monthly team parish service and a mid-week Eucharist.

More benefices were united during Platten's bishopric, including St James's, Hebden Bridge, and St Thomas a Becket and Thomas the Apostle, Heptonstall (2003), St George's, Lupset, and St James's ,Thornes (2005), Holy Trinity and St Jude's, Halifax (2007), St Barnabas's, Crosland Moor, and Christ Church, Linthwaite (2008), and All Saints', Featherstone, and St Thomas's, Purston cum South Featherstone (2009).

In January 2009, in response to a national decision (the Diocesan Pastoral and Mission Measure) the Diocesan Pastoral Committee became the Diocesan Mission and Pastoral Committee as a means of linking Mission with structural planning and further reorganization of parishes. Meanwhile in 2006–07 an ad hoc Deanery Boundaries Working Party met to consider where deanery boundaries might need to be redrawn 'to make more sense of emerging patterns of ministry'. Among its considerations was the equating of deanery boundaries with those of the local government units and the need to maintain viable deanery and chapter units in relation to the number of stipendiary clergy. Its recommendation that the deaneries of Chevet and Wakefield should be merged, with eighteen stipendiary clergy, was accepted.

Changes to the parish structure have not always been a matter of uniting benefices or creating teams. After almost twenty years of deliberations, beginning in 1968, the boundaries of Hanging Heaton and St Thomas's, Batley, were changed in 1984 to bring the mission church of St Luke, Soothill, into the care St Thomas's. The site for St Luke's had been given by Lord Savile, and the mission founded in 1896. In the 1970s, with only one priest at Hanging Heaton, people at St Luke's were complaining that they got a raw deal. St Luke's closed in 2001 and was sold and converted into a private house. A side chapel at St Thomas's provided a means of commemorating it, furnished with its altar and displaying its Mothers' Union banner and processional cross.

Parsonage Houses

In 1972, the *Wakefield Diocesan News* reported that of the 208 parsonage houses in the diocese, fifty had been replaced with modern houses. However, 158 remained large, out of date and difficult to heat. They had been built, the report noted, in the days when clergy could afford servants and servants could be found. Following the establishment of the Diocesan Parsonages Board in 1973, under the 1972 Benefice Buildings Measure, very considerable efforts were made either to modernize existing parsonage houses or to replace them, funding the exercise in part by the sale of the old ones. In 1976, the Church Commissioners asked for a list of basically unsuitable houses and the Board responded with the information that forty-eight were very bad and a further forty-two deemed unsuitable. The Board's 1989 report showed that it had replaced or refurbished ninety-five houses but that there were still twenty-five deemed unsuitable. In a good many cases where benefices were united, one of the parsonages was sold. In 1991, the Board issued a handbook for clergy on the Care and Maintenance of Parsonages and Team Ministry houses. But with the loss of the old houses some parishes also lost a useful facility: Thornes Vicarage, Wakefield, for example, situated on the edge of a large public park, had been built by members of the Gaskell family who already owned the land; committee meetings took place there, social events were held in the large living room and the annual fete was held in the grounds. In 1998, the Board became the Diocesan Houses Committee.

Redundant Churches

While few churches were made redundant in the Wakefield Diocese in earlier periods, the last three decades of the twentieth century and the first decade of the twenty-first have seen the loss of very many more. As noted earlier, some of them became redundant because of urban redevelopment, with slum clearance removing the local population. Some redundancies followed the uniting of parishes and the establishing of group and team ministries or team parishes, as church attendances fell and fewer clergy were available. Some were too costly to maintain. In a few cases, congregations chose to 'downsize', selling their existing church to move to, or even build, a smaller one more suited to contemporary needs. Some were chapels of ease which, as church attendance decreased and transport to the parish church became easier, were surplus to requirements. Some were closed because they had become unsafe or because urgent repairs were too costly.

Recognizing that increasing numbers of churches must be declared redundant, the 1968 Pastoral Measure required dioceses to set up Redundant Churches Uses Committees to seek new uses for the surplus buildings. It also established the Redundant Churches Fund (later renamed the Churches Conservation Trust) to take over some of the most significant of these architecturally. In principle the Redundant Churches Uses Committee sought new uses for the churches that had been closed. The shadow of redundancy was sometimes cast for a considerable period before the Order in Council provided for its demolition or sale. A theatre trust, for example, showed considerable interest in acquiring St George's, Barnsley, and every opportunity was given for this project to be realized, but in the end no sale was made and the church was demolished.

In 1970, Bishop Treacy wrote in the *Wakefield Diocesan News* of the painful task of deciding, on the advice of the Pastoral Committee, that a church is redundant, should be closed, and should be demolished. However, he observed, 'In these days of shifting populations, Civic replanning, and financial shortage, this is something that has to be done.' The Church Commissioners, while agreeing to a redundancy, allowed a period to elapse before approving an Order in Council for demolition, in the hope that new uses could be found for the buildings. Treacy saw the waiting period of a year between redundancy and the order for demolition as disastrous, noting that 'the church becomes a target for gangs of vandals who break into the building and proceed to wreck it'. One way to circumvent the problem was to persuade the Local Authority's surveyor to declare the building unsafe (as happened in 1969 at St Luke's, Middlestown).

As Bishop Hope said in the 1980s in an untitled and undated paper on From Maintenance to Mission, 'We cannot continue to pour vast financial resources into shoring up buildings we do not want. Put bluntly, it would be better to knock them down and clear the site ... Appropriate maintenance has not been carried out over a number of years because parishes simply have not been able to afford it. More radical solutions are now needed. The buildings themselves are inappropriate for worship: they are often too large, they are cold and forbidding.' In advocating redundancy the bishop's declared aim was to 'free God's people in the diocese, both to do and to be that for which we are called'. The authors of the diocesan response to *Faith in the City* wrote in the mid 1980s, 'We do not believe that the diocese should be afraid of declaring a church redundant. There is no particular virtue in leaving a gaunt ecclesiastical building standing unkempt, uncared for and unloved.'

Many of the churches which were closed were ones built in the nineteenth century when church extension was commonplace. They might have taken many years to complete, might be of relatively poor quality in terms, in particular, of materials, and might be of little architectural merit, although dear to their congregations.

The demolition of sub-standard housing and the subsequent redevelopment of the area for industry led to the closure in 1969 of Christ Church chapel of ease, Knottingley, with order given for its demolition the following year.

Proposals for work on a church might be frustrated for some years by the thinking of the Diocesan Pastoral Committee that it was a candidate for redundancy. In the 1970s Eric Treacy halted for some long time the process towards a faculty which was sought by St Luke's, Whitechapel, to extend the space under its chancel to provide lavatories and a kitchen. Still thriving in 2012, St Luke's was by then the only community building in Moorbottom as both the Methodist church and the church school were set to close. It was also 'far and away' the most popular venue for baptisms and weddings in the district.

The sale to other denominations, or to other faiths, proved somewhat problematic. One of the most difficult issues came when St Mary's, Saviletown, was declared redundant in 1970 after services ceased there in 1967. It had begun in 1900 as a mission church founded by the parish of the

Holy Innocents, Thornhill Lees. No use had been found for it and the national Advisory Board for Redundant Churches did not regard it as worth preserving. But then a group of immigrants from Pakistan, now living in Dewsbury, asked to buy it as a mosque. Following the approval of the Diocesan Redundant Churches Uses Committee, the Church Commissioners approved a draft scheme to sell St Mary's 'for prayer and other activities of a religious nature in accordance with the rites and customs of the Muslim religion'. It was a difficult issue for Treacy, but having met the Parochial Church Council of Holy Innocents, he decided to support them in opposition to the sale. His grounds for this were pragmatic. He noted: 'If St Mary's Church were handed over to the Muslims, it would make the district a centre for the immigrants in the whole area of Dewsbury and Batley, and this would make it intolerable for the English residents in the area', and that it would hinder integration since 'the feeling in the area would be so strong that ... there would be anti-racial demonstrations ... and it would become a flash-point in community relations'. Treacy took the issue to the General Synod in July 1972 asking it to articulate a general principle on the question of selling a place of worship to another faith. A Wakefield Diocesan representative on Synod, John Bullimore, wanted an explicit declaration that churches of the Church of England should not be made available to non-Christians for religious purposes. Professor Norman Anderson, then chairman of the House of Laity of the General Synod, who was strongly opposed to the sale, reminded the synod that Muslims denied the deity of Jesus. Treacy suggested that Dewsbury Corporation should find an alternative site for the mosque. The draft scheme was withdrawn and an order for the demolition of the church was made in October 1972. In February 1973, the General Synod voted against the sale of redundant churches to other faiths.

The sale to other Christian denominations was apparently no longer a problem. St Mark's, Dewsbury, was sold in 2000 to Dewsbury Gospel Church. In fact in 1981 Colin James contemplated the closure of St Paul's, Eastthorpe, and asked the Bishop of Leeds whether the Roman Catholics would like it.

The union of the benefices of St John the Divine, Thorpe, and the three Sowerby parishes in 1972 brought the redundancy of the Thorpe church. It was a church which, in the view of at least one Vicar of Halifax, should never have been built. It had been erected in 1880 by his widow as a memorial to Frederick E. Rawson at the immense cost then of £7,000. Designed by the Halifax architect, W. S. Barber, in the Perpendicular style, it was stone built and described as 'very handsome'. It had an elaborately carved reredos of Caen stone presented by Mrs William Henry Rawson, with a bishop's chair and lectern given by the Reverend A. Rawson. Its parish was formed a year later from parts of the parishes of St Peter's and St Mary's, Sowerby, and St Bartholomew's, Ripponden. At least as early as 1934 the possibility of its being united with another benefice was being explored and from the 1940s the living was held in plurality by the incumbents variously of Ripponden and of Sowerby St Peter. An order in Council of 14 August 1972 provided for its demolition.

The formal declaration of redundancy might follow only after some years of closure. St Saviour's, Heckmondwike, was not legally declared redundant until 28 June 1974 but it had by then been closed for almost four years. Deemed the 'Cathedral of the Spen Valley', it was one of two mission churches in the parish of St James and had been closed since July 1970 because of the bursting of the boiler. It had been built in 1927 following the earlier provision of an iron church. In August 1971, the Vicar of Heckmondwike told the Diocesan Secretary that the matter of the redundancy was 'a mixture of the theological/pastoral and financial factors, with the historical and psychological'. He also wrote, 'It is reasonably clear that many of our churches and chapels in this whole area should never have been built, much less dedicated or consecrated. For decades there has been lack of co-operation and rivalry with consequent clogging-up of the work of witness, in the loyalties to lesser things. Even were the building up of three separate congregations possible in this theologically and spiritually uncertain muddled age, it would I believe still be pastorally wrong to attempt it for both laity and clergy.' Nonetheless its closure brought protests. These included reference to its beauty as a building and the fact that the quality Delph stone was in good order while the parish church itself was weathering badly, the strong familial associations, its thriving Sunday School, the loss of facilities for practising the organ, the prospect of renewing the congregation through a housing development in the area, its possible use as an old people's centre, and the distance people would need to travel to worship at the parish church. Among the arguments for its redundancy were the fact that the parish was overweighted by buildings, and the likely shortage of manpower, with Eric Treacy observing that he was entirely unlikely to be able to appoint a curate. The parish buildings included St James Church itself (one of the many Waterloo churches in the diocese), the vicarage, the parish hall, the lower hall, the school house, St Saviour's Church, St Saviour's Sunday School, All Souls Church, and All Souls Hall which had been built on to it in 1969. A protest committee appealed to the Privy Council but was unsuccessful. It was reopened for a short period in 1972 for monthly services. The order for demolition was granted in September 1975.

In 1977, St Thomas's, Bradley, was sold for use as a gymnasium. Its congregation had recognized that it was poorly sited and much too large, and opened a new church in 1974. It was consecrated by Bishop Treacy.

St George's, Barnsley, which had been built in 1833, was declared redundant in 1981, not because its parish had been amalgamated with any other but because the costs of repairing it were held to be better spent on improving the church hall as a parish centre. Its demolition was keenly opposed by SAVE, The Ancient Monuments Society and Barnsley MB Council, on the grounds that it was an important landmark in the town centre and was an example of fine architecture by Thomas Rickman, an architect of national standing who wrote the first systematic treatise on gothic architecture and who coined the terms Early English, Decorated and Perpendicular. Without it the townscape would be irredeemably spoiled, they urged. An offer by a firm of auctioneers to buy it for £500 was turned down by the Church Commissioners after protests from the congregation that it would be offensive to the eye and to the people whose loved ones were interred in its burial ground.

Disposing of the fittings of redundant churches was frequently placed at the decision of the bishop. In 1976, when the church at High Hoyland was made redundant, its high altar was taken to the Walsham How Chapel at the cathedral. In 1981, the church became a centre for outdoor pursuits run by the Bramley Trust, but was later sold to become a private house.

When St Augustine's, Halifax, was declared redundant in the 1970s, worship continued in the school and vicarage.

A report for the Church Commissioners' Redundant Churches Committee for 1982 showed that since the 1968 Pastoral Measure, twenty-five churches in the Wakefield Diocese had been closed. Eleven of these had been demolished, six had been appropriated to new uses, and seven were still to be dealt with. The Report included a section on the use of redundant churches for worship by non-Christian faiths. It noted that the case of St Luke's, Southampton, for use as a Sikh temple, was only the third to be considered, and the previous two proposals – one of which was St Mary's, Saviletown – were not proceeded with.

The closure of All Souls, Haley Hill, which was declared redundant in 1979, was of sufficient interest to merit notice in the Committee's report. It had been built in 1859 to a design by George Gilbert Scott who declared that it was 'on the whole my finest church'. It was a veritable museum of mid-Victorian ecclesiastical art.

A long and difficult search failed to find a new use. The All Souls Haley Hill Preservation Trust was formed in 1981 to take it on a lease for use as a monument and for cultural and community purposes. Grants were obtained from the Historic Buildings Council and the National Heritage Memorial Fund. Substantial repair and conservation took place in the next few years and in 1989 the church was vested in the Redundant Churches Fund (now the Churches Conservation Trust). All Souls had been built at the expense of Edward Akroyd for workers living in his model village of Akroydon. He built a second church at Copley, again for his workers' settlement. This too was declared redundant in 1993 and was accepted by the Redundant Churches Fund.

All Souls, Haley Hill

Some churches have been sold for business or office occupation. In 1990, both Holy Trinity, Halifax, and St John's, West Vale, were sold for office use. At the turn of the century, after its congregation had 'downsized', the church of the Ascension, Kinsley, was sold to S. J. Brown for £40,000, and St Mark's, Huddersfield, was sold to Omega Office Equipment for £50,000. The former church hall at Kinsley was refurbished and licensed in 2000 as the Church of the Resurrection.

St Peter's, Stanley, was of necessity declared redundant in 1999 when, because of the effect of coalmining, the building became unsafe. The congregation happily 'downsized' to lease a local school building, turning it into a community centre as well as a place of worship. It was licensed for worship in October 2001. It proved impossible to find a buyer for the church and in 2012 the diocese proposed its demolition.

If there could be said to be a happy outcome when churches were made redundant, their sale for residential conversion might be accepted as one. Once a source of water had been found, the 1833 hill-top St Paul's, Cross Stone, was sold in 1989 for conversion to a private house. The parochial church council had previously bought the disused National School and the congregation had moved there although subsequently the worship area became a chapel of rest for a funeral director. Emmanuel, Lockwood, sold originally in 1991 to silkscreen printers, later too became a private residence (with its former hymn board fixed beside the west door to display the name, Emmanuel House). All Saints, Paddock, which had been badly affected by dry rot, was sold to become a private house in 1986. Its alteration was hampered for a little while by the discovery of burial vaults beneath rotting floor timbers at its east end.

One of the most satisfying conversions of a redundant church has been that of St Matthew's, Dewsbury, which was acquired by the St Anne's Housing Trust for residential accommodation. It provides supported housing for those who wish for a degree of independence but with the security of regular visits from trained staff.

Two daughter churches built in the 1950s, St Mary's serving the Chequerfield estate at Pontefract, and St Swithun's the Eastmoor estate in Wakefield, were demolished and replaced by community centres (at Chequerfield incorporating the municipal branch library) with facilities for worship.

St Mary's Community Centre, Chequerfield

The mission church of St James the Great, Three Lane Ends, Castleford, closed in 2010. It was the longest used of the old 'tin tabernacles' in the diocese.

St James the Great, Castleford

Bishop Stephen Platten presided at the closing Eucharist on the Feast Day of St James, 21 July, and the Archdeacon of Pontefract, Peter Townley, led a service of thanksgiving on 25 July.

The Dioceses Commission

Some form of reorganization was anticipated when the Bishops of Bradford, Ripon and Leeds, and Wakefield began meeting in 2004 to look at ways of working together. The Dioceses Pastoral and Mission Measure of 2007 increased the role of the Dioceses Commission, which had been charged, *inter alia*, with looking at the 'size, boundaries and number of dioceses'. It was authorized to prepare reorganization schemes which might include the transfer of the whole of the area of a diocese into another diocese. Its first work was to review the boundaries of the dioceses of Peterborough and Ely. It reached no conclusions. However, its second review was of the five Yorkshire dioceses of Bradford, Ripon and Leeds, Sheffield, Wakefield, and, at least as far as its western boundary was concerned, York. It published its recommendations in December 2010. It sought a new 'resilient and sustainable' diocesan structure. It emphasized that its proposals were 'mission-led' rather than 'finance driven', although financial considerations were clearly a strong influence. It also placed immense significance on looking to the West Yorkshire administrative area (albeit founded only in 1974) as requiring coherence in terms of the diocesan structure. At its core was the recommendation that the three dioceses of Bradford, Ripon and Leeds, and Wakefield, should be united, adding to West Yorkshire the part of North Yorkshire covered by the Craven district. It proposed that Wakefield's Barnsley Deanery should be transferred to the Diocese of Sheffield, and made suggestions about the transfer of parishes on the perimeter of the whole area under review to dioceses lying outside this. While proposing the retention of all three cathedrals, it recommended Wakefield as the foremost. Area bishops were suggested centred on Bradford, Kirklees and Calderdale (forming the Huddersfield Episcopal area), Leeds, and Ripon. Wakefield would remain the see but the diocesan bishop would serve also as the fifth area bishop. The new diocese would be styled the Diocese of Wakefield but might be further designated 'the Church of England in West and North-West Yorkshire'.

The proposals were debated at the Wakefield Synod meeting in May 2011. Bishop Platten questioned whether what was needed was really smaller rather than larger dioceses and commented that the Report seemed to him to have insufficient theological analysis in regard to the episcopacy. While narrowly supporting the proposal to unite the dioceses, the synod voted overwhelmingly against Wakefield being its see (41 to 3 with 15 abstentions). Instead it suggested that Leeds would be a more appropriate focus and offered West Yorkshire and the Dales as the new title. Apart from one abstention, it was unanimous in agreeing that the Barnsley Deanery and other individual parishes should have the opportunity to determine their diocesan future.

Following consideration of the Review, the draft scheme itself was put out for consultation in November 2011. The proposed new diocese was to be named the Diocese of Leeds but might also be known by the title suggested at Wakefield, West Yorkshire and the Dales. Leeds Parish Church (which its earlier report had noted was rendered by its configuration and facilities somewhat unsuitable as a cathedral) could become a pro cathedral. Two benefices to the south-west of the Wakefield Diocese, Penistone and Thurlstone, and Silkstone and Hoylandswaine with Stainborough, would, the draft proposed, be transferred to the Diocese of Sheffield, but at the time of writing the latter had chosen to remain with the Wakefield Diocese – whatever its future – and it was thought that the former might do the same.

The diocesan synod considered the draft at its meeting on 10 March 2012. While the synod remained divided over the scheme, members voted overwhelmingly to present an alternative vision, initiated by Bishop Platten and already endorsed by the Bishop's Council, to the Commission.

This suggested reform in terms of a greater sharing of human resources and aspects of administration, but envisaged retaining the three separate dioceses or, alternatively, keeping the Diocese of Wakefield distinct while amalgamating those of Bradford, and Ripon and Leeds.

The Cathedral Chapter submitted its own reservations about the Commission's draft scheme, emphasizing especially the adverse impact it would have on the cathedral's extensive and very successful mission activities. It expressed concern, too, for the rupture of a 125-year tradition in which clergy and laypeople from across the diocese had been brought together in the cathedral on very many significant occasions.

Should the scheme be accepted, the 125th anniversary year of the Diocese of Wakefield, 2013, will be its last.

Appendix
The Diocesan Journals

From its beginning, the diocese was served by its *Gazette*, a substantial journal which came out initially once a quarter and, from January 1898, once a month. The first issue was published in January 1889. The *Gazette* was described as the bishop's official means of communication with his fellow workers. It contained official notices and reports, and regular, and usually lengthy, letters from the successive bishops. It carried details of all ordinations, confirmations, institutions, and licences to perpetual curacies. It listed all faculties granted, noted the consecrations of churches and graveyards, or the licensing for worship of mission churches and mission rooms. It had regular reports from rural deaneries, and occasional obituaries. The April issues were devoted to reports of the diocesan societies (with financial accounts etc.). The November issues provided the reports of the annual diocesan conferences. Items about such bodies as the branches of the Church of England Temperance Society, the Girls' Friendly Society, and the Church Lads' Brigade occurred on a more casual basis. The editorial task must have been heavy but the volumes are a splendid source for the historian. The *Gazette* was distributed free to each vicar, and to one churchwarden in each parish 'for placing within public view'. It was also sent free to every member of each of the diocesan societies, a member being someone who subscribed 5s. a year. Its circulation was thus somewhat limited and its production was comparatively costly. There were not infrequent appeals for donations to help to subsidize it.

The *Gazette* was complemented from 1925 by the much slimmer and distinctly more arbitrary *Wakefield Diocesan News* which had the merit, at least, of being inserted into the individual magazines of the many parishes which paid for it, thus reaching rather more of the people in the pews. (An early issue was satirized in *Punch*.)

The *Gazette* was discontinued in 1948. The *Wakefield Diocesan News* continued. It was edited by a sequence of clergy including, in the 1960s, the then Provost of Wakefield, Philip Pare. The first lay editor, the Diocesan Secretary, C. B. Beverley, had a lengthy spell at the desk in the 1970s. Beverley was followed in 1980 by Christopher Collison, who combined his calling as Vicar of Shepley with serving as the first Diocesan Communications Officer. Collison challenged people to provide a new name for the *News* and from the summer of 1980, as *See Link*, it gained a new look and a new title. It remained of a size to be inserted in parish magazines. Two further members of the diocesan clergy followed as editors. In 1983, the paper passed to Stephen Kelly, curate at St Botolph's, Knottingley, and in 1987, to Hugh Lawrance, curate at St Bartholomew's, Ripponden. Under Bishop Hope, a first attempt was made to recruit an editor with some media experience. He invited Michael Bootes, a priest from Brighton whom he already knew, to become Vicar of Lundwood and help with diocesan communications. Bootes had trained as a BBC engineer, moved into production, become ordained and worked as a freelance broadcaster while serving a series of small parishes. He edited *See Link* for twelve years. Ashley Ellis, who became the Diocesan Secretary in 2000, edited *See Link* for its final years.

From March 1993, *See Link* was complemented by *The Spark*, a quarterly newspaper designed to be handed out in churches rather than inserted in their magazines. It was created by Ian Byfield, a journalist who had become acquainted with Roy Clements, then Vicar of St Matthew's, Rastrick, when Byfield was the editor of the *Brighouse Echo*. Byfield had extensive experience working for newspapers within the diocese, as the arts editor for the *Halifax Courier*, and as deputy editor/news editor, and then chief sub-editor, of the *Wakefield Express*. When Clements became the Diocesan Communications Officer in 1984, he invited Byfield to join the Diocesan Communications Group. He was involved in the centenary celebrations in 1988 and edited the anniversary book. In 1993, Byfield became the Communications Officer himself. The first journalist to hold the post, Byfield responded when a new communications tool was sought, by devising *The Spark*. He wrote, designed and laid it out in a tabloid style, trying to maintain a newspaper feel despite the time-lapse between issues. He undertook other public relations work for the diocese, including dealing with the press at the first ordination service for women at the cathedral in 1994 and the ordination there as a priest in 1995 of the son of Archbishop George Carey. Mark Carey was serving at the time as a curate at Christ Church, South Ossett. Byfield was involved in organizing and running the first conference, at Chester, for the northern diocesan Communications Officers, and visited parochial church councils to give advice on communications. The last issue of *The Spark* was for the winter quarter of 1995.

Byfield's successor in the creation of a diocesan newspaper was another professional journalist but this time one who had been ordained as a deacon. Catherine Ogle had served in the Ripon Diocese in 1988–91 as a curate at Middleton St Mary. She was then invited to take up the ecumenical position of Religious Affairs editor at BBC Radio Leeds. It was a full-time position in which she was given a thorough training in journalism, working with a news agenda across all the Radio Leeds output and, in particular, for the Sunday breakfast programme. Once it became possible for women to be ordained as priests and for her to fulfil what she felt called to do, she hoped to find a parish. She was invited by Bishop McCulloch to take a newly created post which combined the position of Vicar of Woolley with that of editor of the diocesan newspaper. Now named *Outlook*, this was first issued in March 1996. Like *The Spark*, it came out on a quarterly basis. Ogle took the pictures, wrote most of the copy, and learned how to desk-top publish. Roy Clements and Bishop Robinson read the proofs for what she termed 'sensitivity alert' before the paper was printed at the offices of the *Barnsley Chronicle*. When Ogle moved to become Vicar of Huddersfield in 2001, *Outlook* came to an end. Ogle became the Dean of Birmingham in 2010.

Both *See Link* and *Outlook* were replaced in February 2002 by *Flame*. The name was chosen by Bishop McCulloch when it became clear that clergy wanted to retain the Flame logo which had been designed for the centenary celebrations. *Flame*, which came out monthly, was the same size as the *Wakefield Diocesan News* and *See Link* and was designed to be sold to parishes at £5.75p per hundred copies. Its first editor was David Brighton who was working in the communications field for the Diocese of Ripon and Leeds. Brighton was supplied with the content by the Diocesan Communications Committee. He was succeeded in March 2003 by Ashley Ellis, returning for another editorial stint.

Yet another change occurred in April 2004, at Bishop Platten's instigation, with *Flame* replaced by a bi-monthly paper, *Awake,* edited first by Anthony Howe who was both Bishop's Chaplain and Communications Officer. Howe worked with an editorial group which included Robert Cockcroft, editor of the *Barnsley Chronicle,* Catherine Ogle and James Greenfield, a sub-editor with the *Yorkshire Post*. Greenfield undertook the design, producing print-ready copy. The paper had eight pages, was A4 in size and had colour photographs. When Michael Rawson succeeded Howe as the Bishop's Chaplain in 2004, he inherited the editorship, working again with Cockcroft and Greenfield. The editorial group that met before each issue was finalized then included Jonathan Greener and Ashley Ellis. In the summer of 2007, Sally Codman joined the group as the part-time Diocesan Communications Officer. Codman was a professional journalist who had begun her career on the *Dewsbury Reporter*. She served for many years on the *Huddersfield Daily Examiner.* When she joined the diocesan team she was working for Kirklees Council as the Features Editor of the Kirklees Recorder *Talking News,* a digest for blind and partially sighted people of the seven local papers in the Kirklees area. Shortly after she came, she assumed further responsibility for *Awake* and by 2008 it was being produced by Greenfield and herself. Codman left to become overall News and Features Editor for *Talking News.* In 2012, this was distributed in the form of CDs, tapes, and as a podcast.

The turnaround project at Lundwood brought contact with Jane Bower, the producer for Channel 4's *Priest Idol* series and thus brought another professional journalist to the *Awake* editorial desk. Bower had been a crime reporter with the *Yorkshire Evening Post* and later a Chief Reporter with the *Yorkshire Post,* before spending ten years as a television producer. She came to the diocese in the winter of 2008, as the Communications Adviser and editor of *Awake,* on a three-day-a-week basis, allowing her time to continue writing for radio and television. Recognizing that a bi-monthly paper could not carry 'news', she relaunched *Awake* with the summer issue of 2009 as a meatier 12-page quarterly colour magazine. Her aim was to provide articles that would support mission in many ways, reflecting the varied life of the diocese, sharing good practice and helping to foster the sense of being one active family. For a time Bower was assisted by Jenny Lowery as part of her mission and evangelism work for the diocese.

In 2012 *Awake* was written and edited in-house but laid out and printed in Leeds.

Sharing ideas and thoughts on the bigger projects beyond her responsibility for *Awake,* Bower was working in 2012 with the Diocesan Communications Group.

Bibliography

Advisory Group on Full-time Theological Training (1992), *Theological Training: A Way Ahead*, Church House Publishing.

Bancroft, Harry, Asa Briggs and Eric Treacy (1948), *One Hundred Years: The Parish of Keighley 1848–1948*, The Rydal Press.

Blackmore, Henrietta (2007), *The Beginning of Women's Ministry: The revival of the deaconess in the nineteenth-century Church of England*, Church of England Record Society 14, Boydell Press.

Carless, Frank (reprint, 1988), *William Walsham How 1823–1897: The first Bishop of Wakefield*, F. Carless.

Chandler, Andrew (2006), *The Church of England in the Twentieth Century*, Boydell Press.

Commissioners appointed by the Right Reverend the Lord Bishop of Wakefield (1890), *The Report*, Diocese of Wakefield.

Commissioners appointed by the Archbishop of Canterbury (1985), *Faith in the City: a Call for Action by Church and Nation*, Church House Publishing.

Dale, W. L. (1946), *The Law of the Parish Church*, Butterworth and Co.

Donne, William (1908), *Wakefield Cathedral in the Making 1897–1908* (n.p.).

Dransfield, John N. (1906), *History of Penistone*, The Don Press.

Foulkes, Simon, Christine Smith and Anne Wood (2003), *Turnaround Teams*, Grove Books.

Foundation Member (1964), *Fulfilled in Joy: The Order of the Holy Paracleet, Whitby, and its Foundress Mother Margaret*, Hodder and Stoughton.

Foster, Barbara, et al. (eds) (2011), *St Hilda's Church 1911–2011: 100 Years of Faith, Hope and Love* (n.p.).

Furlong, Monica (2000), *The C of E: The state it's in*, SPCK.

Giles, Richard (2004), *Re-Pitching the Tent*, third edition, Canterbury Press.

Green, Simon J. D. (1996), *Religion in the Age of Decline: Organisation and Experience in Industrial Yorkshire 1870–1920*, Cambridge University Press.

Hall, M. Penelope and Ismene V. Howes (1965), *The Church in Social Work: A Study of the Moral Welfare Work undertaken by the Church of England*, Routledge and Kegan Paul.

Hampson, Michael (2006), *Last Rites: The End of the Church of England*, Granta Books.

Hansen, Astrid (1994), *One Small Corner: a History of Bradford Diocese*, The Bradford Diocesan Board of Finance.

Hargreaves, John (1992), *The Church of England in late-Victorian Halifax 1852–1914*, Halifax Antiquarian Society.

BIBLIOGRAPHY

How, F. D. (1898), *Bishop Walsham How: A Memoir*, Ibister.

Jackson, Bob (2002), *Hope for the Church: Contemporary strategies for growth*, Church House Publishing.

Jagger, Peter J. (1978), *A History of the Parish and People Movement*, The Faith Press.

Jones, Bill (2008), *Shoulder to Shoulder: The Making of the Mara Link*.

Keily, Pamela (1986), *Memoirs: Haphazard Recollections of a Lifetime of Religious Drama*, Smith Settle.

King, T. G. (1973), *Readers: A Pioneer Ministry*, The Central Readers' Board.

Leach, John (2009), *Renewing Charismatic Worship*, Grove Books.

Lloyd, Roger (1966), *The Church of England 1900–1965*, SCM Press.

McCaslin, Patrick and Michael G. Lawler (1986), *Sacrament of Service: A Vision of the Permanent Diaconate Today*, Paulist Press.

Marchant, James, et al. (1926), *The Future of the Church of England*, Longmans Green and Co.

Marshall, Rob (2004), *Hope the Archbishop: a Portrait*, Continuum.

Middleton, Richard A. (2006), *The Church at Dewsbury: A History of the Ancient Parish of Dewsbury*, third edition, Richard A. Middleton.

Morrish, P. S. (1994), 'Leeds and the Dismemberment of the Diocese of Ripon', Thoresby Society Second Series, Leeds.

Palmer, Bernard (2003), *Serving Two Masters: Parish Patronage in the Church of England since 1714*, The Book Guild.

Paul, Leslie (1964), *The Deployment and Payment of the Clergy*, Church Information Office.

Pearson, Geoff (2005), *Towards the Conversion of England*, Grove Books.

Peart-Binns, John (1980), *Eric Treacy*, Ian Allan.

Peart-Binns, John (2007), *Gordon Fallows of Sheffield*, The Memoir Club.

Pigou, Frances (1898), *Phases of My Life*, second edition, Edward Arnold.

Platten, Stephen (2007), *Vocation: Singing the Lord's Song*, SPCK.

Rogers, Canon T. Guy (1931), *The Church and the People: Problems of Reunion, Sex and Marriage, Women's Ministry etc.*, Sampson Low, Marston & Co.

Slater, Terry (2005), *A Century of Celebrating Christ: The Diocese of Birmingham, 1905–2005*, Phillimore.

Speak, Harold and Jean Forrester (1981), *For All the Saints: An Outline History and Guide to The Cathedral Church of All Saints, Wakefield*, self published.

Straton, Norman (1888), *The Wakefield Bishopric Movement*, Elliot Stock.

Swain, E. P., ed. (1939), *Bishop Seaton of Wakefield: Addresses and a Memoir*, SPCK.

Vaughan, Patrick (1987), 'Non-Stipendiary Ministry in the Church of England', unpublished PhD thesis.

Walker, J. W. (1934), *Wakefield its History and its People*, The West Yorkshire Printing Company.

Wassell, Joyce (2009), *A History of Airedale with Fryston and a Guide to Holy Cross Church*, Pen2Print.

Welsby, Paul (1984), *A History of the Church of England 1945–1980*, Oxford University Press.

Whittle, Tyler (1985), *Solid Joys and Lasting Treasure: An historical companion to many favourite hymns*, Ross Anderson Publications.

Wilkinson, Alan (1992), *The Community of the Resurrection: A Centenary History*, SCM Press.
Yelton, Michael (2006), *Alfred Hope Patten and the Shrine of our Lady of Walsingham*, Canterbury Press.
New DAWM Two: Women in Ministry 2008 Report, P Church & Society, Liverpool Diocese.

Issues of the *Wakefield Diocesan Gazette*, the *Wakefield Diocesan News*, the *Cathedral Magazine*, *The Times*, the *Yorkshire Post*, the *Wakefield Herald*, the *Wakefield Express*, the *Halifax Courier*, the *Huddersfield Examiner*.

Index

Accra, Bishop of 88
Ackworth 66, 192, 197
Adair, Ray 82
Additional Curates Society 148
Adelaide 109, 191
Adult Education Officer 150
Advisory Board for Redundant Churches 224
Advisory Council for the Church's Ministry 131-2
Agbrigg 182
Age Concern 188-9
Aglen, Elizabeth Sarah 92, 101, 121
Airedale 32; High School 133
Airedale with Fryston 32-3, 75, 133
Akroyd, Edward 47, 227
Akroydon 227
Alberius, Anders Bertil 177
Alford, John 151
All God's Children 158
All Souls Haley Hill Preservation Trust 226
Allen, John 153, 184
Allen, Roland 131
Allendale, Lord 29, 52
Allison, James 190
Almondbury 160, 167, 192, 197, 204-5, 216, 219; High School 143
Almondbury with Farnley Tyas 189, 219
Alpha Course 104, 141
Alternative Service Book 149
Altofts 182
Alverthorpe 31, 92, 152, 170
Ampleforth Abbey 177
Ancient Monuments Society 226
Anderson, Norman 224

Andrew, David 137, 140
Anglican Accredited Lay Workers Federation 129
Anglican Communion 58, 190
Anglican Covenant 119
Anglican-Methodist Covenant 97, 119, 144, 176
Anglican-Roman Catholic 168, 173
Anglo-Catholic xvi, 10, 36, 47-52, 63, 90, 93, 105-7, 121, 123, 126-8, 137, 191-3, 195-6, 198, 212
Anglo-Methodist Unity 114-5, 119
Anniversary, golden 55-6; ninetieth xv, 146; centenary 190, 233-4; 125th xi, 125, 164, 166, 210, 231
Apostolic Church, The 89, 90
Apsley 160
Archbishop Holgate Hospital 66, 138, 158, 193
Armitage Bridge 43, 143, 145, 171-2, 204, 220
Armley 10
Armley Gaol 34
Armytage, Lady 40
Armytage, George 29
ARP 70
Ashton, Mary 42
Asian Christians 111
Athersley 76, 78, 188, 207
Australia 87, 191
Auxiliary Pastoral Ministry 131-3
Awake 234-5

Back to Church Sunday 104
Badsworth 53, 182
Bailiff Bridge 27

Baker, Donald 193–4
Baker, Hugh 189
Bamford, Geoffrey 137
Bamford, Marion 128
Bands of Hope 43
Baptist Church/Baptists 97, 108, 145, 162, 173, 176–7, 186, 193
Baptist Church of Georgia 177
Barber, W. S. 224
Barclay's Bank 208
Barkisland 126
Barnett, Anne 122
Barnsley 6, 8, 24, 28, 31, 44, 45, 51–2, 55, 64, 66, 68, 76–8, 96, 109, 115, 120, 125, 153, 171, 177, 183, 87, 194, 212, 215, 219, 222; Exodus Project 153; Labour Party 183; Rescue house 45; shelter 44
Barnsley Chronicle 234
Barrow in Furness 109
Basingstoke, Bishop Suffragan of 106
Basutoland, Diocese of 87
Bath and Wells, Diocese of 63
Batley 6, 43, 51, 86, 93, 141, 190, 206–7, 217, 221, 224
Batley Carr 217
Battie-Wrightson, Robert 53
Battyeford 35, 48, 70, 115, 190
Baxter, David 155
BBC 86, 106–7, 233–4; Radio Leeds 234; Radio Sheffield 142
Beacroft-Mitchell, Jo 165
Beaumont, Stuart 206
Beaumont, Wentworth Blackett 51
Bedale 42
Bede Home 9
Bedford, Bishop of 8, 110
Belgium 102
Bell, Brian 197
Bell, Maurice 32
Belle Vue 182
Bevan, Kenneth 193
Beverley, Bishop of 127
Beverley, C. B. 232
Biafra 114
Bible Study 85, 104, 114–15, 117, 141, 186
Bickersteth, Robert 1, 5

Bielby, Jonathan 155, 211
Biggard, Frank 37
Bingley 42
Birchencliffe 218
Birkby 30, 143, 217–18
Birkenshaw 50, 75–6, 137, 140, 207
Birmingham 61, 124, 183; Cathedral 124; Dean of 234
Birstall 7, 55, 93, 126
Bishop of Wakefield's Spiritual Aid Fund 17, 20
Bishop's Adviser on Community Relations 179; Adviser for Deliverance and Healing 194; Centenary Fund 152, 179, 204; Chaplain 39, 138, 234; Chaplain in Evangelism 159
Bishop's Lodge xi, xiii, 17, 79, 100, 108
Bishopgarth 11, 16–17, 22, 29, 56, 79
Bishoprics Act 1, 4
Bishop's breakfasts 109
Bishopthorpe 164, 175
Black, William 68
Blackburn, Bishop of 55; Diocese of 8, 133
Blackmoorfoot 118
Blackmore, David 161
Blair, James 38
Blinco, Joe 90
Bodley, George Frederick 26
Bolton, Bishop of 149
Bootes, Michael 233
Bournemouth 61, 106
Bower, Jane 235
Box, Linda Mary 130
Boyd Carpenter, William 5, 15
Boys' Brigade 68
Bradford 140, 175, 230; Bishop of 110, 155, 229; Diocese of 8, 91, 105, 120, 133, 153, 230–1
Bradley 226
Bradnum, Margaret 121, 126, 134–5, 137
Bradshaw 52, 197, 216
Bramley Trust 226
Branch, Clarence 79
Bray, Mary 27; Hannah 27

INDEX

Bryanwood 178
Bread, not Stones 151-3, 166, 176, 185
Brereton, John Lloyd 24
Bretton Hall 51, 172
Bretton Hall College of Education 102, 172, 193
Brighouse 6, 19, 26, 42, 52, 60, 133, 158, 179, 219
Brighouse Echo 233
Brighouse and Rastrick Band 85
Bristol 61-2, 88; Cathedral 13
British and Foreign Bible Society 87
British Council of Churches 169, 175, 181
British Empire 97
British Expeditionary Force 61
British Legion 113, 188
British National Party 167
British Trust for Conservation Volunteers 188
Broadhurst, John 67
Broadmoor 194
Brook, Charles 52
Brooke, Joshua Ingham 5. 9. 15. 26
Brooke, William 52
Browell, Maureen 189
Brown, Robin 150
Brumpton, John Charles Kenyon 115
Bruntcliffe 23, 126, 220
Bryanwood 178
Buchanan, Stephanie 190
Bullimore, Christine 125, 136
Bullimore, John 224
Bullimore, Matthew 190, 177
Bullivant, Ronald 117
Bulmer, William 207
Burge, Richard 165
Burnley, Bishop of 55
Burton, Lewis 175-6
Butler, Josephine 210
Butterworth, Gill 129
Butterworth, Frank 92
Butterworth, Joseph 69
Byfield, Ian 233
Byram, Angela 165

Calder, River 1, 65, 201
Calderdale 120, 178, 186, 130; Ecumenical Housing Association 186; Hospice 148
Call to the North 144-5, 168
Call to Worship and Witness 72, 89
Cambridge 5, 9, 32, 53, 61-3, 211
Canada 68, 87
Cannon Hall 51, 164
Canon Missioner 54, 72, 141-2, 160, 165, 167, 197
Canon Parochial 96
Canterbury 9, 98; Archbishop of 12, 29, 47, 62, 106, 109, 151, 155, 160, 168, 184, 189, 195, 205; Province of 127
Canterbury Pilgrim Players 98
Capetown, Bishop of 37
Carbutt, Ron 152
Cardigan, Countess of 51
Carey, George 233
Carey, Mark 233
Carlecote 218
Carleton 69, 216
Carlinghow 93
Carlton 66, 76
Carnegy, Patrick Charles Alexander 58
Carter Charity 51
Cashmore, Thomas Herbert 89
Castleford 31-2, 43, 66-7, 69, 92, 96, 101, 115, 183, 220, 228-9; Women's Centre 183
Cater, Derek 96
Cathedral, Wakefield 2, 4, 6, 10, 11-14, 18, 19, 20, 23, 31, 34, 39, 49, 50, 54, 55, 56, 70, 71, 74, 75, 83, 85, 87, 90, 92, 93, 96, 101, 109, 120, 122, 126, 128, 130, 136, 146, 149, 150, 155, 157, 158, 162, 163, 166, 174, 177, 184, 187, 191, 192, 194, 196, 197, 198, 199, 207-12, 233; bells 73-4, 83; Boys' School 56, 94; Centre 210; choir 54, 101, 191, 209; Development Fund 207; rood screen 93; School 94, 118, 150; Sustentation Fund 20
Cathedral Magazine 10, 50, 93
Cathedrals Measure 15, 96, 209
Cavell, Edith 102

Centurion, HMS 87–8
Chamberlain, Bernard 149, 179–80, 193
Chancellor, Lord 51
Channel Islands 72
Chantry Chapel of St Mary the Virgin 65, 116, 197–8, 209
Chapelthorpe 50, 79, 101
Charismatic Movement/Renewal 104, 109, 147, 150, 156, 175, 191–3, 195, 199
Chatfield, Albert 65
Chelmsford 110; Bishop of 160
Chequerfield 78, 228
Chester 34, 233; Bishop of 55, 155; deanery synod 161; Diocese of 133
Chesters, Jennie 184
Chevet, Deanery of 118, 221
Chevet Hall 159
Chichester 159; Bishop of 62
Chickenley Heath 25, 135
Children's Adviser, Diocesan 141
Children's Special Service Mission 105
China 193
Choppards Mission Church 204
Chorlton-cum-Hardy 127
Chota Nagpur, Diocese of 114
Chrism Eucharist 104, 196
Christ Our Light 158, 162–3, 166, 171, 206
Christadelphians 97
Christian Aid 88, 114, 175
Christian Pakistani 181
Christian Parity Group 124
Christian Scientists 97
Christian Stewardship 58–9, 148–50, 165–6, 168
Church Army 39, 44–6, 66, 72, 89, 92, 115, 133, 143, 148
Church Assembly 21, 59, 60, 73, 92, 103, 118, 123, 131
Church Association 47, 50
Church Commissioners 77–9, 103, 158, 165, 214, 221–2, 224, 226
Church in the Eighties, The 120, 146–51, 166, 179
Church in Wales 19, 191
Church Lads Brigade 31, 43, 55, 232

Church Lite 142
Church of England Children's Society 183; Education Committee 10; Liturgical Commission 109; Men's Society 40, 70, 148; Schools Council 62; Society for Waifs and Strays 9; Temperance Society 43, 232; Zenana Missionary Society 38, 87–8
Church of Ireland 191
Church Missionary Society 38, 87
Church Times 185
Church Urban Fund 88, 107, 162, 179, 184, 186–7, 202
Churches Conservation Trust 222, 227
Churches Council of Healing 194
Churches Together in Britain and Ireland 169–70, 177
Churches Together in Wakefield 176
Churches Unity Commission 168
Civil Defence 70
Clare, Charlotte 189
Claremount 170, 196
Clark's Brewery 188
Clarke, David 140
Clarkson, George William 64, 84
Clayton West 96, 98, 193, 220
Cleckheaton 26, 152
Clements, Roy 154, 160, 189–90, 233–4
Clergy Training, Director of 137
Clerk of the Closet to the Queen 62
Clifton 7, 90, 219
Cluny 197
Cobb, Mark 189
Cockcroft, Robert 234
Codman, Sally 234–5
Coggan, Donald 144
Coggins, Glenn 169, 177
Cole, Brian 169
Coles, Vincent Stuckey Stratton 49
Coles, William Henry 23
Coley 30, 173
College of the Resurrection 36, 63, 123, 128, 133, 142, 165, 211
Collison, Christopher 149, 232
Colonial and Continental Church Society 88

INDEX

Common Worship 141
Communications Group, Diocesan 235
Community Industry 182
Community of the Resurrection,
   Mirfield 7, 19, 34–5, 39–40, 48, 50,
   54, 56, 70–1, 84, 86, 90, 99, 127,
   131, 148–9, 155, 158, 165, 173, 179,
   193–4, 196, 210
Community of St Mary the Virgin,
   Wantage 207
Community of St Peter, Horbury 7,
   34–5, 37, 44, 46, 128, 148, 150,
   158, 178
Community of St Peter Chains,
   Manchester 35
Community of the Holy Paraclete,
   Whitby 34, 37, 194
Community Relations, Bishop's Advisor
   on 179–80; Officer 180
Comper, Ninian 93
Coney, Harold Robert Harvey 86
Confirmation 1, 16, 40–1, 60, 66,
   70–1, 116, 133, 158, 163, 192, 232
Confraternity of the Blessed
   Sacrament 197
Congregational Church 97, 174
Congregationalism 112, 184
Conrad, Mr 76
Cooper, Arthur 69
Coote, Roderic Norman 87
Copley 47, 169, 227
Cornholme 27, 51, 137, 203
Cottrell, Stephen 159–62
Coventry Cathedral 97
Counselling, Advanced Diploma in 136
Cowcliffe 217–18
Cowperthwaite, John 116
Cragg Vale 134, 219
Craig-Wild, Dorothy (Dhoe) 126
Cranmer Hall, Durham 161
Craston, Colin 192
Craven, Archdeacon of 1;
   Archdeaconry of 6–7
Credit Union 188
Croft, Steven 159–60, 162
Crofton 6, 72, 115, 197
Cromer Convention 61
Crosland Moor 25, 51, 67, 87, 174

Crosland, Joseph 25
Cross Stone 101, 227
Cross, Richard Assheton 4
Crowe, Effie 74
Cuddesdon 10
Cuddesdon Theological College 10,
   108, 134
Cudworth 70, 93, 117
Cumberworth 52, 65
Cursillo 197–8
Cusworth Hall 53

Dad's Army 107
Daily Offices 113
Daily Telegraph 157
Dale, Alison 66
Daly, John Charles Sydney 32, 56, 75
Darrington 219
Dartmouth, Earl of 23, 29
Darton 31, 51, 195
Davidson, Randall 29
Davies, Peter 148
Daw Green 7, 84
Dawson, George 69
Dawtry, Anne 127
Deaconess Committee 129
Deaconesses 41–3, 66. 92, 101, 120–2,
   124, 126, 133–4, 169; Order of 122
Dearing, Trevor 195
Deliverance 194–5; Bishop's Adviser
   for 195
Denby Dale 65
Derby, Lord 53
Development Education Officer 175
Dewsbury 5–7, 20, 25, 43, 45, 55,
   84–5, 101, 148, 180, 185, 201,
   224, 228; Gospel Church 224;
   Minster 153, 168, 189, 201–2; team
   parish 217
Dewsbury Reporter 234
Dilapidations, Diocesan Board 21, 71
Diocesan
   Advisory Committee 200;
   Chancellor 18, 200, 203;
   Conference 3, 5, 10, 18–19, 21, 37,
   48, 58–9, 71, 95, 97, 103, 118, 232;
   Pastoral Committee 81, 212,
   215–16, 218, 220, 222–3;

243

Registrar 13, 18, 23, 130, 219;
Reorganization Committee 73
Dioceses' Commission xi, 168, 211, 229
Distinctive Diaconate 129
Dodson, Peter 150
Dodworth 93, 183
Dolan, Mary 177
Donne, William 7, 13, 15, 43, 55
Dover, Bishop of 9
Dransfield, John 47
Drighlington 6, 207
Durham 9, 32; Bishop of 9, 55; Cathedral 32, 124; Diocese of 99
Dykes, Frederick 47
Dykes, John Bacchus 47

Earey, Mark 165
Easdale, Robert Geoffrey 77–8
East Ardsley 69, 207
East Bierley 76
East Hardwick 215
East Knottingley 66
Eastern Orthodox Church 63
Eastmoor Estate 76, 116, 228
Eastthorpe 220, 224
Ebbsfleet, Bishop of 127
Ecclesiastical Commissioners 2, 3, 7, 15–17, 25, 82
Ecumenical Affairs, Adviser for 169; Archbishop's Secretary for 109
Ecumenical Canons 177, 209; Centre, Woodhall 179; Chaplaincy Centre 174; Commission (Roman Catholic) 173; Council, West Yorkshire 175, Housing Association, Calderdale 186; Officer 173, 175
Ecumenical Review 97
Ecumenical Society of the Blessed Virgin Mary 177
Ede, William Moore 19
Eden, Constance Mary 13
Eden, George Rodney 8–9. 10, 13, 16, 19, 22–3, 25–6, 28–31, 35–6, 38, 40, 42, 44, 48, 52, 54, 56, 59–60, 62, 92
Edinburgh 34
Edinburgh, Bishop of 134; Duke of 58

Edmondson, Christopher 134, 149–50
Education
 Act 1870 19; Act, 1944 60, 73, 95, 131; Church Assembly Council of 60; Committee, Diocesan 89; Department of 95; Diocesan Board of 17, 18, 148; Diocesan Director of 130; Diocesan Officer for 149; Diocesan Society 19, 20; Diocesan Director of 130; Diocesan Officer for 149; Ministry of 96; Parish Adviser for 127
Edwards, Henry 2–3
Egerton, Frederick 66
Eggborough Methodist Church 170
Egypt, Bishop of 157
El Salvador 188
Electoral Roll 21, 41, 66, 114
Elizabeth II, Queen 58, 62, 210
Eliot, Thomas Stearns 101
Elland 26, 48, 49, 66–7, 132, 158, 174, 217
Ellis, Ashley 233–4
Ellis, Bryan 150, 193
Ely, Diocese of 229
Emley 51, 74, 86, 193, 207, 220
Emmaus Course 161, 171
Emmerson, Ralph 150
English Heritage 205
Ennis, Lesley 137
Environment, Department of 73
Episcopal Visitor 127, 129, 196
Erringden 219
Established Church xv, xvi, 45, 57, 90, 120, 184
Estonia 191
European Union 184
Evangelism, Adviser in 134, 150; Bishop's chaplain in 159; Decade of 104, 108, 110, 158; National Officer for 159; Parish Adviser for 141, 160
Evans, Stan 152
Everyday God 165
Exorcism 194–5

Faisalabad, Bishop of 191; Diocese of 109, 111, 190–1, 200

INDEX

Faith in the City (1985) 104, 107, 137, 151, 155, 157, 169, 179, 184–5, 188, 199, 214, 223
Fallows, William Gordon 109
Family Life and Marriage (FLAME) 126, 186
Family Welfare Council, Diocesan 104, 178
Farnley Tyas 20, 189, 216, 219
Farrer, Harriet Louisa 34
Featherstone 53, 90, 174, 220
Felkirk 72, 89, 93
Fellowship of Marriage 68
Fellowship of St Sergius and St Alban 63
Fellowship of Vocation 89
Fellowship of Worship and Witness 72
Ferguson, Robert 182
Ferry Fryston 79–80
Festival of Britain 1951 86
Finance, Diocesan Board of 19–21, 130
Finland 191
Finney, John Thornley 110, 151, 159, 160, 162
Fire Guards 70
First World War 30, 35, 37, 39, 40–1
Fisher, Gordon 133
Fitzwilliam 78
Fitzwilliam, Earl 9
Fixby 76–7, 98, 217–18
Flack, John 192
Flame 234
Fletcher, David 189
Flockton 50–1, 220
Foljambe, E. W. S. 52
Folkestone 34
Ford, Peter 183
Forshaw, Oliver 80
Forsyth, J. Nesfield 13
Foster, Toby 142
Foulkes, Simon 141, 160
Four Square Gospellers 69
Fowler, C. Hodgson 27–8
Franciscans 108
Free Churches 90, 96–7, 145, 168–9, 179
Freedom from Hunger Appeal 101

Freeman, Robert 165–6
Freemasonry 61, 65, 113
Frere, Walter Howard 19, 36–7, 54, 131
Fresh Expressions 104, 143, 197
Fryston 32, 133
Fryston Hall 79–80

Gaisford, John 127
Gallagher, Liam 185
Gambia, Bishop of 32, 56, 75, 87; Diocese of 11, 32, 55, 68
Garbett, Cyril 59, 85–6
Garfield Weston Foundation 211
Gartside, Oswin 212
Gaskell, Charles George Milnes 29
Gaskell family 222
Gaskell, Ian 183, 188–9
Gaskell's School 107
Gawber 114–15, 194–5
Gawthorpe 25, 135, 167, 207
Genders, Anselm 127, 196
Georgia 109, 191
Georgia (SA), Bishop of 75
Georgia, Bishop of Baptist Church of 164
Germany 96, 191
Gibson, Abraham 80
Gildersome 130, 169, 186–7
Giles, Richard 154, 191, 202–4, 206
Gill, Philip 195, 208
Gill, William Henry 2
Girls' Friendly Society 22, 31, 55, 66, 98, 101, 232
Glasshoughton 93, 220
Golcar 203
Goldthorpe, Shirley 122
Gomersal 52, 207
Goole 87
Gore, Charles 35, 50, 210
Graham, Billy 90
Graham, Nicholas 99
Grahamstown 62
Gray, Angela (Kit) 122
Gray, James 69
Greaves, Alfred Ernest 93
Green, Edward 29
Green, Pamela 130

Green, Sydney F. 47
Greenbelt Festival 167
Greener, Jonathan 128, 142, 165, 234
Greener, Pamela 211
Greenfield, James 234-5
Greenhead College 143
Greenman, Irene 137
Greenwood Lee 80
Gribben, John 196
Griffin, Keith 189-90
Grimethorpe 52-3, 113, 155, 183
Grimethorpe Colliery Band 183
Group Ministries xv, 79, 104, 117, 129, 137, 212-17, 220, 222
Group Rhodes 211
Grundy, Thomas 43
Guides, Girl 55, 68
Guild of St Raphael 193-4
Guildford Cathedral, Dean of 64
Guiver, George 165

Haigh, Nicholas 143
Haileybury 63
Haley Hill 47, 66, 216, 226-7
Halifax 1-7, 25-6, 28-30, 41, 44, 48, 50-2, 66, 69-70, 81-2, 87, 92-3, 96, 109-10, 120, 122, 134-5, 141, 148, 150, 165, 170, 174, 176-82, 185, 197-8, 200, 202, 206, 216-7, 220, 224, 226-7 220, 224, 226-7; Archdeacon of 7-9, 55, 64, 105, 131, 151; Minster 4; War Hospital 41
Halifax Courier 3, 233
Halifax, Lord 30
Hall Croft 15, 36
Hallam, Diocese of (RC) 177
Hallett, David 218
Halling, Bill 189
Handley, Dennis 189
Hanging Heaton 114-15, 170, 221
Hannam, Stephen 140
Hare, Richard 106, 109-10, 124, 133-4, 155, 169, 173, 192, 195
Harewood, Earl 29
Harley Wood 27, 101, 215
Harringay Arena 90
Harris, Cedric 115

Harrison, Ian 149, 173, 175
Harrogate 161
Hartley, Cyril 193
Hartshead 7
Harvey, Richard Charles Musgrave 23, 46, 55
Hawley, Anthony 184
Hawley, John 201
Healing Ministry 141, 186, 193-6
Heath 16
Hebden Bridge 220
Heckmondwike 17, 24, 26, 66, 207, 225
Hellawell, Keith 188
Hemsworth 7, 38, 53, 66, 115, 148, 197
Helme 27
Heptonstall 6, 80-1, 155, 203, 220
Hepworth 219
Hepworth Wakefield 109
Hereford, Bishop of 63, 75
Heritage Lottery Fund 211
Herne (Ruhrgebiet) 109
Hickleton Hall 89
Higgins, Godrey 193
High Hoyland 193, 226
Hightown 31, 220
Hill, John Brown 49
Hinchliffe Mill 171
Hirst, Edwin 10
Hitch, Nathaniel 14
Hoare, A. H. 30
Hodgkin, Alice 169
Hofbauer, Andrea (Andi) 126
Hoggard, Jean 125
Holmbridge 86, 93, 171, 219
Holme 27
Holme Moss TV Station 86
Holmes, John 141-2, 160, 165, 167
Holmfield 186, 216
Holmfirth 6, 171, 198, 204, 219
Home Guard 70
Homelessness Officer 185
Hone, Campbell Richard xvi, 8, 16, 42, 53, 55, 59-60, 63-6, 71-3, 75, 82, 85, 87, 105
Hone, Evelyn 59
Hope, Anne 107

INDEX

Hope, David Michael 107–8, 110, 124–5, 130, 135–7, 151–2, 154–5, 157, 164, 175–6, 183–4, 186, 197, 202–3, 206, 217, 219, 223, 233
Hope Hospital 45
Hope-Urwin, Mark 168
Hopkins, Noel T 50, 60, 71, 75, 91, 93–4
Horbury 7, 25, 34–5, 37, 40, 44, 46, 49, 55, 84–5, 95, 116, 128, 179, 197, 217; School 160; Bridge 34, 51, 84, 114–16, 217; Junction 25, 34, 84, 116, 154, 182
Horne, William Francis Lovell 13
Hostel of the Resurrection, Leeds 99
House of Bishops 21, 109, 124, 134, 196, 211
House of Clergy 21, 122–3, 125, 128–9
House of Laity 21, 92, 119, 122–3, 125, 128, 224
House of Lords 10, 52, 60, 109
House of Mercy, Horbury 35, 40, 44, 95, 178
Hove Edge 27, 219
How, Edith 22
How, Henry Walsham 9, 36, 40
How, William Walsham 3, 8–9, 11–18, 22, 24–9, 31, 36, 39, 51, 60, 64, 155, 207, 226
Howard, John 193
Howe, Anthony 234
Hoylandswaine 51, 189, 230
Huddersfield 3, 6–8, 25, 33, 40, 43, 45–6, 51–2, 66, 70, 76, 82, 86–7, 91, 97, 107, 109, 123, 142, 155, 162, 164, 176–81, 185, 191, 199, 202–5, 208, 210, 216, 220, 227, 234; Archdeacon of 7–8, 55; Corporation 52, 82, 86; Council of Churches 97, 181; Episcopal area 230; football ground 155; George Hotel 142; Labour Home 43; Methodist Mission 143; Polytechnic 82, 174; Technical College 82; Town Hall 86, 160; University 109
Hull, Bishop of 55

Hume, Cardinal Basil 183
Humphrey, Betty 121
Humphrey, George 121
Hunsworth 75, 137, 140
Hunter, John 101–2
Hunter, John Gaunt 144

Iceland 191
Illingworth 77, 94, 121, 200, 215–17
Industrial Christian Fellowship 88
Ingamells, Harold 117, 149–50, 192
Investing in our Faith 164–6
Inwood, Richard 110
Islam xv, 179, 224

Jackson, Bob 143, 168
Jagger, Peter 91
Jamaica 87
James, Colin Clement Walter xv, 103, 106–7, 110, 123, 134–6, 146–51, 154, 173–4, 179–81, 183–4, 192, 196–7, 208, 214, 216, 224
James, David Charles 110, 191
James, Eric Arthur 157
Japan 38
Jaray, Tess 209
Jarrett, Martyn 127, 129
Jarrow, Bishop of 55, 63, 99
Jennings, Anne 126, 128
Jerusalem and the East Mission 87–8
Jerusalem Trust 142
Johannesburg, Archdeacon of 10
John Paul II, Pope 169
Jones, Bill 180, 190–1
Jones, Peter 208
Joppa 34
Jubb, William 116
Judaism 179
Judkins, Mary 165
Julian of Norwich 198
Julian Meetings 198

Keily, Pamela 98–102, 148
Kellington 53, 121, 124, 170
Kelly, Stephen 233
Kensit, John 48
Kensitites 48–9
Kent, Duke of 210

Kenya, Christian Council of 122
Kenyan High Commission 157
Keresforth Hall 28
Kettlethorpe Estate 182
Kettlethorpe Hall 54
Kilner, Celia 210
King Cross 26, 28-9, 52, 66, 92, 216
King, Edward 47
Kinsley 78, 227
Kirk Smeaton 197, 219
Kirkburton 50, 118, 139
Kirkhamgate 117
Kirkheaton 69, 78, 143, 149-50, 192
Kirklees 120, 187, 230; Council 235
Kirklees and Calderdale Faith Fellowship 181
Kitchen Miners' Support Group 183
Knaresborough, Bishop of 150, 155
Knottingley 66, 68, 101, 113, 179-80, 182, 223, 233
Konstant, David 175
Kowak 190

Labour Party 182-3
Laleham Abbey 35, 37
Lamb, Philip 86
Lambeth Conference 10, 22, 29, 42, 50, 75, 131-2, 157, 191
Lambeth Palace 10, 109
Lancaster, Duchy of 51
Lancaster, Edward 28, 51
Lancaster University 157
Lang, Cosmo Gordon 37
Lawrance, Hugh 233
Lawrence, George 115
Lawson, Felicity 130, 160 162
Lawson, John 140, 165
Lawson, June 177
Lay Education and Training Committee 121
Lay Pastoral Ministry 135-6, 140, 165
Lay Workers, Licensed 121, 216
Lee, Elizabeth 150
Leeds 5, 10, 34, 44, 69, 86, 101, 120, 175-6, 181, 193, 204, 230, 235; Bishop of (Roman Catholic) 174, 177, 224; Clergy School 10, 59-60; Crown Court 194; Diocese of (proposed) 105, 119, 168, 230; Diocese of (Roman Catholic) 173-5, 177; Episcopal Area (proposed) 230; Grammar School 10; Methodist College 96; Methodist District 177; Metropolitan University 183; University 36
Leicester 110
Lent courses 68, 89-90, 92, 104, 145, 147-8, 158, 165, 169, 170, 175, 177
Lepton 199
Lichfield 88
Lightcliffe 190
Lightfoot, Joseph Barber 9
Lincoln, Achdeacon of 212; Bishop of 47; Theological College 109
Lindley 190
Lindley, Milton 123
Link Dioceses 111, 157, 190-1, 210
Linthwaite 177, 208, 220; Methodist Church 177
Lister Kaye, Beatrice 50
Lister, John xv, 76, 105, 151
Lithuania 191
Liturgical Movement 90
Liverpool 28, 61-2, 108, 144; Bishop of 55, 67; Cathedral 61; Diocese of 2, 4-5, 133
Liversedge 197
Loan Fund, Diocesan 17, 20
Local Ecumenical Partnership 171-2, 174-5
Lockwood 67, 145, 220, 227; Baptist Church 145
Lodge, John 216-17
London 2, 26, 32, 34-5, 61-3, 107-8, 185; Bishop of 8, 183
Longworth, Tom 63, 75, 85
Lowe, Christopher 84
Lowery, Jenny 198, 235
Lowles, Martin 140
Luddenden 43, 52, 143, 163
Luddendenfoot 27, 163
Lundwood 32, 66, 78, 142, 171, 233, 235
Lunt, Geoffrey Charles Lester 55
Lupset 30-1, 33, 82, 101, 182, 188, 220

INDEX

Lutheran Church 176, 191, 209
Luwum, Janani 210
Lux Mundi 10
Lydon, Barbara 124, 170

McAlpine Stadium 142
McCaskill, James 142
McCulloch, Nigel Simeon 107-8, 110, 125-8, 137, 140-1, 158-64, 169, 183, 188, 191, 196, 198, 203, 206, 210-1, 220, 234
MacDonald, Catherine 190
Macdonald-Bosville, Alexander Wentworth 52
MacFarlane, Jean 158
McGowan, Henry 58, 60-1, 74-5, 85, 95
McLean, Maggie 189
Macleod, William Arthur 15, 49-50
Macpherson, Anthony Stuart (Tony) 165, 168, 183, 197
McTighe, Mick 143
Maddocks, Morris 67
Male, David 142-3
Malik, Ghais Abdel 157
Manchester 24, 34-5, 59, 101, 133; Bishop of 8, 36, 59, 101, 133; Diocese of 1, 8, 99, 110, 133
Manpower Services Commission 182, 204
Manygates House, Sandal 21
Mara, Bishop of 157; Diocese of 107, 109, 157, 190, 210; Issenye Secondary School, 190; Primary School 190
Mara Link Committee 164, 190
Marsden 6
Marsh 25, 152
Marsh, John 136
Marshall, Edmund 169
Marshall, Peter 205, 208
Martyn, Henry 210
Masham 40
Masih, Yacub 191
Master-Whitaker, Arthur 51
Master-Whitaker, Mary Charlotte 51, 27
Maundy Thursday 196

Maundy, Royal 210
May, Edith 43
Maybury, Paul 167
Medicine Hat, Canada 68
Melanesian Mission 88
Meltham 139, 170
Methley, Violet 98
Methodism/Methodist Church 1, 30, 90, 97, 114-15, 117, 119, 143-5, 154, 163, 168-77, 181, 186, 194, 209, 223
Middle East 72
Middlestown 34, 84, 223
Middleton, Bishop of 155
Middleton St Mary 126, 234
Midgley 27
Midhope 8, 33, 52, 218
Millennium 158, 161-4, 171, 207
Millward, Paula Freda 120
Milnsbridge 68
Miners' strike 104, 106, 182, 184
Mining Industry 95, 107, 112, 115, 142, 183, 227
Ministerial Training, Director of 130
Ministry
  Development Officer 129; Diocesan Board of 131, 134, 136, 148; Diocesan Dean of 160; Diocesan School of 140, 211; Training Officer and Tutor to Readers 134; Wakefield scheme 137, 138-41
Ministry of Public Buildings and Works 73
Ministry of Works 73
Ministry Training Officer and Tutor to Readers 134
Mirfield Centre 211-12
Mirfield team parish 220
Missa 197
Mission, Board of 22, 37-8, 148-9, 151, 182
Mission and Unity, Board for 159, 169, 186, 204
Mission to Seafarers/Seamen 87-8, 127
Missionary Diocese of Wakefield 108, 110, 141, 158, 161
Mixenden 77, 83, 153, 176, 179, 216
Moldgreen 78, 204

Monk Bretton 78, 116, 142, 149, 192, 206; Priory 171
Moorbottom 223
Moore, Simon 177
Moore, Temple Lushington 24
Moorhouse, Walter 101
Moral Welfare, Diocesan Council for 46, 104, 178
Moravian Church 173
Morgan, A. E. C. 49
Morgan, Barry 164
Morisy, Ann 165
Morley 6, 43, 101, 141, 155, 160, 207, 220; team ministry 126, 142
Morley Report 58, 114
Morris, Arthur Harold 63–4
Morris, Brian 165
Mother Dora 79
Mother Robina 161
Mother Superior 45
Mothers' Union 31, 55, 66, 68, 115, 148, 155–6, 191, 221
Mount Pellon 26, 52, 60
Moverley, Gerald 174
Moxon, C. F. 64
Murder in the Cathedral 98, 100–1
Musgrave, Charles 1
Musgrove, Walter 66, 68
Muslim xv, 167, 179–81, 189, 224
Mytholmroyd 52, 219

Nairn-Briggs, George 185, 187–8, 209
Nairobi 122
Nash, James Oakey 37, 56
Nassau 35
National Coal Board (NCB) 95, 115
National Coal Mining Museum 189
National Delivery Advisory Team 195
National Diaconal Association 129
National Health Service 41
National Mission of Hope and Repentance 39
National Society for Promoting Religious Education 60
National Society for the Protection of Children 9
Neighbourhood Watch 154
Nesham, George 116

Net, The 142–3
Netherthong 219
Netherton 84
New Crofton 115
New Mill 200, 219
New Pilgrim Players 798–9
New Zealand 87
Newcastle, Bishop of 55; Cathedral 124; Diocese of 2, 4–5, 63
Newsome 171–2, 220
Newsome South Methodist Church 171–2
Nicaragua 175
Nicholson, Charles 15, 30, 32, 65
Nicholson, David 189
Nicholson, Norman 99, 101
Nonconformity 1, 67–8, 82, 144
Non-Stipendiary Minister (NSM) 126, 130–3, 136, 139–41, 215
Norfolk 105
Norland 33
Normanton 53, 66, 192, 206; Baptist Church 101; music group 156
Norris, William Foxley 9, 24, 42, 55
North Elmsall 66
North Featherstone 206
North Huddersfield tea parish 217
North Light Gallery 143
North West Ordination Course 131, 133
Northern Ordination Course 133, 140, 211
Northowram 26, 30, 125
Nortonthorpe 79
Norway 191
Norwich, Bishop of 145; Dean of 108; Diocese of 198; Diocesan Missioner 108
Norwood Green 27
Nostell Priory 164
Nyaronga, Gershom 157

Oates, John 82
Ockenden House 180
Ogle, Catherine 234
On the Deployment and Payment of the Clergy 58, 104, 212

INDEX

Ordained Local Minister (OLM) 133, 136–7, 139
Ordination Candidates Fund 20
Ossett 6, 43, 68, 167, 207
Oswestry 10
Outlane 217
Outlook 234
Ovenden 149–51, 159, Hall 55
Oxford 9–10, 36, 51, 53, 60, 62, 73, 107–8, 122, 211; Cathedral 10; Committee for Famine Relief (Oxfam) 88; Diocese of 109; Mission to Calcutta 38, 88; Movement 9, 47, 50
Oxspring 218

Packer, Goodwin S. 28
Paddock 171, 196, 228
Pakistan 111, 179, 181, 190–1, 210, 224
Pan Anglican Congress 19
Pare, Philip Norris 58, 196, 232
Parish and People Movement 63, 90–1, 157
Parish Development Officer 154, 168, 202
Parish Education Adviser 127
Parish Eucharist 91
Parish Evangelism Adviser 141, 160
Parker, Alice 38
Parker, Susan 168
Parochial Church Councils 21, 58–9, 90, 114, 118, 130–1, 135, 150, 160, 212, 216, 233
Parsonage Boards 104
Parsonage Board, Diocesan 221
Parsonage Houses 17, 21, 24, 29, 54, 57, 73, 75, 85, 104, 112, 221
Partners in Ministry 58
Pastoral Measure of 1968 58, 104, 212–13, 222, 226
Patronage, Diocesan Board of 21, 52–3
Patten, Alfred Hope 35, 37
Paul VI, Pope 168
Paul, Lesley 212
Paul Report 58, 104, 114, 117, 212–13
Paulinus 14, 201
Pawley, Bernard 132

Pawson, Godfrey 173
Peache Trustees 51, 65, 84
Peacock, Elizabeth 183
Pearson, Frank Loughborough 12, 14
Pearson, John Loughborough 12
Pearson, Stuart 148–9, 180, 182, 194
Pedley, Betty 127, 141, 153
Penistone 6, 8, 27, 33, 38, 47, 52, 66, 200, 218, 230; Grammar School 38; team ministry 218
Penrith, Bishop of 165
Pentecostal Movement 191–2
Peterborough, Bishop of 55; Diocese of 229
Philippines 175
Phipps, Richard 19, 21, 39
Pigou, Frances 1–3
Pilkington, Lionel 201
Pilkington, Thomas 29
Pilgrim Trust 58
Pinderfields Hospital 71, 79, 198
Platten, Stephen (Bishop) 108, 110, 119, 129, 139, 142, 164–6, 176, 183, 189–91, 202, 209, 211, 220, 229–30, 234
Pobjoy, Harold Norman 74, 86
Pobjoy, Lorna 86
Pobjoy, Marion 86
Pobjoy, Nada 86
Police Court Missioners 44
Pollock, Hugh Gillespie 144
Pontefract 31, 38, 46, 55, 66, 71, 78, 93, 97, 107, 115, 178, 194, 228; Archdeacon of 8, 16, 60, 63–4, 110, 142, 165; Archdeaconry of 8; Bishop of 8, 55, 59, 63, 65, 72, 75, 84, 88–9, 105, 109–10, 127, 159, 169, 214, 229; Centre for Preventive and Rescue Work 46; Corporation 78; Barracks 71
Porvoo Agreement of 1996 191
Porvoo Communion 191
Portobello Estate 176, 182
Portsmouth 143; Diocese of 109
Potter, John 29
Powell, Frances Sharpe 5
Prayer, Diocesan Cycle of 106
Pretoria, Bishop of 87

Preventive and Rescue Work, Diocesan
   Council for 44–5
Preventive and Rescue Work,
   Pontefract Centre for 46
Priest Idol 142, 235
Private Eye 205
Privy Council 47, 217, 225
Protestant Church Association 47
Protestant Truth Society 48
Provincial Episcopal Visitor 127, 196
Prynne, George Halford Fellowes 26
Public Worship Regulation
   Act 1874 47
Purdy, Debbie 189
Punch 232
Purlwell 25, 28, 30, 51, 69, 187
Purston 93, 220
Pusey House, Oxford 35
Pye Nest 216

Quakers 175, 186 (see also Society of
   Friends)
Quarmby, Arthur 200
Quarry Hill (Almondbury) 77, 219
Queen Victoria Clergy Fund 20

Radcliffe, Dorothy Una 49
Radcliffe, John 74
Ramsey, Michael 62, 168
Ramsbotham, David 188
Ramsbotham, John Alexander 58, 63,
   77, 79, 84, 92, 94, 96–102, 146,
   193, 196
Ramsden, John 9, 29, 52
Ramsey, Michael 62, 168
Ranchi 87, 114
Rangoon 87
Rank, Nicholas (Nick) 206
Rashcliffe 66, 92, 220
Rastrick 27, 101, 139, 170, 233
Ravensthorpe 37, 67, 114
Rawalpindi 191
Rawson, A. 225
Rawson family 51
Rawson, Frederick E. 224
Rawson, Michael 165, 234
Rawson, Mrs William Henry 224
Rawthorpe 78, 92, 122, 155

Raynes, Raymond 37, 99
Readers 22–3, 28, 66, 85, 89, 103,
   120–1, 130, 133, 135–6, 140, 150,
   165, 192, 211; Committee 131;
   Diocesan Association of 22;
   Diocesan Board of 23; Tutor to 134;
   Warden of 23, 126
Rebuilding Jerusalem 166
Redundant Churches 58, 73, 75,
   81, 84, 104, 170, 212–13, 215,
   218, 220, 222–8; Advisory Board
   for 224; Church Commissioners
   Committee 226; Fund 222, 227;
   Uses Committee, Diocesan 222, 224
Reed, Malcolm 138
Registry of Deeds, Wakefield 31
Rei, Prio Manget 181
Religious Drama 86, 99–102,
   148; Diocesan Adviser for 98;
   Manchester Diocesan Committee
   for 101; Northern Province
   Committee for 97–8, 101; Ripon
   Diocesan Committee for 101;
   Sheffield Diocesan Commmittee
   for 97; Society (Radius) 97, 102;
   Spenborough group 102
Reordering 77, 80–1, 109, 148, 152,
   163, 186, 199–207, 210
Repton, Bishop of 155
Reynolds, George 68–9
Rhodesia 35
Richborough, Bishop of 127
Richmond 9, 40
Rickman, Thomas 226
Ridley Hall, Cambridge 61
Ripon 17, 40, 73; Bishop of 1, 5, 55,
   75, 154, 181; Bishopric of 4;
   Diocese of 1–2, 5–7, 22, 41, 47, 91,
   99, 101, 126, 133, 148, 153, 160;
   Diocesan Board of Education 17;
   Diocesan Communications
   Officer 154
Ripon and Leeds, Bishop of 229;
   Diocese of 105, 119, 168, 189,
   229–31, 234
Ripon College, Cuddesdon 134
Ripon Episcopal Area 230
Ripon Hall, Oxford 109

INDEX

Ripon Training College 17, 73
Ripponden 6, 52, 126, 225, 233
Rishworth 31, 126
Rishworth School 133, 192
Robin, John Bryan Calvert 133
Robinson, Anthony (Tony) 110–11, 127, 167, 196–7, 234
Robinson, John 132
Robinson, Michael P. 203
Robinson, Rebecca Disney 51, 82
Roche, Arthur 177
Roe, Thorley 150–1
Rolfe, Tony 158
Roman Catholicism/Roman Catholic Church 30, 69, 77, 101, 104, 123–4, 144–5, 168–70, 173–7, 181, 186, 209, 224
Roman Catholic Justice and Peace Commission 175
Roman Catholic Mass 174
Rome, Anglican Centre 177
Romero, Oscar 188
Romero Project 188
Rorya, Diocese of 190
Roseveare, Reginald Richard 98
Rosse, Lord 53
Rotary 113
Rowntree Trust 186
Royal Almoner 196, 210
Royal British Legion 188
Royston Christian Council 117
Rugby League 59
Runcie, Robert 155
Ryhill 116

Sacramental Confession 50
St Aidan's College Birkenhead 61
St Albans, Bishopric of 2
St Andrew's College, Grahamstown, South Africa 62
St Austin's Roman Catholic Church 101, 174
St Gabriel's House 34
St John's College, Nottingham 130
St John's Home 44–6, 95, 178
St Oswald, Lord 29, 53
St Paul's Cathedral 8, 124
St Paulinus 14, 201
St Peter's Convent 13, 45, 79, 84, 150, 158, 161, 178, 207
St Stephen's House, Oxford 107
Salterhebble 25, 206
Salvation Army 145, 173, 175
Samaritans 216
Sampson, Gerard 37
Samuel, John 191
Sandal 21, 51, 66, 88, 101, 163, 176, 186, 200
Sanderson, Michael Edwin 15, 53–4, 64
Sanderson, Thomas Kemp 2–4, 54
Sarum and Wells Theological College 110
SAVE (Save Britain's Heritage) 226
Savery, George Ernest 67
Savile, Lord 26, 29, 51, 77, 221
Saviletown 115, 223, 226
Sawyer, Ken 158
Scarborough, Lord 29
Scissett 26, 220
Scott, George Gilbert 15, 211, 226
Scottish Episcopal Church 191
Scouts, Boy 55, 66, 68
Seaton, James Buchanan xiii, 8, 10, 16, 23, 25, 31–7, 46, 52, 55–6, 76, 82, 99, 107, 132
Second World War xv, 35, 41, 57, 61, 69–72
Sedgewick, J. N. 94
See Link 137, 148–9, 233
Self-Supporting Minister (SSM) xvi, 133, 139–41, 166, 189
Selly Oak College 63
Selwood, Evelyn Mary 120, 122
Sentamu, John Mugabi Tucker 164
Shackleton, Anthea 129
Shared Ministry Project 103, 133–5, 137, 139–40, 146, 149–51, 175, 185
Sharlston 7, 66, 69 207; Colliery 183
Sharp, John 34, 51
Shaw, Fanny Jane 28
Sheffield 2, 34, 98–9, 102, 198; Bishop of 55, 99, 109, 155; City Training College 98; Diocese of 8, 99, 120, 126, 133, 218, 229–30; Provost of 56; teaching hospitals 189

Sheffield Formula/Scheme 103, 109, 133-4, 164, 214
Shelley 67
Shelter 114
Shepley 170, 233
Shepley, Richard 150
Siddal 27, 141
Sikhs 179, 226
Silcoates School 110, 157, 170, 174
Silkstone 7, 8, 189, 230
Simeon, Charles 47
Simeon Trustees 47-8, 51
Simpson, Edward 26
Simpson, William 88
Sister Barbara 150
Sister Jean Mary 207
Sister Mary Clare 128
Sister Millicent Olga 207
Sister Sara Maureen 207
Sister Ursula 193
Skara, Dean of 177; Diocese of 109, 190-1, 210
Skelmanthorpe 26, 193; Group Ministry 220
Slater, Eileen 181
Slater, Timothy 125
Smith, Arthur 212
Smith, Brian 134-5, 149
Smith, Christine 141
Smith, Elizabeth (Lissa) 175
Smith, Elizabeth Ann 177
Smith, Raymond 194
Snapethorpe 30
Snowden Hill Farm Chapel 218
Social Responsibility 43-6, 140, 147, 149, 157, 177-90, 216; Adviser/officer 148, 180, 182, 185, 188-9, 194, 210; Diocesan Board for 186; Department of 183; Commission on Christian 180; Co-ordinator 189; Group for 181
Society for the Promotion of Christian Knowledge 87
Society for the Propagation of the Gospel 38, 87-8
Society of Friends, The (see also Quakers) 175
Society of St Francis 108

Sodor and Man 7
Songulashvili, Malkhaz (Bishop) 164, 177
Soothill 114, 221
South Africa 10, 35, 63, 75, 175, 179
South American Missionary Society 88
South Crosland 68, 220
South Elmsall 34, 66, 183
South Featherstone 93, 220
South Kirkby 32, 68, 87, 123
South Ossett 52, 68, 115, 233
South Parade 15, 21-2, 54
South Yorkshire 2, 4, 120, 175
Southampton 226
Southowram 7, 128, 170
Southport 28, 61
Southwark, Bishop of 132
Southwark Ordination Course 132
Southwell, Bishop of 151; Chancellor of 130; Diocese of 2, 4-5, 130, 198
Sowerby 137, 215, 224-5
Sowerby Bridge 33
Spain 198
Spark, The 233
Spencer, Stephen 190
Spencer Stanhope, Walter 2, 29, 51
Spivey, Peter 170
Spring End, Horbury 179
Stainborough 7, 66, 230
Stainborough Hall (Wentworth Castle) 27
Staincliffe 87
Staincross 31, 51, 167
Stainland 217
Stanley 114, 227
Stepney 131
Sterry, Christopher 136
Strategy for the Church's Ministry 104
Stevenson, J. L. 97
Stipends, Central Authority 103
Stockwood, Mervyn 132
Storthes Hall Hospital 216
Straton, Norman 2, 5, 7, 15
Sullivan, Arthur 16
Sunday School 26, 34, 43, 55, 68, 70, 78, 92, 113, 114, 115, 116, 122, 154, 159, 171, 225; Association 20; Organizer 71; Teachers'

INDEX

Association 22; Wakefield Diocesan Association 20
Sutherland 54
Swallow, Gillian 126
Swallow Hotels 138
Sweden 177, 191, 210
Sykes, Jean 217
Synod, Chester Deanery 161; General 118, 123, 124, 125, 129, 131, 158, 168, 192, 224; Ripon and Leeds 176, 215; Wakefield Diocesan 18, 22, 73, 97, 109, 118, 119, 123, 125, 128, 130, 134, 135, 137, 146, 158, 159, 162, 166, 168, 176, 177, 180, 181, 186, 196, 206, 230

Talbot, Neville 131
Tanzania 107, 157; Anglican Church in 190
Tarime, Diocese of 190
Taunton, Bishop of 107
Taylor, Michael 194–5
Team Parishes xv, 104, 116, 189, 212, 213, 217, 218, 219, 220, 222
Tear Fund 88
Tempest, Robert 14
Tempest, Tristram 14
Temple, Frederick 12
Temple, William 55, 96
Tew, Margaret Percy 15
Thompson, Canon 54
Thompson, Henry 174
Thompson, Mary 22
Thompson, Robert of Kilburn 15, 32, 79
Thomson, Cyril 196
Thomson, William 11
Thongsbridge 219
Thorner 193
Thornes 31, 34, 81–2, 107, 115, 199, 220, 221
Thornes House 15
Thornhill 5, 9, 15, 51, 70, 77, 85, 86, 87, 112, 145, 180, 224
Thornhill Edge 145
Thornhill Lees 77, 93, 115, 145, 180, 224

Thorpe 215, 224
Thurgoland 218
Thurlstone 27, 218, 230
Thurstonland 219
Tiller, John 104
Todmorden 8, 25, 66, 68, 101, 215
Tong 8
Tong Hall 14
Townley, Peter 229
Trades Union Congress 183
Trades Unions 88, 145, 179
Traditionalists 188
Transformational Plan 166
Transforming Lives 164–6, 177, 182, 194, 197
Treacy, Eric xv, xvi, 64, 89, 102, 105–6, 109, 111–17, 118, 120, 121, 122, 131, 145, 146, 169, 170, 179, 195, 196, 199, 207, 215, 216, 217, 222, 223–4, 226, 226
Treacy Hall 188, 210
Treacy, May 106, 208
Triangle 51
Truro, Bishop of 37; Cathedral 12; Diocese of 2
Turner, Eileen 126
Turner, Philip 101
Tweedy, Mark 90

United Missionary Festival 38
United Reformed Church 168, 170, 171, 173, 174, 175, 181, 186
United Society for Christian Literature 88
Unity House 74
University Mission to Central Africa 87
Unwin, Kenneth 214
Upper Holme Valley team 137, 171, 219
Upper Hopton 182, 220
Upperthong 52, 150, 219
Upton 32
Urban Community Adviser 128
Urban Priority Areas 110, 135, 151, 155, 184–5

Vaughan, Patrick 131
Venn, Henry 210

Venn, John 210
Verity, Bill 193
Vietnamese refugees 180
Vincent, Peter 194
Vincent, Sally 194
Wainstalls 27
Wakefield 2–11, 15, 19, 29, 31, 34, 42, 43, 44, 45, 49, 53, 54, 60, 61, 62, 67, 74, 78, 82–4, 85, 87, 88, 90, 95, 96, 109, 110, 114, 116, 122, 128, 150, 175, 177, 180, 181, 182, 188, 193, 195, 198, 208, 221, 228; Awake (festival) 176; Bishopric Fund 5–6, 7; Central School 38; Charities 3, 93, 207; Church Extension Society 17, 54; Church Institute 6, 17; Church Organization Society 17; City Council 94; Civic Society 63; Clergy Pensions Fund 20; College 183, 188; College of Technology 183, 188; Corporation 30, 120; Dilapidations Board 21. 71; Diocesan Association of Church Schools 20; Diocesan Conference 3, 59, 118; *Diocesan Gazette* 22, 35, 45, 232; *Diocesan News* 22, 58, 70, 89, 90, 91, 92, 118, 131, 145, 146, 147, 148, 151, 176, 194, 195, 221, 222, 232, 234; Garden Suburb Trust 10, 45; Girls High School 71; Historical Society 14; in Flowers 210; Metropolitan District Council 120, 152, 157, 178, 211; Mechanics Institute 18; Primary Care Trust 188; Prison 34, 163, 174, 182Rent Deposit Scheme 187; Sanitary Aid Society 10; Spiritual Aid Fund 17, 19; Theatre Royal 153; Town Hall 29, 85, 174; Trinity Football Club 211; Fund 17, 19; Loan Fund 17; Union of Men's Bible Classes 37
Wakefield Express 199, 233
Wakefield Herald 2, 29
Wales, Archbishop of 164
Wales, Church of 191
Wales, Prince of 205

Walpole, Neil 143
Walsden 8, 79, 92
Walsingham 35, 37, 93, 107, 196
Walton 26; Hall 26
Wardman, Carol 189
Warley 194
Warmfield 6, 7, 53
Warren, Robert 159, 160, 162
Warship Week 72
Watkinson, George 30
Watkinson, S. L. 30
Way, Thomas 43
Weatherall, Theo 123
Wells Theological College 63, 110
Welsby, Paul 132
Welsh, Charles 67
Welsh Suspensory Bill 19
Went Valley 219
Wentworth, Vernon 27
West Africa 87
West Bretton 7, 172
West Indian Community 197
West Riding xi, 5, 207; Charitable Society 20; Constabulary 120; County Council 16, 17, 70, 95, 120; Education Committee 60; Pauper Lunatic Asylum 71; Police Band 156; Police Training School 114
West Town 84
West Vale 227
West Yorkshire Methodist District 175
Westmorland Centre 210
Westmorland, Archdeacon of 109
Weston, Judith 150
Westwood, Miss M. G. 180
Wheatley, David 138
Wheatley-Balme, Edward 3, 6, 26
Wheeler, Gordon 174
Whirlow Grange, Sheffield 198
White, Colin 170
White, Frank 96
White, William 15
Whitechapel 68, 223
Whitley 53, 112, 121, 124, 170
Whittaker, Peter 177
Whittington 8, 9
Whittington, Richard Piers 52

INDEX

Whitwood 31, 220
Widdows, John Christopher (Kit) 197
Wilby, Wendy 165
Wilkinson, Alan 35
Wilkinson, Marlene 122
Willett, Geoffrey 116
Williams, Frank 107
Williams, John 137
Williams, Rowan 158, 189
Wilson, Bill 153
Wilson, Roger Plumpton 62, 64, 75, 76, 77, 78, 79, 81, 82, 85, 87–8, 89, 90, 91, 146, 208
Wilson, John 177
Wilton, Earl 51
Winchester, Diocese of 106, 107, 151, 184
Winchester School 62
Winter, Ernest 48
Women, Ordination of 107, 108, 110, 119, 120, 122–9, 139, 159, 163, 169, 233, 234; consecration as bishops 125, 128, 130
Women Workers 40, 41, 42, 89, 121, 133; Association of 42
Women's Work, Board of 92, 122
Womersley 53, 219
Wood, Anne 141
Woodhall 179
Woodhead, Mrs 24
Woodhouse 218; schools 187
Woodhouse, David 149
Woodhouse Hall 45
Woodkirk 68, 69, 116
Woodthorpe Lodge 16
Woolley 6, 51, 172, 182, 193, 194, 234; Colliery 79
Workers' Educational Association 188
World Call to the Church 38
World Council of Churches 96
Wortley 218
Wragby 53
Wrangbrook 32, 66, 67, 115
Wrenthorpe 52, 117
Wyke 8, 52

Yew Tree Theatre 188
York 14, 229; Convocation 22; Dean of 56; Diocese of 2, 6, 7, 32, 121, 133; Minster 10, 60, 63, 109, 110, 164; Province of 127
Yorkshire Ministry Course 133, 140, 211
Yorkshire Philosophical Society 14
Yorkshire Evening Post 235
Yorkshire Post 48, 145, 234, 235
Yorkshire Regional Training Partnership 212
Yorkshire Sculpture Park 172
Yorkshire Weekly Newspaper Group 207
Young, Anne 130
Young, David 181
Youth, Chaplain for 127
Youth Opportunities Programme 182